AF798940

Law and Religion in a Global Context

Volume 3

Series Editor

Frank S. Ravitch, College of Law, Rm 315, Michigan State University,
East Lansing, MI, USA

Law and Religion in a Global Context will focus on law and religion issues from a global perspective at a time when that field is of increasing importance and relevance around the world. Designed to be broad, the scope allows for books on the relationship between religion and government as well as on religious law. Focus will be placed on comparative law issues, but also on issues within single countries. Representative areas of focus will be:

- the relationship between government and religion ranging from laicete to theocracy
- religious freedom in pluralistic societies
- the relationship between religious freedom and other freedoms such as freedom of speech and sexual freedom
- regulation of religion by government
- original contributions on religious law

The series seeks to highlight up and coming voices in the field alongside those of established scholars. We encourage scholars from a wide range of geographic perspectives to apply. Purely doctrinal analysis of law and religion is not preferred. Nor is analysis of religious law issues without any original contribution or insights. The only exception to this rule might be books on legal doctrine from a region that has been under analyzed in English language literature.

More information about this series at http://www.springer.com/series/15625

Rodrigo Vitorino Souza Alves
Editor

Latin American Perspectives on Law and Religion

Springer

Editor
Rodrigo Vitorino Souza Alves
Brazilian Center for Studies in Law
and Religion
Federal University of Uberlândia
Uberlândia, Minas Gerais, Brazil

Law and Religion in a Global Context
ISBN 978-3-030-46716-6 ISBN 978-3-030-46717-3 (eBook)
https://doi.org/10.1007/978-3-030-46717-3

© Springer Nature Switzerland AG 2020
This work is subject to copyright. All rights are reserved by the Publisher, whether the whole or part of the material is concerned, specifically the rights of translation, reprinting, reuse of illustrations, recitation, broadcasting, reproduction on microfilms or in any other physical way, and transmission or information storage and retrieval, electronic adaptation, computer software, or by similar or dissimilar methodology now known or hereafter developed.
The use of general descriptive names, registered names, trademarks, service marks, etc. in this publication does not imply, even in the absence of a specific statement, that such names are exempt from the relevant protective laws and regulations and therefore free for general use.
The publisher, the authors and the editors are safe to assume that the advice and information in this book are believed to be true and accurate at the date of publication. Neither the publisher nor the authors or the editors give a warranty, expressed or implied, with respect to the material contained herein or for any errors or omissions that may have been made. The publisher remains neutral with regard to jurisdictional claims in published maps and institutional affiliations.

This Springer imprint is published by the registered company Springer Nature Switzerland AG
The registered company address is: Gewerbestrasse 11, 6330 Cham, Switzerland

Acknowledgements

This book brings together leading scholars from Latin America. It grows from debates and dialogues that took place in the region for the past years, most of them sponsored by the Latin American Consortium for Religious Freedom and national bodies and academic institutions, such as the Brazilian Center of Studies in Law and Religion and the Faculty of Law of the Federal University of Uberlandia.

This book is a part of the series *Law and Religion in a Global Context*, which aims to focus on law and religion issues from a global perspective. A special thanks to Frank S. Ravitch and to the editorial board of the series for allowing the inclusion of Latin American matters in this important collection. Christi Jongepier-Lue, Ambrose Berkumans, Anja Trautmann, Raghavy Krishnan and the editorial team of Springer offered indispensable support since the beginning of this project.

The publication would not have been possible without the generosity and commitment of its authors, as well as the assistance provided by Anaisa Almeida Naves Sorna and Stefanie Schegoscheski Viotto Ferraz, from the Brazilian Center of Studies in Law and Religion.

Rodrigo Vitorino Souza Alves

Contents

Latin American Perspectives on Law and Religion: An Introduction 1
Rodrigo Vitorino Souza Alves

Law and Religion in the Encounter of Cultures: The Normative Conflicts Between Freedom of Religion or Belief and the Rights of Indigenous Peoples 5
Rodrigo Vitorino Souza Alves

Secular or Multi-confessional, that Is the Question: Tensions Within the Argentinean Protestantism During the Religious Freedom Act Negotiations 35
Juan Martin Vives

The 2017 Proposed Law on Religious Freedom for Argentina: Comparative Perspectives 47
Juan G. Navarro Floria

Secular State and Religious Education in Public Schools: The Brazilian Case 73
Jayme Weingartner Neto

Religious Intolerance in Brazil: An Analysis of the Social Reality 95
Alexandre Brasil Fonseca

Mexican Law of Religion at 28 Years of the Constitutional Reform on Religious Matters 117
María Concepción Medina González

Colombia as a Secular State 145
Vicente Prieto

Contributors

Rodrigo Vitorino Souza Alves The Brazilian Center of Studies in Law and Religion, Federal University of Uberlandia, Uberlândia, Brazil

Alexandre Brasil Fonseca Federal University of Rio de Janeiro, Rio de Janeiro, Brazil

María Concepción Medina González National Autonomous University of Mexico, Mexico City, Mexico

Juan G. Navarro Floria Pontifical Catholic University of Argentina, Buenos Aires, Argentina

Vicente Prieto Universidad de La Sabana, Chía, Colombia

Juan Martin Vives Center for Studies on Law and Religion, Adventist University of Plata, Libertador San Martin, Argentina

Jayme Weingartner Neto Rio Grande do Sul Court of Justice, LaSalle University, Porto Alegre, Brazil

Latin American Perspectives on Law and Religion: An Introduction

Rodrigo Vitorino Souza Alves

Abstract In this new collection of essays, Latin American scholars discuss several issues regarding religion–state relations and the exercise of freedom of religion or belief in the region. This chapter provides an introduction to the book.

Keywords Law and Religion · Latin America · Freedom of religion or belief · Religion-state relations

Law and Religion has been internationally consolidated as a specific area of study in the previous years. However, due to language barriers, most of the regional and national debates within Latin America has not been accessible to the interested audience from other parts of the world.

The present volume aims to contribute to the fascinating global debate on the meaning and scope of freedom of religion or belief and the relations between state, society and religion. Despite the particularities of the Latin American context, the series of issues, arrangements and processes that have been negotiated and developed in this part of the Global South potentially adds new insights and perspectives to the challenges that have been arisen in other regions.

"Latin American Perspectives on Law and Religion" analyzes the intersections and interactions between religion and other far-reaching subjects, such as politics and democracy, traditional cultures, national and ethnic groups, majorities and minorities, public education, management of diversity, intolerance and violence, secularism and equality.

The first chapter explores the significance of religious freedom for indigenous groups and analyzes the normative conflicts between the indigenous collective right to self-determination, religious freedom and other human rights. Rodrigo Vitorino Souza Alves investigates these conflicts from different perspectives, including the right of indigenous groups to maintain their own religious and cultural traditions in spite of their relative incompatibility with the national legislation, their protection

---

R. V. S. Alves (✉)
The Brazilian Center of Studies in Law and Religion, Federal University of Uberlandia, Uberlândia, Brazil
e-mail: rodrigo@direitoereligiao.org

© Springer Nature Switzerland AG 2020

R. V. S. Alves (ed.), *Latin American Perspectives on Law and Religion*, Law and Religion in a Global Context 3,
https://doi.org/10.1007/978-3-030-46717-3_1

against cultural assimilation by the majority religious culture, the individual right to leave or not to practice the indigenous community's religion, and the right of indigenous persons to hold a belief that is different from the orthodox beliefs of the community.

The debate on church–state relations in Argentina is addressed by Juan Martin Vives and Juan G. Navarro Floria. In his chapter, Vives highlights that the current model of church–state relations adopted by Argentina violates the principle of equality, as it guarantees a privileged position for the Roman Catholic Church. Meanwhile, the country experiences a rapid growth of the Protestant community, which claims the protection not only of freedom but also equality in matters of religion or belief. However, as there is no consensus on the meaning of religious equality, the author focuses on the arguments and tensions within the Argentinean Protestantism related to the negotiations of the proposed Religious Freedom Act. In its turn, Floria examines the content of that bill and compares it with the current legislation in place in Spain, Portugal, Chile, Colombia, Peru and Mexico. Furthermore, he analyzes various aspects of the proposed legislation, including the regulation of conscientious objection and reasonable accommodation, the creation of a registry for churches and religious communities as well as the protection of autonomy of religious bodies.

Jayme Weingartner Neto and Alexandre Brasil Carvalho da Fonseca explore two relevant issues connected to the Brazilian context: religious education and religious intolerance. Weingartner Neto's chapter investigates the debate on the place of religion in Brazilian elementary public schools. Despite neither the Constitution nor the legislation determine the nature of religious education in public schools, the Federal Supreme Court has ruled that denominational teaching in public schools is not forbidden by the Constitution, a conclusion that is shared by the author as long as the Government is not excessively entangled with religion and religious plurality is respected. The latter issue is analyzed by Fonseca from a sociological perspective. His chapter examines data gathered during the production of the Report on Religious Intolerance and Violence in Brazil (2011–2015) by the Federal Government and identifies that acts of intolerance occur once every two days on average in Brazil, a total of almost one thousand cases in five years.

Interactions between religious freedom, equality and state secularity are considered by María Concepción Medina González and Vicente Prieto. González analyzes the legal regulation of religion in Mexico under the principles of religious freedom, "*laicidad*" and the separation of religion and state. Her chapter focuses on the amendments to the Mexican Constitution and the New Constitution of Mexico City, the legal protection of religious freedom, public policies regarding religious diversity, and recent legal cases, such as the Native American Church and the Blood Transfusion for Jehovah Witnesses cases. Prieto's chapter describes the meaning and scope of secularity in Colombia. The principle of secularity has its foundations in the Constitution of 1991, it was explicitly established by the Religious Freedom Act in 1994 and it has been affirmed by the Constitutional Court in several cases for the past three decades. However, there are different approaches developed by national courts, which depend on the specific case and the personal convictions of the judges. Prieto identifies that most of the decisions of the Constitutional Court has the Catholic Church as reference point and that there are difficulties in explaining the relationship between equality, secularity and pluralism. His chapter addresses these issues considering religious freedom as the basis for both secularity and equality.

This new collection of essays brings together examples of the religion–state models prevailing in Latin America (from strict separation in Mexico to preferential treatment in Argentina) in addition to a selection of significant issues and recent developments concerning the exercise of religious freedom in this area. The book is certainly of interest not only to legal scholars and practitioners but also to sociologists, political scientists and theologians, as well as to policymakers and civil society organizations.

Law and Religion in the Encounter of Cultures: The Normative Conflicts Between Freedom of Religion or Belief and the Rights of Indigenous Peoples

Rodrigo Vitorino Souza Alves

Abstract There are over 300 million indigenous people in the world and they are in every continent. The United Nations, regional human rights systems, and numerous countries have already recognized that indigenous people are specifically entitled to several rights, which include the right to freedom of religion or belief, and at least some dimensions of the collective right to self-determination. According to the United Nations Declaration on the Rights of Indigenous Peoples of 2007, the latter ensures that indigenous peoples may freely determine their political status and pursue their economic, social and cultural development. In relation to the former, freedom of religion or belief is a human right that might be exercised individually or collectively with others, comprising the right of indigenous people to manifest, practice, develop and teach their spiritual and religious traditions, customs and ceremonies, the protection of their religious sites and ceremonial objects, and the right to the repatriation of their human remains. This paper provides a critical evaluation of the potential normative collisions between the right to self-determination, minority rights and freedom of religion or belief, and concludes that self-determination advances freedom of religion or belief and, at the same time, self-determination is limited by freedom of religion or belief. At the intersection of these norms lies the right of indigenous groups to maintain their own religious and cultural traditions without external coercive intervention (freedom for religion), their protection against cultural assimilation by the majority religion (external freedom from religion), the individual right to leave or not to practice the community's religion (internal freedom from religion), and the freedom against religious internal oppression and persecution (freedom within religion).

A draft version of this chapter was presented at the Fourth ICLARS Conference "Freedom of/for/from/in Religion: Differing Dimensions of a Common Right" of the International Consortium for Law and Religion Studies, which was held at St. Hugh's College, University of Oxford, United Kingdom, September 8–11, 2016.

R. V. S. Alves (✉)
The Brazilian Center of Studies in Law and Religion, Federal University of Uberlandia, Uberlândia, Brazil
e-mail: rodrigo@direitoereligiao.org

© Springer Nature Switzerland AG 2020

R. V. S. Alves (ed.), *Latin American Perspectives on Law and Religion*, Law and Religion in a Global Context 3,
https://doi.org/10.1007/978-3-030-46717-3_2

Keywords Freedom of religion or belief · Self-determination · Cultural rights · Minority rights · Individual and collective rights

1 Introduction

While much of the development of political and constitutional theory has occurred in the Global North, especially in countries such as the USA, France, England, Italy, and Germany, major transformational processes have been taking place in the South. In the past thirty years, social movements have caused immense changes, especially when applying those theories to their social reality (Santos 2007).

Maybe the clearest example is related to indigenous issues. The strenuous opposition of indigenous peoples to the historical conditions of injustice and discrimination implemented since the period of colonization contributed to the gradual recognition of their collective claims as rights in the legal system. In Latin America, indigenous peoples have sought to improve the living conditions in their communities, on equal terms with other social groups.

Indigenous peoples possess valuable ancestral cultures, which make important contributions to society in general. However, despite the recognized value of these peoples and their cultures, they have been violated in their most essential rights for a long time. The post-colonial era did not put an end to the internal colonization, since in many places the natives remain being treated as inferior to the other inhabitants of the State territory. Nonetheless, international law moves toward the opposite direction, to recognize the dignity and the rights not only of individuals, but also of indigenous peoples, ensuring them cultural security. Relevant international documents have been adopted in the past decades, which inspired constitutional reforms and human rights initiatives for the protection of indigenous peoples.

One of the most recent developments in the global protection of indigenous rights is the United Nations Declaration on the Rights of Indigenous Peoples of 2007, which protects the right to freedom of religion or belief and the collective right to self-determination. The latter ensures that indigenous peoples may freely determine their political status and pursue their economic, social and cultural development. In relation to the former, freedom of religion or belief is a human right that might be exercised individually or collectively with others, comprising the right of indigenous peoples to manifest, practice, develop, and teach their spiritual and religious traditions, customs and ceremonies; the protection of their religious sites and ceremonial objects; and the right to the repatriation of their human remains. In the Americas, the Organization of the American States Declaration on the Rights of Indigenous Peoples of 2016 also advanced the protection of indigenous group autonomy together with freedom of religion or belief.

The following sections of this chapter aim to investigate, firstly, the legal recognition of indigenous self-determination by international law and by five Latin American countries, which have adopted a multiethnic and multicultural perspective toward indigenous groups, namely the constitutions of Brazil (1988), Colombia (1991), Bolivia (1994, 2009), Ecuador (1998), and Venezuela (1999).

2 The Self-determination of Indigenous Peoples

According to Jose R. Martinez Cobo's study on the problem of discrimination against indigenous populations,[1] indigenous peoples are characterized primarily by having a bond of ancestry with the original people (historical continuity), by differentiation from the dominant social group (they are not hegemonic groups), and by their cultural identity (individuals partake of traditions, customs, language, etc.). Although these people live in situations normally associated with the violation of rights, especially the rights of minorities under international law, their representatives demand recognition of self-determination as the basis for all human rights that are provided to them, and not just their condition as minorities or vulnerable groups.

Human rights systems and numerous countries have already recognized that indigenous people are specifically entitled to several rights. Within the United Nations (UN) and the Organization of American States (OAS), a distinction is drawn between the rights of persons belonging to minorities and those of indigenous peoples.

Indigenous peoples have concerns that are not properly addressed by the minority rights framework.[2] Although the 1992 UN Declaration on the Rights of Persons Belonging to National or Ethnic, Religious and Linguistic Minorities proclaimed rights and protections for ethnic minorities, in which category indigenous peoples are included, it was not comprehensive enough.

Advancing the principles brought by the Convention concerning Indigenous and Tribal Peoples in Independent Countries (1989) of the International Labor Organization (ILO), the UN Declaration on the Rights of Indigenous Peoples (2007) proclaimed some additional dimensions of human rights in accordance with their special needs. Similarly, after decades of debate, the OAS has adopted the American Declaration on the Rights of Indigenous Peoples, on June 2016. It will certainly be an important instrument for the interpretation of human rights conventions within the Inter-American Human Rights System.

The most important right that was recognized by both declarations is the right of indigenous peoples to self-determination, which allows the community to exercise control over its own future, and thus survive and thrive. It is a central component of group identity, which carries a strong political meaning (Foster 2001), and implies,

[1] UN Doc.E/CN.4/Sub.2/1986/7/Add.1-4.

[2] UN Doc. E/CN.4/Sub.2/AC.5/2005/2, 4—Commentary of the Working Group on Minorities to the United Nations Declaration on the Rights of Persons Belonging to National or Ethnic, Religious or Linguistic Minorities, April 2005, para. 16.

inter alia, autonomy, self-government, recognition and protection of diversity, protection of the territory, participation policy, protection of language, art and traditional practices as well as the recognition of indigenous customary law.[3]

Unlike the policies of assimilation or integration, which are monocultural and ethnocentric, self-determination requires respect for cultural diversity by State and social powers, so that the indigenous people are not treated as inferior to the other people or as mere objects of public policies and paternalistic protection, especially by the mechanism of tutelage. Indigenous peoples are subjects of rights in the legal order, which shall have the right to political participation, including but not limited to matters affecting their *status quo*. In this case, the most powerful way to participate is through the expression of consent (or, to a lesser extent, consultation), so that indigenous peoples should acquiesce to policies that affect their situation. This treatment given to indigenous peoples is justified primarily by their existence in the territory before the State came to form—ancestry. In addition, the accommodation of indigenous difference is the most appropriate way to avoid the emergence of political violence organized by the minority—democratic stability (Dutter 2012).

Self-determination is also opposed to a "traditionalist" model, as designated by Will Kymlicka (2011). This perspective affirms that cultural relativism would require the preservation of the authenticity and purity of cultures, which would be achieved by maintaining the identity of ethnic groups, their practices understood as traditional or sacred. However, this position is politically dangerous because it implies that cultural development is abnormal and that intercultural contact is harmful, what would justify xenophobic feelings, forced isolation of ethnic groups, and disrespect for individual rights of group members to preserve the collective identity. Contrary to the dynamic and dialogical reality of cultures, the traditionalist perspective could be described not as a defense of cultural rights, but as the imposition of cultural duties, which is not compatible with the current conception of human rights in international law.

3 The Legal Protection of the Self-determination of Indigenous Peoples

3.1 Self-determination of Indigenous Peoples in the International Law

An understanding of human rights that reduces them to individual freedoms takes away the possibility of protecting the collective rights of indigenous peoples. However, such a reductionist approach is unsustainable given the fact that human beings, by their nature, are dependent of collective life. In addition, there is a relationship of interdependence and complementarity between the different dimensions of

[3] See also Alves (2015a, b).

human rights. On the one hand, the protection of collective or corporate rights, which includes the right to self-determination, allows for the correct application of individual rights of indigenous peoples and avoids their subjection to oppression or assimilation. On the other, any system or institution internal to indigenous peoples, which existence or continuation is made possible because of the recognition of self-determination, must respect the human rights of every indigenous individual (Musafiri 2012).

Individual rights establish the foundation and the limit to self-determination. The foundation, because the right to self-determination is based on the principle of equality between individuals and peoples (in opposition to the ideas of racial or ethnic hierarchy/superiority), which removes any supposed right to promote assimilation or subjugation. The limit, because the right to self-determination does not invalidade or reject the other dimensions of human rights, so it cannot become a justification for the violation of individual rights. Therefore, no one may invoke cultural diversity to infringe upon human rights guaranteed by international law, nor to limit their scope, as stated in the General Comment n. 21 of the UN Committee on Economic, Social and Cultural Rights and in the Article 4 of the Universal Declaration on Cultural Diversity of the United Nations Educational, Scientific and Cultural Organization (UNESCO), an idea that may be called "liberal multiculturalism" (Kymlicka 2011).

Under the international law, legal instruments and other documents from different organizations recognize self-determination of indigenous peoples. This study will highlight three international organizations, namely ILO, UN and OAS.

3.1.1 The Protection of Indigenous Peoples by the ILO

One of the most important instruments related to the recognition of collective rights of indigenous peoples is the above-mentioned ILO Convention of 1989, also known as Convention n. 169. This document promoted multiculturalism and made obsolete the ILO Convention n. 107 of 1957, which had an integrationist character.

The Convention n. 169 proclaims that, in applying national law to indigenous peoples, States must have due regard to their customs and customary law (Article 8). In doing so, the ILO and the ratifying States recognize the legitimate power of indigenous peoples to create disciplinary norms of internal affairs to their communities, which should be respected by the State. Certainly, the Convention ensured the indigenous peoples' right to self-determination, however without express use of the term.

It should also be underlined that the collective rights guaranteed to indigenous peoples do not constitute sovereignty. The Convention expressly excluded any interpretation of their provisions as a right to independence or secession, by the limitation of the scope of the term "people." Indigenous peoples are not sovereign nations, as they sit on the territory of sovereign States. Therefore, national legislation is applicable to indigenous peoples, albeit in attenuated form. Moreover, the exercise of self-determination is also limited by human rights and fundamental freedoms, under national and international law. On the one hand, individuals and groups receive protection against human rights violations by external agents; on the other, the internal human rights violations should also be curbed (Article 3).

As the Convention n. 169 is a legally binding instrument, the rights guaranteed therein must be respected by the States that have ratified it. For this reason, the Convention has been of great importance in promoting the rights of indigenous peoples not only from the perspective of international law, but as domestic rule within the States. To date, twenty-three States have ratified the Convention, mostly Latin American countries—the last country to ratify was Luxembourg, on June 5, 2018.

3.1.2 UN Human Rights System

Within the UN human rights system, the Declaration on the Rights of Indigenous Peoples was adopted in 2007 by the UN General Assembly and represents an important political breakthrough at the global level regarding the protection of indigenous rights. The Declaration sets out the right to self-determination, which includes: the right to freely determine their political status and to pursue freely their economic, social, and cultural development (Article 3), the right to autonomy or self-government with respect to their internal and local affairs, as well as ways and means for financing their autonomous functions (Article 4), and the right to maintain and strengthen their distinct political, legal, economic, social, and cultural institutions, while maintaining their right to participate fully—if they so desire—in the political, economic, social, and cultural life of the State (Article 5).

The recognition of self-determination is especially important to ensure that indigenous peoples may govern their communities autonomously, *i.e.*, the right to exercise administrative and regulatory activities. Therefore, the right to self-determination was not ensured in the full sense of Article 1 of the International Covenant on Civil and Political Rights, independence as a State, but rather the right to autonomy and self-government under the rule of the sovereign State (cf. Musafiri 2012). The expression of Hurst Hannum (1996) aptly describes this concept: it is the "less-than-sovereign self-determination."

The Declaration also seeks to promote the freedom from forced assimilation or destruction of indigenous culture (Article 8). Consequently, it fell to States to develop mechanisms to avoid acts detrimental to the right of self-determination. However, although cultural identity is protected by the Declaration, it does not remove the right of indigenous people to get in contact with other cultures, establish intercultural dialogue or assimilate elements of different cultures, provided that this is done voluntarily (Anaya 1996; Kymlicka 2011). The condition of material vulnerability that indigenous peoples face does not deprive them the capacity for political and cultural self-determination (Article 33). For this reason, it is for indigenous peoples to decide their own cultural identity, what makes State interventions in this matter unwelcome and paternalistic welfare policies. Rather, the task of the State is to adopt effective measures that ensure the exercise of the right to self-determination by indigenous peoples.

However, it should be noted that indigenous peoples, although autonomous, remain subject to the human rights system. Every indigenous person is entitled to all human rights (Article 1), such as the rights to life, equality, freedoms, and property. In this sense, any existing minority group within an indigenous community must also be safeguarded in their human rights, particularly the right to enjoy their culture, to profess and practice their religion and use their language (Wheatley 2005).

3.1.3 Indigenous People and the Inter-American Human Rights System

Within the Organization of American States, in 1989, its General Assembly requested that the Inter-American Commission on Human Rights prepare a legal instrument for the protection of indigenous peoples, which adoption was scheduled for 1992. However, the proposal was approved by the Commission only in February 1997, and there was no consensus among States on the matter. In 1999, a Working Group was established and all member States were entitled to the rights of participation and to vote, aiming to continue the analysis and preparation of the project. In June 2016, during the meeting of the General Assembly, the American Declaration on the Rights of Indigenous Peoples was adopted.

The objective of the Working Group had not been achieved earlier for it had to obtain the complete agreement and support of all member States on the text. Several points were discussed by the parties, but those expressing the strongest resistance against the approval of the project were the USA and Canada, which had not signed the UN Declaration of 2007. One of the main issues that caused the long delay in the adoption of the American Declaration was the provision of the right to self-determination.

The American Declaration provides that "States recognize and respect the multicultural and multilingual character of indigenous peoples, who are an integral part of their societies" (Article 2) and that "Indigenous peoples have the right to self-determination. By virtue of that right, they freely determine their political status and freely pursue their economic, social, and cultural development" (Article 3). The rights advanced by the Declaration, however, do not authorize indigenous peoples to take any action that would impair the territorial integrity or political unity of a sovereign State.[4]

In addition to that Declaration, issues related to self-determination were addressed under the American Convention on Human Rights of 1969, by the two bodies with jurisdiction to hear issues related to compliance with the commitments undertaken

[4] "Article 4. Nothing in this Declaration may be interpreted as implying for any State, people, group, or person any right to engage in any activity or to perform any act contrary to the Charter of the Organization of American States or the Charter of the United Nations or construed as authorizing or encouraging any action which would dismember or impair, totally or in part, the territorial integrity or political unity of sovereign and independent states."

by States Parties to the Convention, namely the Inter-American Commission and the Court of Human Rights.

Some cases indicate the position of these organs in relation to indigenous peoples' rights. In the 80s, there were conflicts in Nicaragua among the Miskito Indians and the Sandinista government because of a new agrarian reform program. The Miskitos believed that the program did not take into account the indigenous ownership of many lands distributed. The Miskitos filed a representation before the Inter-American Commission on Human Rights, arguing that the group's right to the land with their resources should be ensured, as well as the right to self-determination. One of the lawyers of the indigenous people claimed that the community had the qualities that made it an independent State: territory, population, government, and ability to establish international relations (Engle 2011).

In casu, the Commission recognized that international law guarantees the right to self-determination, but it would not be applicable at the time because the Miskito had no political independence (the Commission interpreted self-determination as sovereignty). Nevertheless, the decision did not allow Nicaragua to assimilate the indigenous culture. Rather, the State should have to protect all aspects related to the cultural identity of the people.

Two reports on Colombia underscore the Commission's concern to protect indigenous peoples. In 1981, the Commission recommended that the Colombian government should take the necessary measures for the protection of indigenous people during the execution of military operations. In 1993, the Commission stressed the importance of the constitutional provision of judicial autonomy of indigenous authorities for the development of the independence of ethnic minorities.

Besides the Commission, the Inter-American Court of Human Rights plays an important role in the transformation of social reality in the region. Regarding the autonomy of indigenous peoples, in Aloeboetoe peoples and others v. Suriname (1993), the Court ensured that the existence of tribal customary law should prevail over the laws of Suriname, provided it was not contrary to the terms of the American Convention. In Saramaka people v. Suriname (2007), the Court recognized the right of indigenous people to promote their own socio-economic development, to freely dispose of natural wealth and resources, and not to be deprived of the means of survival. In Xákmok Kásek people v. Paraguay (2010), the Court affirmed the State's responsibility to recognize and respect the legal personality of the indigenous community, and not to violate their self-determination. Finally, in Kichwa Sarayaku people v. Ecuador (2012), after a long legal battle, the Court decided in favor of the indigenous people and it mentions the UN Declaration on the Rights of Indigenous Peoples in support of its orders related to the right to prior consultation of the indigenous peoples.

3.2 The Self-determination of Indigenous Peoples in Latin America

This study has shown that, under the international law, self-determination is a principle applicable to all peoples. As for the indigenous peoples, the ILO Convention

n. 169 of 1989 and UN Declaration of 2007 afirmed the indigenous peoples' right to a "less-than-sovereign self-determination" (Hannum), which allow them to choose their way of life and how they will develop economically, socially, and culturally. Regarding the Inter-American system, there is a strong tendency to recognize their right to self-determination, which is reinforced by the adoption of the OAS Declaration in 2016. However, domesticaly, there is a variety of ways State legal systems treat indigenous rights in Latin America. In this third section, the paper discusses five Latin American constitutions, namely the Venezuelan, Bolivian, Colombian, Ecuadorian, and Brazilian constitutions, with some notes on national legislation and relevant jurisprudence.

3.2.1 Overcoming the *Regimén de Excepción* in Venezuela

The Venezuelan Constitution of 1961, driven by an integrationist ideology, considered indigenous individuals culturally inferior to the others. The Constitution provided that indigenous communities would be tutored in a "regime of exception," and that the State would promote the progressive incorporation of the communities to the life of the nation (Article 77). Therefore, the Venezuelan State was to protect indigenous peoples and promote their inclusion in civilized life.

However, the Venezuelan legislation moved to exclude the tutelage mechanism. This was replaced by the principle of interculturalism in the Constitution of the Bolivarian Republic of Venezuela of 1999 (Article 100). In addition to the ideological break with the colonial heritage, this Constitution brought a long list of rights of indigenous peoples, as well as imposed duties to the State (Articles 119-126).

The Constitution also provided that the State is to recognize the existence of indigenous peoples and communities, their social, political, and economic organization, which includes customs, languages, and religions, as well as the right to the land they traditionally occupy. It also assured that indigenous peoples have the right to maintain and develop their ethnic and cultural identity, worldview, values, and religion, and the right to express their own culture and to receive education according to their socio-cultural particularities and traditions. These rights are accompanied by the possibility of political participation in the National Assembly and other organs of political representation.

These standards demonstrate that the Venezuelan Constitution historically progressed to recognize the right of each indigenous people to decide their *modus vivendi*, i.e., the right to self-determination. This, however, does not consist in the affirmation of their sovereignty, since the indigenous peoples form part of Venezuela, as a sole, sovereign and indivisible State.

According to Ñáñe (2009), the Constitution of 1999 marked the creation of a new citizenship status for the indigenous people, recognizing that they are, at the same time, members of their ethnic group and citizens of the Venezuelan State, which is a culturally diverse country: multiethnic, multicultural, and plurilingual.

3.2.2 The Right to *Libre Determinación* in the Bolivian Constitution

As a result of the Constituent Assembly of 2007, which was organized by the first indigenous President, Juan Evo Morales Ayma (elected two months before that event), the new Bolivian Constitution (2009) recognizes the plurinational State (Article 1) and ensures the self-determination of indigenous peoples within the State, consisting of the right to autonomy, self-government, culture, recognition of institutions, land, among others (Article 30). For the situations of greater vulnerability, the Constitution expressly provides that indigenous peoples at risk of extinction, in isolation or not contacted, will be protected and respected in their forms of individual and collective life (Article 31). Certainly, the Constitution of Bolivia became the fundamental document that grants possibly the greatest relevance for the rights of indigenous peoples, even when compared to international standards. The Constitution affirms the right of indigenous peoples to exercise their political, legal and economic systems according to their worldview, within the framework of legal pluralism and interculturalism (Aguilar et al. 2010).

Concerning the right to participation, this includes consultation of indigenous communities on matters of their interest and participation in State organs, including the adoption of a process for the election of representatives according to the norms established by the people (Article 26, II, 4).

Regarding the exercise of jurisdiction, the Bolivian Constitution establishes the equal hierarchy both to the ordinary and indigenous jurisdictions, recognizing the traditional law and the courts of indigenous peoples. At the top of the judicial system, the Constitution places the Constitutional Court, as a plurinational body comprising judges from the ordinary as well as the indigenous traditional systems (Articles 196-199). While recognizing the legitimacy of the indigenous law and courts, the Constitution limits the scope of the self-determination, since they are obliged to respect and promote the constitutional rights guaranteed to all individuals (Articles 17, 190-192).

Clavero (2010), the former Vice-President of the UN Permanent Forum on Indigenous Issues, praises the existence of a Plurinational Constitutional Court and affirms that the combination of indigenous institutions with the central institutions and other autonomous territorial entities contributes to the process of decolonization and consolidation of the Plurinational State. The Constitutional Court is the only Bolivian body which presides over the entire judicial system, as it is the only court that is hierarchically superior to the indigenous jurisdiction. The existence of this body coupled with indigenous representation in the Constitutional Court and the constitutional writ of interculturalism make Bolivia a unique and maybe the most advanced case in Latin America.

3.2.3 Self-determination in the Colombian Constitutional Court

The Political Constitution of the Republic of Colombia, in force since 1991, guarantees the rights of indigenous peoples. Although the right to self-determination is not expressly provided, the Constitution protects cultural diversity (Articles 1, 7, and 70), provides the right to political participation (Articles 171 and 176), and recognizes the special jurisdiction (Article 246) as well as territorial rights (Articles 286, 329, and 330) in relation to indigenous peoples. Regarding the latter issue, the Colombian Constitution recognizes the indigenous territory as a territorial entity of the State, which was confirmed by the Colombian Constitutional Court in 2011 (Sentence T-693).

In this case, the Court faced the issue of the right to self-determination and participation of ethnic communities in order to identify the scope of protection of that right. The Court affirmed the existence of the right to self-determination in the Colombian Constitution on grounds of the intrinsic value of ethnic communities as culturally differentiated groups, which had already been laid down by international instruments ratified by the government, including the ILO Convention n. 169. The Court also relied on the constitutional jurisprudence, which has recognized the right to self-determination of indigenous peoples (especially Sentence C-030 of 2008). The Court ruled that self-determination includes the right to determine their own institutions and government authorities, to develop and maintain their own rules, customs, worldview, ways of development and life projects, to make internal decisions they consider more appropriate for the preservation or protection of their purposes.

In addition, for the Court, the right to self-determination of indigenous peoples comprises, at least, two specific dimensions. The external dimension includes the right to participate in decisions that affects the indigenous groups, which require prior consultations with the respective communities. It also includes the right to political participation of indigenous communities in the national Congress. The internal dimension comprises the recognition of the autonomy and self-governance of communities, so that they may create and apply the rules in their constituency, as well as the judicial power, although subject to constitutional standards (Sentence T-973 of 2009).

Because of conflicts of jurisdiction arising between the ordinary and indigenous courts, the Constitutional Court recognized that indigenous jurisdiction was not subject to the issuance of a law of coordination (Sentence T-254 of 1994). The Court also held that constitutional provisions have immediate applicability and the indigenous jurisdiction is subject to the procedural rules established by traditional authorities and by the Constitution (Sentence C-139 of 1996).

3.2.4 Indigenous People's Rights in the Ecuatorian Constitution

The Constitution of Ecuador is a cutting-edge document in terms of politics of recognition. When compared to other countries, the Ecuadorian Constitution is certainly among the most advanced when it comes to respecting cultural diversity.

Among the fundamental principles of the Republic of Ecuador are sovereignty, interculturalism and plurinationality, as well as the recognition of indigenous languages as official languages for the intercultural relations and the duty of the government to promote national unity in the face of diversity (Articles 1-3).

Since Ecuador is a multinational State, the constituent laid down the rules on dual citizenship, which allow individuals to hold both the Ecuadorian and the indigenous nationality, and the exercise of constitutional rights was ensured to every individual and people inside the country (Articles 6 and 10).

Concerning the rights of welfare, the Constitution secured the individual right to develop and maintain a cultural identity, to decide about one's membership to a cultural community, as well as the right to express the cultural identity and to have access to diverse cultural expressions (Articles 21 and 23).

It also provided collective rights related to the groups of priority attention, including children, youth, seniors, people with disabilities, and people with serious illnesses and other (Title II, Chap. 3). Those groups have in common the need for State protection because of their situation of vulnerability (Article 35). However, it is important to note that ethnic groups are not mentioned among vulnerable groups, but as a separate category (Title II, Chap. 4). Cultural difference does not imply vulnerability; it is the basis double-nationality (Article 56), which requires a specific set of rules, comprising rights and duties arising from this special condition.

The Article 57 of the Ecuatorian Constitution brings a long list of indigenous peoples' collective rights. The most relevant rights for the self-determination of indigenous peoples are the rights to maintain and develop their own ways of life and social organization, to create and exercise authority, to enact and enforce their law, to establish and maintain representative organizations, to participate in official bodies and in the development of public policies, to be consulted before the adoption of a legislative measure that might affect them, and the right to maintain and develop cooperative relations with other peoples. It must be highlighted, however, that the right to self-determination does not allow indigenous peoples to violate fundamental rights of any person (indigenous or not), especially the rights of women, children, and adolescents.

Finally, the Constitution also recognizes the indigenous peoples the power to establish courts (Article 171). They interpret and apply the law of the cultural group in their territorial scope, bearing in mind the respect for constitutional norms and international instruments, while the ordinary jurisdiction exercises the judicial review.

3.2.5 The Protection of Indigenous People in the 1988 Brazilian Constitution

The Constitution of the Federative Republic of Brazil was enacted in 1988, in the context of revision of international standards on the rights of indigenous peoples (it predates the adoption of the ILO Convention n. 169). Although the Brazilian constituent has not used the term "indigenous peoples," but only "Indians," and the term "self-determination" has been used only as a principle of international relations (Article 4, III), the rights of indigenous peoples are constitutionally recognized in line with the new international paradigms.

The socio-cultural rights, which are essential for the exercise of self-determination, are ensured by the Constitution to indigenous peoples. It recognizes indigenous social organization, their customs, languages, beliefs, and traditions (Article 231). To guarantee them, the State should support and encourage the appreciation and dissemination of cultural expressions, giving specific protection to expressions of indigenous culture, which is part of the "national civilizing process," along with popular and African-Brazilian cultures (Article 215). Regarding the right to education, although the Portuguese language is the official language of Brazil (Article 13), there is a command for accommodation of diversity. Indigenous communities are allowed to use their mother tongues and their own learning processes in elementary education (Article 210, §2), which is free and characterized by compulsory attendance (Article 208, I).

A key factor for the promotion of indigenous self-determination is the right to land, and it is expressly provided by the Constitution (Article 231, §1). Although considered property of the Union (Article 20, XI), the permanent possession of the land and the use of its resources are provided to indigenous peoples (Article 231, §2).

Indigenous people, their communities, and their organizations have also the right to take legal action to defend their rights and interests (Article 232). Although there is an institutional duty of prosecutors to intervene in all stages of the proceedings, once the Constitution recognizes the procedural capacity of indigenous people, it rejects the integrationist ideology and the tutelage mechanism, which was prevalent in the system that preceded it.

As for the judiciary, there is no recognition or creation of an indigenous jurisdiction. The Constitution gives the Union the power to legislate on indigenous people's issues (Article 22, XIV), to the Public Prosecutor Office is given the power to defend the interests and rights of indigenous peoples in court (Article 129, V), and Federal Courts are assigned jurisdiction to adjudicate the dispute over indigenous rights (Article 109, XI).

Although the Constitution was promulgated in 1988, Law n. 6.001 of 1973 is still in force despite its assimilationist inspiration. "The Indian Statute," as it is called, regulates the legal status of indigenous people and their communities, "in order to preserve their culture and integrate them progressively and harmoniously to the national communion" (Article 1).

According to the Indian Statute (Articles 7-9), the integrationist ideal should be accomplished through the tutelage regime, which is exercised by the Union through the official Indian agency (the Indian Protection Service (SPI) from 1910 to 1967, which was succeeded by the National Indian Foundation (FUNAI), by means of Law n. 5.371 of 1967). In establishing the tutelage regime, the Statute reproduced the same ideology that guided the drafting of the former Civil Code of 1916 (Article 6), which considered indigenous people as "relatively incapable" individuals (the 2002 Civil Code does not consider them as such).

However, this system is clearly incompatible with the new Constitution, the ILO Convention n. 169 and the UN and OAS Declarations on the rights of indigenous peoples, in which cultural otherness does not imply inferiority nor inadequacy. For this reason, the integrationist mechanisms provided by the Indian Statute should be regarded as unconstitutional. As an example of the implementation of the new multicultural perspective is the National Policy for the Territorial and Environmental Management of Indigenous Lands (PNGATI), which defines as one of its guidelines the socio-cultural autonomy of indigenous peoples (Decree n. 7.747 of 2012, Article 3).

In respect of indigenous self-determination in Brazil, there is a recent decision of the Federal Supreme Court, known as the "Raposa Serra do Sol" case (Petition n. 3388 RR of 2009). In deciding a question of demarcation of indigenous land in the State of Roraima, the Supreme Court, besides setting 19 parameters or safeguards that give legitimacy to the definition of the protected area, it made some considerations that are relevant to this study. Firstly, the Court explained that the term "lands," which is used by the Constitution, clearly assumes a socio-cultural meaning and cannot be used as the grounds for the recognition of political independence of indigenous peoples. Secondly, indigenous lands are not independent territories or States of the Federation, so that indigenous groups neither form a federated entity nor they have normative stature to appear before the international legal order. Thirdly, the court ruled that the land demarcation is an affirmative action to ensure the rights of indigenous peoples over the occupied areas, thus promoting the compensation of historically accumulated disadvantages and the protection of cultural identity, as part of a fraternal constitutionalism.

This decision provoked intense controversy that prompted the filing of a Motion for Clarification, requiring a new manifestation of the Supreme Court mainly in relation to the 19 parameters, which occurred on October 2013. In this ruling, the Court clarified the parameters for the demarcation process, affirming that these standards are not binding on other cases of demarcation, although they constitute an important judicial precedent. In addition, the Supreme Court recognized the impact of its decision on other relevant cultural dimension of self-determination. In spite of not being judicially binding to other cases, the Presidency of the Republic approved the Opinion n. 001/2017/GAB/CGU/AGU on July 2017, in order to apply those standards to all cases regarding demarcation of indigenous lands. However, the President also adopted the controversial thesis of the "time frame" ("*marco temporal*"), which means that only the lands occupied by indigenous communities and those lands under legal or factual dispute at the time of the promulgation of the Federal Constitution (October 05, 1989) are protected.

To face the question of the permanence of non-indigenous religious temples and authorities in indigenous lands, the Court pointed out that although the constitutional rules aim to ensure a unique space where indigenous people can maintain their traditions and live, it does not mean a duty of necessary or complete isolation. On the one hand, the constituent rejected the integrationist ideal of assimilation of the indigenous culture by the majority one, on the other, it has not prevented them to decide whether to contact with other groups and ideas. The court also stated that the government has the duty to protect indigenous peoples and their lands, as well as to organize and supervise the entry, stay, and exit of non-indigenous people (including missionaries). However, the court made clear that this duty may not be understood as cultural dirigisme promoted by the State, since public authorities must respect the autonomy of indigenous individuals and communities, which hold the power to decide on these matters.

Although the Brazilian Constitution cannot be ranked among the most protective when compared to other Latin American constitutions, it implicitly establishes the self-determination as the paradigm to be observed by the State and the majority society in their relationship with indigenous peoples. This new paradigm also requires the immediate elimination of the system of tutelage provided by the Indian Statute and the removal of any policies of integrationist or traditionalist nature.

3.3 Final Remarks on the Right to Self-determination

The right to self-determination of indigenous peoples plays an increasingly central role in the international legal order. The OAS and UN declarations on the rights of indigenous peoples reinforced the aspiration that indigenous people and their communities should have the right, *inter alia*, to freely determine their ways of life and cultures, and to practice their languages and traditions. Self-determination is a collective right, which is limited by individual human rights and regarded as a necessary condition for the protection of indigenous peoples within independent and sovereign States, as well as for the accommodation of ethnic diversity.

Concerning the Latin American countries, the right to self-determination has been incorporated into domestic legal systems over the past three decades. There was, therefore, a departure from colonizing ideologies, characterized by the differentiation of civilization/savagery that prompted the promotion of policies either of assimilationist or of isolationist nature. In a comparative way, it might be stated that the Bolivian, Ecuadorian, Colombian, and Venezuelan constitutions have a higher level of constitutional recognition of indigenous peoples and their collective rights. On a lower level should be positioned the Brazilian constitution, for it has brought a less protective set of rules (at least formally). What is needed, then, is to reshape the legislation (especially the Brazilian Indian Statute) according to the Federal Constitution and international standards to recognize the equality of cultures and to explicitly abolish the indigenous tutelage regime. There should be special protections for indigenous peoples based on their vulnerability, without, however, treating them as incapable or inferior.

4 Freedom of Religion or Belief and the Rights of Indigenous Peoples

4.1 The Protection of Freedom of Religion or Belief

The core of democracy is civil and political rights, and one of the most important of these rights is freedom of religion and belief. National constitutions and international covenants on human rights have regarded religious liberty as a freedom so foundational and precious that it should be guaranteed by law. By protecting all dimensions of freedom of religion or belief as well as equality and non-discrimination, the freedom to believe and to manifest religion or belief is guaranteed not only to members of majority and long-established religions, but also to members of minority groups, new religious movements, and indigenous religious traditions.

4.1.1 Freedom of Religion or Belief Within the UN Human Rights System

Within the UN system, the basic sources for the protection of freedom of religion or belief include the Universal Declaration of Human Rights, the International Covenant on Civil and Political Rights,[5] the Declaration on the Elimination of All Forms of Intolerance and of Discrimination Based on Religion or Belief, the International Covenant on Economic, Social and Cultural Rights, the International Convention on the Protection of the Rights of All Migrant Workers and Members of Their Families, and the Convention on the Rights of the Child. Resolutions of the Human Rights Council, General Assembly and other organs of the UN, in conjunction with the Human Rights Committee General Comment n. 22 are also important for the understanding of the several dimensions recognized or attributed to this right by the UN.[6]

Freedom of religion or belief includes the protection of:

1. Freedom to adopt, change, or renounce a religion or belief,[7]

---

[5] Article 18.

[6] See International Standards on Freedom of Religion or Belief—Digest on Freedom of Religion or Belief. Available at http://www.ohchr.org/EN/Issues/FreedomReligion/Pages/Standards.aspx. For a comment on this catalogue, see Bielefeldt, Ghanea and Wiener (2016).

[7] Universal Declaration, Article 18. "Everyone has the right to freedom of thought, conscience and religion; this right includes freedom to change his religion or belief [...]."

International Covenant on Civil and Political Rights, Article 18.1: "Everyone shall have the right to freedom of thought, conscience and religion. This right shall include freedom to have or to adopt a religion or belief of his choice [...]."

Declaration on the Elimination of All Forms of Intolerance and of Discrimination Based on Religion or Belief, Article 1.1: "Everyone shall have the right to freedom of thought, conscience and religion. This right shall include freedom to have a religion or whatever belief of his choice [...]."

2. Freedom from coercion,[8]
3. The right to manifest one's religion or belief,[9]

Human Rights Committee general comment 22, para. 3: "Article 18 does not permit any limitations whatsoever on the freedom of thought and conscience or the freedom to have or adopt a religion or belief of one's choice"; para. 5: "The Committee observes that the freedom to 'have or to adopt' a religion or belief necessarily entails the freedom to choose a religion or belief, including the right to replace one's current religion or belief with another or to adopt atheistic views, as well as the right to retain one's religion or belief."

[8]Universal Declaration, Article 18. "Everyone has the right to freedom of thought, conscience and religion; this right includes freedom […] either alone or in community with others and in public or private, to manifest his religion or belief in teaching, practice, worship and observance."

International Covenant on Civil and Political Rights, Article 18.2: "No one shall be subject to coercion which would impair his freedom to have or to adopt a religion or belief of his choice."

Declaration on the Elimination of All Forms of Intolerance and of Discrimination Based on Religion or Belief, Article 1.2: "No one shall be subject to coercion which would impair his freedom to have a religion or belief of his choice."

General Comment n. 22, para. 5: "Article 18.2 bars coercion that would impair the right to have or adopt a religion or belief, including the use of threat of physical force or penal sanctions to compel believers or non-believers to adhere to their religious beliefs and congregations, to recant their religion or belief or to convert. Policies or practices having the same intention or effect, such as, for example, those restricting access to education, medical care, employment or the rights guaranteed by Article 25 and other provisions of the Covenant, are similarly inconsistent with Article 18.2. The same protection is enjoyed by holders of all beliefs of a non-religious nature."

[9]International Covenant on Civil and Political Rights, Article 18.1: "Everyone shall have the right to freedom of thought, conscience and religion. This right shall include freedom […] either individually or in community with others and in public or private, to manifest his religion or belief in worship, observance, practice and teaching."; Article 18.3: "Freedom to manifest one's religion or beliefs may be subject only to such limitations as are prescribed by law and are necessary to protect public safety, order, health, or morals or the fundamental rights and freedoms of others."

Declaration on the Elimination of All Forms of Intolerance and of Discrimination Based on Religion or Belief, Article 1.1: "Everyone shall have the right to freedom of thought, conscience and religion. This right shall include freedom to have a religion or whatever belief of his choice, and freedom, either individually or in community with others and in public or private, to manifest his religion or belief in worship, observance, practice and teaching"; Article 1.3: "Freedom to manifest one's religion or belief may be subject only to such limitations as are prescribed by law and are

4. Freedom to worship,[10]
5. Places of worship,[11]

necessary to protect public safety, order, health or morals or the fundamental rights and freedoms of others."

General Comment n. 22, para. 4: "The freedom to manifest religion or belief in worship, observance, practice and teaching encompasses a broad range of acts. The concept of worship extends to ritual and ceremonial acts giving direct expression to belief, as well as various practices integral to such acts, including the building of places of worship, the use of ritual formulae, and objects, the display of symbols, and the observance of holidays and days of rest. The observance and practice of religion or belief may include not only ceremonial acts but also such customs as the observance of dietary regulations, the wearing of distinctive clothing or head coverings, participation in rituals associated with certain stages of life, and the use of a particular language, customarily spoken by a group. In addition, the practice and teaching of religion or belief includes acts integral to the conduct by religious groups of their basic affairs, such as freedom to choose their religious leaders, priests and teachers, the freedom to establish seminaries or religious schools and the freedom to prepare and distribute religious texts or publications."

[10]Declaration on the Elimination of All Forms of Intolerance and of Discrimination Based on Religion or Belief, Article 6.a: "In accordance with Article 1 of the present Declaration, and subject to the provisions of Article 1, para. 3, the right to freedom of thought, conscience, religion or belief shall include, inter alia, the following freedoms: To worship or assemble in connection with a religion or belief […]"; Article 6.c: "To make, acquire and use the necessary articles and materials related to the rites or customs of a religion or belief."

Commission on Human Rights resolution 2005/40 (para. 4.d), Human Rights Council resolution 6/37 (para. 9.g) and General Assembly resolution 65/211 (para. 12.g) urges States "To ensure, in particular, the right of all persons to worship or assemble in connection with a religion or belief […]."

General Comment n. 22, para. 4: "The concept of worship extends to ritual and ceremonial acts giving direct expression to belief, as well as various practices integral to such acts, including […] the use of ritual formulae, and objects […]."

[11]Declaration on the Elimination of All Forms of Intolerance and of Discrimination Based on Religion or Belief, Article 6.1: "To worship or assemble in connection with a religion or belief, and to establish and maintain places for these purposes."

Human Rights Council Resolution 6/37, Article 9.e: "The Human Rights Council urges States […] To exert the utmost efforts, in accordance with their national legislation and in conformity with international human rights and humanitarian law, to ensure that religious places, sites, shrines and

6. Religious symbols,[12]
7. Observance of holidays and days of rest,[13]

symbols are fully respected and protected and to take additional measures in cases where they are vulnerable to desecration or destruction;" 9.g: "To ensure, in particular, the right of all persons to worship or assemble in connection with a religion or belief and to establish and maintain places for these purposes […]."

General Comment n. 22, para. 4: "The concept of worship extends to […] the building of places of worship."

[12]Declaration on the Elimination of All Forms of Intolerance and of Discrimination Based on Religion or Belief, Article 6.c: "To make, acquire and use to an adequate extent the necessary articles and materials related to the rites or customs of a religion or belief."

Commission on Human Rights Resolution 2005/40, Article 4.b: "The Commission on Human Rights urges States […] To exert the utmost efforts, in accordance with their national legislation and in conformity with international human rights law, to ensure that religious places, sites, shrines and religious expressions are fully respected and protected and to take additional measures in cases where they are vulnerable to desecration or destruction"; Article 4.c "The concept of worship extends to […] the display of symbols […] The observance and practice of religion or belief may include not only ceremonial acts but also such customs as […] the wearing of distinctive clothing or head coverings […]."

[13]Declaration on the Elimination of All Forms of Intolerance and of Discrimination Based on Religion or Belief, Article 6.h: "To observe days of rest and to celebrate holidays and ceremonies in accordance with the precepts of one's religion or belief."

General Comment n. 22, para. 4: "The concept of worship extends to […] the observance of holidays and days of rest."

8. Appointing clergy,[14]
9. Teaching and disseminating materials (including missionary activity),[15]
10. The right of parents to ensure the religious and moral education of their children,[16]

[14]Declaration on the Elimination of All Forms of Intolerance and of Discrimination Based on Religion or Belief, Article 6.g: "To train, appoint, elect or designate by succession appropriate leaders [...]."

General Comment n. 22, para. 4: "In addition, the practice and teaching of religion or belief includes acts integral to the conduct by religious groups of their basic affairs, such as the freedom to choose their religious leaders, priests and teachers [...]."

[15]Declaration on the Elimination of All Forms of Intolerance and of Discrimination Based on Religion or Belief, Article 6.d: "To write, issue and disseminate relevant publications in these areas"; Article 6.e: "To teach a religion or belief in places suitable for these purposes."

Commission on Human Rights Resolution 2005/40, para. 4.d and Human Rights Council Resolution 6/37, para. 9.g: "Urges States [...] To ensure, in particular, [...] the right of all persons to write, issue and disseminate relevant publications in these areas."

General Comment n. 22, para. 4: "In addition, the practice and teaching of religion or belief includes acts integral to the conduct by religious groups of their basic affairs, [...] the freedom to establish seminaries or religious schools and the freedom to prepare and distribute religious texts or publications."

[16]International Covenant on Civil and Political Rights, Article 18.4: "The States Parties to the present Covenant undertake to have respect for the liberty of parents and, when applicable, legal guardians to ensure the religious and moral education of their children in conformity with their own convictions."

Convention on the Rights of the Child, Article 14.2: "States Parties shall respect the rights and duties of the parents and, when applicable, legal guardians, to provide direction to the child in the exercise of his or her right in a manner consistent with the evolving capacities of the child"; Article 29.1.c: "The development of respect for the child's parents, his or her own cultural identity, language and values, for the national values of the country in which the child is living, the country from which he or she may originate, and for civilizations different from his or her own."

International Covenant on Economic, Social and Cultural Rights, Article 13.3: "The States Parties to the present Covenant undertake to have respect for the liberty of parents and, when applicable, legal guardians to [...] ensure the religious and moral education of their children in conformity with their own convictions."

International Convention on the Protection of the Rights of All Migrant Workers and Members of Their Families, Article 12.4: "States Parties to the present Convention undertake to have respect for the liberty of parents, at least one of whom is a migrant worker, and, when applicable, legal

11. Registration,[17]
12. Communicate with individuals and communities on religious matters at the national and international level,[18]
13. Establish and maintain charitable and humanitarian institutions/solicit and receive funding,[19]
14. Conscientious objection.[20]

Although restrictions or limitations are not allowed to the internal component of freedom of religion or belief (*forum internum*), which includes the right to form, adopt, hold or change inner convictions and beliefs, the freedom to manifest religion with all its dimensions (*forum externum*) is not an absolute right, as it is subject to

---

guardians to ensure the religious and moral education of their children in conformity with their own convictions."

Declaration on the Elimination of All Forms of Intolerance and of Discrimination Based on Religion or Belief, Article 5: "1. The parents or, as the case may be, the legal guardians of the child have the right to organize the life within the family in accordance with their religion or belief and bearing in mind the moral education in which they believe the child should be brought up. 2. Every child shall enjoy the right to have access to education in the matter of religion or belief in accordance with the wishes of his parents or, as the case may be, legal guardians, and shall not be compelled to receive teaching on religion or belief against the wishes of his parents or legal guardians, the best interests of the child being the guiding principle. [...] 4. In the case of a child who is not under the care either of his parents or of legal guardians, due account shall be taken of their expressed wishes or of any other proof of their wishes in the matter of religion or belief, the best interests of the child being the guiding principle [...]."

[17]Commission on Human Rights Resolution 2005/40, para. 4.c and 4.e, Human Rights Council Resolution 6/37, para 12.e and 12.h: "Urges States [...] To review, whenever relevant, existing registration practices in order to ensure the right of all persons to manifest their religion or belief, alone or in community with others and in public or in private" and "Urges States [...] "To ensure that, in accordance with appropriate national legislation and in conformity with international human rights law, the freedom for all persons and members of groups to establish and maintain religious, charitable or humanitarian institutions is fully respected and protected."

[18]Declaration on the Elimination of All Forms of Intolerance and of Discrimination Based on Religion or Belief, Article 6.i: "The right to freedom of thought, conscience, religion or belief includes the freedom, "To establish and maintain communications with individuals and communities in matters of religion and belief at the national and international levels."

[19]Declaration on the Elimination of All Forms of Intolerance and of Discrimination Based on Religion or Belief, Article 6.b: "To establish and maintain appropriate charitable or humanitarian institutions"; Article 6.f: "To solicit and receive voluntary financial and other contributions from individuals and institutions."

Commission on Human Rights Resolution 2005/40, para. 4.e and Human Rights Council Resolution 6/37, para. 12.h: "Urges States [...] To ensure that, in accordance with appropriate national legislation and in conformity with international human rights law, the freedom for all persons and members of groups to establish and maintain religious, charitable or humanitarian institutions is fully respected and protected."

[20]General Comment n. 22, para. 11: "Many individuals have claimed the right to refuse to perform military service (conscientious objection) on the basis that such right derives from their freedoms

limitations.[21] Article 18.3 of the International Covenant on Civil and Political Rights states that "Freedom to manifest one's religion or beliefs may be subject only to such limitations as are prescribed by law and are necessary to protect public safety, order, health, or morals or the fundamental rights and freedoms of others." Therefore, although limitations on the right to manifest religion are permitted, they must meet the requirements of the following legitimacy test: (1) Is the limitation justified by a legitimate ground (public safety, order, health, or morals or the fundamental rights and freedoms of others)? (2) Is the limitation prescribed by law? (3) Is the limitation necessary or proportionate?

In addition, there are specific restrictions imposed to those external dimensions of freedom of religion or belief, such as the limitations to the rights of the parents to organize the life within the family in accordance with their religion or belief[22] as well as the prohibition of any advocacy of religious hatred that constitutes incitement to discrimination, hostility, or violence (religiously motivated hate speech).[23]

---

under Article 18. In response to such claims, a growing number of States have in their laws exempted from compulsory military service citizens who genuinely hold religious or other beliefs that forbid the performance of military service and replaced it with alternative national service. The Covenant does not explicitly refer to a right to conscientious objection, but the Committee believes that such a right can be derived from Article 18, inasmuch as the obligation to use lethal force may seriously conflict with the freedom of conscience and the right to manifest one's religion or belief. When this right is recognized by law or practice, there shall be no differentiation among conscientious objectors on the basis of the nature of their particular beliefs; likewise, there shall be no discrimination against conscientious objectors because they have failed to perform military service. The Committee invites States parties to report on the conditions under which persons can be exempted from military service on the basis of their rights under Article 18 and on the nature and length of alternative national service."

[21]General Comment n. 22, para. 3 "Article 18 distinguishes the freedom of thought, conscience, religion or belief from the freedom to manifest religion or belief. It does not permit any limitations whatsoever on the freedom of thought and conscience or on the freedom to have or adopt a religion or belief of one's choice. These freedoms are protected unconditionally, as is the right of everyone to hold opinions without interference in Article 19.1. In accordance with Articles 18.2 and 17, no one can be compelled to reveal his thoughts or adherence to a religion or belief."

[22]Declaration on the Elimination of All Forms of Intolerance and of Discrimination Based on Religion or Belief, Article 5.3: "The child shall be protected from any form of discrimination on the ground of religion or belief. He shall be brought up in a spirit of understanding, tolerance, friendship among peoples, peace and universal brotherhood, respect for freedom of religion or belief of others, and in full consciousness that his energy and talents should be devoted to the service of his fellow men"; Article 5.5: "Practices of a religion or beliefs in which a child is brought up must not be injurious to his physical or mental health or to his full development, taking into account Article 1, para. 3, of the present Declaration."

[23]International Covenant on Civil and Political Rights, Article 20.2: "Any advocacy of national, racial or religious hatred that constitutes incitement to discrimination, hostility or violence shall be prohibited by law." See also the Rabat Plan of Action on the prohibition of advocacy of national, racial or religious hatred that constitutes incitement to discrimination, hostility or violence."

4.1.2 Freedom of Religion or Belief Within the OAS

There are three core documents that protect freedom of religion or belief within the OAS.[24] Firstly, the American Declaration is a source of international obligations for the member States and contains the fundamental human rights referred to in the OAS Charter (cf. Advisory Opinion OC-10/89, para. 42-48). Secondly, by the American Convention, states undertook an obligation to respect and ensure to all persons subject to their jurisdiction rights and freedoms without any discrimination for reasons of religion, among other reasons (Articles 1 and 12). Lastly, the Additional Protocol to the American Convention on Human Rights in the Area of Economic, Social, and Cultural Rights also known as "Protocol of San Salvador" (adopted in San Salvador, El Salvador, 1988), protects the exercise of social, economic, and cultural rights without discrimination of any kind (Article 3).

Freedom of religion and belief is a right that might be exercised individually or collectively. The American Declaration establishes that every person is entitled to the right to religious freedom, which includes freedom to adopt, manifest and practice religion both in public and in private (Article 3). The right to associate with others to promote, exercise, and protect legitimate interests, including interests of a religious nature, is also protected (Article 22, American Declaration). Moreover, freedom of religion and conscience is affirmed as one of the civil and political rights in the American Convention, which includes freedom to maintain or to change religion or belief, to profess or disseminate religion or belief, either individually or together with others, in public or in private, and not to be subject to restrictions that might impair his/her freedom to maintain or to change his religion or beliefs (Article 12.1-2). Additionally, the Convention affirms that every person may associate freely for religious purposes (Article 16.1).

Other documents also protect individuals or groups from violations of their freedom of religion or belief and from discrimination, such as Inter-American Convention on the Prevention, Punishment and Eradication of Violence against Women also known as "Convention of Belem do Para" (1994), the Declaration of Principles on Freedom of Expression (2000), the Inter-American Democratic Charter (2001), and the Principles and Best Practices on the Protection of Persons Deprived of Liberty in the Americas (2001). Furthermore, there are several joint statements that cover issues on religion-state relations and religious freedom, which were signed by the UN Special Rapporteur for Freedom of Expression, the Representative on Freedom of the Media of the Organization for Security and Co-operation in Europe (OSCE), the Special Rapporteur for Freedom of Expression of the OAS, and the Special Rapporteur on Freedom of Expression and Access to Information of the African Commission on Human and Peoples' Rights, namely the Joint Declaration on International Mechanisms for Promoting Freedom of Expression (2006), the Joint Declaration on Defamation of Religions, and Anti-Terrorism and Anti-Extremism Legislation (2008), and the Tenth Anniversary Joint Declaration: Ten Key Challenges to Freedom of Expression in the Next Decade (2010).

[24] See Alves (2016).

4.1.3 Freedom of Religion or Belief in Latin America

Concerning the Latin American countries discussed in the present study, freedom of religion or belief is broadly protected by the domestic legislation.

The Brazilian Constitution states that "freedom of conscience and belief is inviolable, assuring free exercise of religious beliefs and guaranteeing, as set forth in law, protection of places of worship and their rites" (Article 5, VI) and guarantees the right to conscientious objection, since "no one shall be deprived of any rights because of religious beliefs or philosophical or political convictions, unless invoked in order to be exempted from a legal obligation imposed upon all by one refusing to perform an alternative service established by law" (Article 5, VIII).

Colombia ensures that "freedom of religion is guaranteed. Every individual has the right to freely profess his/her religion and to disseminate it individually or collectively." The Constitution adds that "All religious faiths and churches are equally free before the law" (Article 19).

The Bolivian Constitution requires that "The State respects and guarantees freedom of religion and spiritual beliefs, according to their view of the world. The State is independent of religion" (Article 4) and that "Bolivians have the following rights: [...] 3. To freedom of belief, spirituality, religion and worship, expressed individually or collectively, in public and in private, for legal purposes. 4. To freedom of assembly and association, publicly and privately, for legal purposes" (Article 21).

In Ecuador, Article 66.8 of the Constitution recognizes the "right to practice, keep, change, profess in public or private one's religion or beliefs and to disseminate them individually or collectively, with the constraints imposed by respect for the rights of others." It also requires that "The State shall protect voluntary religious practice, as well the expression of those who profess no religion whatsoever, and shall favor an environment of plurality and tolerance."

Finally, Article 59 of the Venezuelan Constitution states that "The State guarantees the freedom of worship and religion. All persons have the right to profess their religious faith and cults, and express their beliefs in private or in public, by teaching and other practices, provided such beliefs are not contrary to moral, good customs and public order," and adds that "No one shall invoke religious beliefs or discipline as a means of evading compliance with law or preventing another person from exercising his or her rights." It protects religious organizations as it affirms that "The autonomy and independence of religious confessions and churches is likewise guaranteed, subject only to such limitations as may derive from this Constitution and the law." Regarding the moral education of children, "Father and Mother are entitled to have their sons and daughters receive religious education in accordance with their convictions" (Article 59).

4.2 *Freedom of Religion or Belief, Minority Rights, and the Rights of Indigenous Peoples*

Besides the significant guarantees that International Human Rights Law and the National Constitutions provide for the free exercise of religion or belief, human rights instruments add special safeguards to members of indigenous groups.[25] Within the UN, Article 27 of the International Covenant on Civil and Political Rights[26] together with the Article 2.1 of the Declaration on the Rights of Persons Belonging to National or Ethnic, Religious and Linguistic Minorities[27] allow the adoption of special measures to address discrimination and inequality,[28] while provide each member of indigenous minority groups with the right to practice and profess his or her own religion in community with other members of his or her group,[29] a protection that Article 30 of Convention on Rights of the Child[30] grants to indigenous children in particular.

In addition to the protections under the freedom of religion or belief framework and minority rights framework, due to the specific characteristics of indigenous groups (for instance, that they have suffered from historic injustices and discrimination as a result of colonization and land dispossession[31] as well as their special and

---

[25]For a discussion on the intersections of religious and minotiries protections, see Ghanea (2008, 2012).

[26]"In those States in which ethnic, religious or linguistic minorities exist, persons belonging to such minorities shall not be denied the right, in community with the other members of their group, to enjoy their own culture, to profess and practise their own religion, or to use their own language."

[27]"Persons belonging to national or ethnic, religious and linguistic minorities (hereinafter referred to as persons belonging to minorities) have the right to enjoy their own culture, to profess and practise their own religion, and to use their own language, in private and in public, freely and without interference or any form of discrimination."

[28]Recommendations on Guaranteeing the Rights of Religious Minorities (A/HRC/25/66): "16. States should consider, where appropriate, special measures that address discrimination and inequality experienced by persons belonging to religious minorities. Institutional attention to religious minorities should be strengthened as appropriate to facilitate such measures and improve the mainstreaming of minority issues in national-level bodies, including government ministries or departments working on central concerns for minorities, national human rights institutions, consultative bodies and mechanisms, and other relevant national entities."

[29]See also Wheatley (2005).

[30]"In those States in which ethnic, religious or linguistic minorities or persons of indigenous origin exist, a child belonging to such a minority or who is indigenous shall not be denied the right, in community with other members of his or her group, to enjoy his or her own culture, to profess and practise his or her own religion, or to use his or her own language."

[31]See, for example, the Report submitted by the Special Rapporteur on Freedom of Religion or Belief (Mrs. Asma Jahandir) to the Human Rights Council (A/HRC/13/40 2009, para. 37): "There are also further issues of concern in relation to her mandate, which seem to be more prevalent in particular regions or countries. For example, some domestic registration procedures for religious communities are applied in a discriminatory manner by the authorities, often curbing the freedom of religion or belief of minority communities such as new religious movements or indigenous peoples. In addition, she is concerned about undue State interference in religious teaching and dissemination of related publications, for example when the authorities censor, monitor and write

spiritual connection with their lands and resources[32]), the Declaration on the Rights Indigenous Peoples protect the collective dimension of the indigenous life, including their self-determination (as seen above) and their spiritual and religious traditions. Article 12.1 states that "Indigenous peoples have the right to manifest, practice, develop and teach their spiritual and religious traditions, customs and ceremonies; the right to maintain, protect, and have access in privacy to their religious and cultural sites; the right to the use and control of their ceremonial objects; and the right to the repatriation of their human remains."

Within the Inter-American System, along with the general human rights protections under the American Declaration on the Rights and Duties of Man and the American Convention on Human Rights, which include *inter alia* freedom of religion or belief, prohibition of discrimination, and the right to take part in the cultural life of the community, Article 16 of the American Declaration on the Rights of Indigenous Peoples provides for the right of indigenous peoples to freely "exercise their own spirituality and beliefs and, by virtue of that right, to practice, develop, transmit, and teach their traditions, customs, and ceremonies, and to carry them out in public and in private, whether individually or collectively" (Article 16.1). They are also protected from "pressures or impositions, or any other type of coercive measures that might impair or limit their right freely to exercise their indigenous spirituality and beliefs" (Article 16.2), and they "have the right to preserve, protect, and access their sacred sites, including their burial grounds, to use and control their sacred objects and relics, and to recover their human remains" (Article 16.3). States shall adopt effect measures to advance respect for indigenous beliefs and practices, their symbols, ceremonies,

sermons or persecute religious leaders. Furthermore, the Special Rapporteur has noticed a number of restrictions imposed on different forms of religious expression, for example, on the wearing of distinctive clothing or head coverings. At the same time, she is concerned about reports of women who are forced to wear religious dress in public in certain countries."

[32] See, for example, the Report submitted by the Special Rapporteur on Freedom of Religion or Belief (Mr. Abdelfattah Amor) after his country visit to Argentina, presented to the Comission on Human Rights (E/CN.4/2002/73/Add.1, para. 112-113 and 150): "C. Situation of indigenous peoples [...] 112. The principal problem regarding freedom of religion and freedom to manifest one's religion or belief relates to the question of land. Land is the sine qua non for the maintenance and development of an indigenous identity. A Mapuche tenet holds that 'the land does not belong to the Mapuche, the Mapuche belongs to the land'. The land, the source of identity, thus has a religious dimension and meaning for indigenous peoples. It constitutes the matrix for their beliefs and a support for the manifestation of those beliefs. 113. The claims of the indigenous communities regarding the restitution of property thus implicitly embody a religious dimension, namely, access to sacred sites and to graves. The situation varies widely in practice: some provinces have granted definitive community property title to land, others have recognized indigenous lands without granting property title; disputes involving private property have led to instances of expropriation or have yet to be resolved. Serious disputes remain, particularly involving companies (for example, in Patagonia, the expropriation by multinational companies, including Benetton, of land belonging to the Mapuche community), as well as State institutions (for example, the army). In this connection INAI has been criticized for a lack of consultation with indigenous groups, the meagre results obtained and, above all, in the view of some, a paternalistic approach to indigenous issues. [...] 150. [...] The process of returning land to indigenous people, as the touchstone of their identity, is thus a precondition for providing access to holy sites and burial grounds and hence for legitimate religious or spiritual activities."

expressions and protocols, in accordance with international law (Article 16.5), and shall ensure the full enjoyment of the civil, political, economic, social, and cultural rights of indigenous peoples, including "their right to maintain their cultural identity, spiritual and religious traditions, worldview, values and the protection of their religious and cultural sites, and human rights contained in this Declaration" (Article 31.1).[33]

Therefore, the religious life of indigenous peoples is protected under three different frameworks. Firstly, as human beings, they are entitled to freedom of religion or belief. Secondly, as members ethnic, religious or linguistic minority groups, they are protected by the minority rights regime. Finally, as indigenous groups, they are entitled to a group or corporate right to freely determine their own culture and religion, as a result of their group right to self-self-determination. While the former frameworks advance individual aspects of freedom of religion or belief, including the exercise of religion in community with others, the latter protects indigenous peoples *qua* peoples or collective entities.

The three frameworks should be regarded as complementary and interdependent. Although self-determination is ensured by those instruments, it is not an absolute right and may not be used to suppress freedom of religion or belief nor to prevent the existence of religious minorities within indigenous groups—the protection of "minorities within minorities" (Eisenberg and Spinner-Halev 2005). The core of indigenous "less-than-sovereign self-determination" is the autonomy to determine their political status and to pursue their economic, social, and cultural development, which does not include the authority to prohibit or violate individual and minority rights. Article 46.2 of the UN Declaration on the Rights of Indigenous Peoples provides that "In the exercise of the rights enunciated in the present Declaration, human rights and fundamental freedoms of all shall be respected." Similarly, Article 35 of the OAS Declaration on the Rights of Indigenous Peoples states that "Nothing in this Declaration may be interpreted so as to limit, restrict, or deny human rights in any way, or so as to authorize any action that is not in keeping with international human rights law." Furthermore, the International Covenant on Civil and Political Rights

---

[33] In two cases, the Inter-American Court of Human Rights found violations on the rights of members of indigenous groups to freedom of religion and belief: *Plan de Sánchez Massacres vs. Guatemala* (2004, para. 36 and 52) and *Río Negro Massacres v. Guatemala* (2012, para. 153-165). In the latter, the Court considered that Guatemala had violated Article 5.1 of the American Convention, in relation to Articles 12.1 and 1.1 thereof, to the detriment of the members of the community of Río Negro, by failing to protect the right to bury the deceased, to live in their sacred lands and, to freely maintain their social and family structures. In the former, the Court recognized that the state violated Articles 12.2, 12.3, 13.2, and 13.5, since it failed to guarantee freedom to manifest religious, spiritual, and cultural beliefs of the families of the massacre victims and community members. In *Río Negro Massacres v. Guatemala*, the Court also recognized that farewell rites for the dead in accordance to religious beliefs were an important element for the Mayan religion and culture and that, even if the American Convention does not explicitly establish the right to "bury the dead," it had to be protected. The Court also reaffirmed that the special relationship of the indigenous peoples with their ancestral lands is not merely because they constitute their main means of subsistence, but also because they are an integral part of their worldview, religious beliefs ("*sacred* lands") and, consequently, their cultural identity or integrity, which is a fundamental and collective right of the indigenous communities that must be respected in a multicultural, pluralist, and democratic society.

excludes freedom of religion or belief from the rights subject to derogation[34] and the Recommendations on Guaranteeing the Rights of Religious Minorities requires the prohibition of harmful practices based on traditional religion or belief, a protection that limits the power of the group over the individual.[35]

5 Conclusion and Final Remarks

The addition of self-determination to the human rights legal framework poses the problem of how to equate group autonomy and other human rights, which includes issues related to self-determination *vis-à-vis* State intervention to regulate religious practices within an indigenous community, self-determination *vis-à-vis* freedom of religion or belief of the members of other groups (including the majority one) and, self-determination *vis-à-vis* freedom of religion or belief of the members of the indigenous group. Concerning the first issue, self-determination requires the recognition of the individual and collective capacity of indigenous people and that they should not be treated as incapable or mere objects of public policies. States should grant indigenous peoples autonomy and self-government, so that they might freely decide whether they preserve, modify or abandon their ancestral ways of life (the negative dimension of self-determination, or respect for cultural and religious diversity). Secondly, the condition of vulnerability or susceptibility to risks that usually characterizes indigenous peoples demands from States to ensure that communities can exercise the right to self-determination, by means of special measures[36] (the positive dimension of self-determination, or protection of ethnic, religious and linguistic minorities). Finally, the constitutional rules and human rights are legitimate limits to the exercise of the right to self-determination within an independent State. The collective rights of indigenous peoples are not placed above the individual rights of each indigenous person; on the contrary, they are granted to ensure that indigenous individuals are respected as human begins that are "free and equal in dignity

[34]"Article 4.1. In time of public emergency which threatens the life of the nation and the existence of which is officially proclaimed, the States Parties to the present Covenant may take measures derogating from their obligations under the present Covenant to the extent strictly required by the exigencies of the situation, provided that such measures are not inconsistent with their other obligations under international law and do not involve discrimination solely on the ground of race, colour, sex, language, religion or social origin. 2. No derogation from Articles 6, 7, 8 (para. I and 2), 11, 15, 16 and 18 may be made under this provision. [...]."

[35]Recommendations on Guaranteeing the Rights of Religious Minorities (A/HRC/25/66): "25. Harmful traditional religion- or belief-based practices that violate the human rights of any individual should be prohibited by law and addressed in conformity with international standards. Where appropriate, consultations should be undertaken with leaders and members of religious communities to address such issues and their causes."

[36]See also the General Recommendation n. 32 on The meaning and scope of special measures in the International Convention on the Elimination of All Forms [of] Racial Discrimination of the UN Committee on the Elimination of Racial Discrimination.

and rights" (recognition of human freedom, equality and dignity as the limits to self-determination).

Considering the different dimensions and the limits of self-determination, freedom of religion or belief gains a group perspective in the context of the indigenous communities and should include freedoms for, from and within religion or belief:

1. Freedom for religion or belief, or the right of indigenous groups to maintain or change their own religious and cultural traditions without external coercive intervention. For example, the principle of secularism in public institutions: as the group's ("less-than-sovereign") power and authority would be comparable with State's power and authority, one could argue that the indigenous authority should be secular; however, the recognition of self-determination means the recognition of some degree of legal pluralism, as the traditional legal systems should be enforced. Nevertheless, the same documents that recognize freedom for religion limits its extension by protecting individual human rights, which means that the indigenous authorities cannot force someone to follow the traditional religion.
2. External freedom from religion or belief, or their protection against cultural assimilation by the majority culture or religion. It does not mean, however, an obligation of isolation or a requirement of "cultural purity," as self-determination protects not only the maintenance, but also the freedom to decide about their own future in terms of culture and religion. And here is also placed the debate on the limits of intercultural dialogue, cross-cultural exchanges, missionary activities, and proselytism.
3. Internal freedom from religion or belief, or the right to leave or not to practice the community's religion. This dimension protects apostates and non-religious indigenous individuals and practices.
4. Freedom within religion or belief, or the freedom against religious internal oppression and persecution. It allows indigenous persons to dissent, to hold a belief that is different from the orthodox beliefs of the community, which can be exercised individually or in community with others. It ensures that indigenous individuals are free to be dissenters or non-conformists.

While freedom for religion and external freedom from religion protect indigenous peoples against forced assimilation, illegitimate interference and abuses from alien agents, internal freedom from religion and freedom within religion protect individuals against abuses practiced by their own people, also granting protection for the "minorities within minorities." In this sense, any existing religious minorities and other vulnerable population within indigenous communities must also be safeguarded in their human rights, particularly the right to enjoy their culture, to profess and practice their religion and use their language.

References

Aguilar G, Lafosse S, Rojas H, Steward R (2010) The constitutional recognition of indigenous peoples in Latin America. International Law Review Online Companion 2(2):44–96

Alves Rodrigo Vitorino Souza (2015a) Pueblos indígenas, diversidad cultural y el derecho a la autodeterminación: desde el derecho internacional al constitucionalismo latinoamericano. Derecho PUCP, pp 119–138

Alves Rodrigo Vitorino Souza (2015b) Diversidade cultural e o direito à autodeterminação dos povos indígenas. Rev Jurídica da Presidência 16:725–749

Alves Rodrigo Vitorino Souza (2016) Organization of American States. In: Robbers G, Durham WC, Thayer D (eds) Encyclopedia of law and religion. Brill Nijhoff, Leiden and Boston, pp 208–216

Anaya J (1996) Indigenous peoples in international law. Oxford University Press, New York

Bielefeldt H, Ghanea N, Wiener M (2016) Freedom of religion or belief: an international law commentary. Oxford University Press, Oxford

Clavero B (2010) Tribunal Constitucional entre Estado Plurinacional y Pueblos Indígenas: Um Reto Inédito en Las Américas. Memoria Conferencia Internacional Hacia la Construcción del Tribunal Constitucional Plurinacional. Programa de Fortalecimiento a la Concertación y al Estado de Derecho (CONCED-GTZ), La Paz, pp 1–21

Santos BS (2007) La reinvención del Estado y el Estado plurinacional. Obs Soc América Lat VIII:25–46

Dutter LE (2012) Return of the natives: explaining the development and non-development of political action by Indigenous peoples in democratic political systems. Int J Minor Gr Rights 19:453–480

Eisenberg A, Spinner-Halev J (eds) (2005) Minorities within minorities: equality, rights and diversity. Cambridge University Press, Cambridge

Engle K (2011) On fragile architecture: the UN declaration on the rights of Indigenous peoples in the context of human rights. Eur J Int Law 22:141–163

Foster CE (2001) Articulating self-determination in the draft declaration on the rights of Indigenous peoples. Eur J Int Law 12:141–157

Ghanea N (2008) Religious or minority? Examining the realisation of international standards in relation to religious minorities in the Middle East. Relig State Soc 36:303–325

Ghanea N (2012) Are religious minorities really minorities? Oxford J Law Relig 1:57–79

Hannum H (1996) Autonomy, sovereignty and self-determination: the accommodation of conflict in rights. University of Pennsylvania Press, Philadelphia

Kymlicka W (2011) Multicultural Odysseys: navigating the new international politics of diversity. Oxford University Press, Oxford

Musafiri PN (2012) Right to self-determination in international law: towards theorisation of the concept of indigenous peoples/national minority? Int J Minor Gr Rights 19:481–532

Ñáñe OG (2009) Interculturalidad y ciudadanía. Los pueblos indígenas de Venezuela: excluídos origiarios. Anu Grhial, pp 61–68

Wheatley S (2005) Democracy, minorities and international law. Cambridge University Press, Cambridge

Secular or Multi-confessional, that Is the Question: Tensions Within the Argentinean Protestantism During the Religious Freedom Act Negotiations

In Memoriam

Juan Martin Vives

Abstract Argentine law establishes a system of religious freedom without religious equality: It guarantees a privileged status to the Catholic Church, while other churches and religious communities are ruled by a detrimental legislation. Since the restoration of democracy (1983), there have been around twenty bills aimed to rule over religious minorities. This determination to amend the law dealing with Church-State relations coincides with the demographic explosion of religious minorities, particularly Protestantism (*lato* sensu). Protestant churches have played a central role in the demand for revision of the legal system. They claim the Government for a law that ensures both religious freedom and equality. However, the Argentine Protestant churches do not have a unified approach to what "religious equality" means. Some of them seek to obtain benefits like those of the Catholic Church, while others propose a model of separation of Church and State in which no religion obtains such benefits. This has generated an internal tension within the Argentine Protestantism. On the one hand, an attempt has been made to generate a strategy for unity that allows for a unified representation for negotiations with the Government. On the other hand, there is no actual internal agreement on what the outcome of these negotiations should be. This paper addresses the process of legal amendment, from the 1990s to the bill being debated currently, focusing on the tension produced inside Argentine Protestantism.

Keywords Freedom of religion or belief · Equality · Argentina

1 Introduction

As it occurs with many Latin American countries, the Argentinean law poses a system of liberties, but without equality: It guarantees a privileged status for the Catholic

J. M. Vives (✉)
Center for Studies on Law and Religion, Adventist University of Plata, Libertador San Martin, Argentina
e-mail: juanmartin.vives2@e-campus.uab.cat

© Springer Nature Switzerland AG 2020

R. V. S. Alves (ed.), *Latin American Perspectives on Law and Religion*, Law and Religion in a Global Context 3,
https://doi.org/10.1007/978-3-030-46717-3_3

Church, while the other churches and religious communities are ruled by detrimental laws.

Since the reinstatement of democracy in 1983, there have been approximately twenty bills and drafts aimed at ruling religious minorities. They either confirmed or modified the current system.

This intention of modifying the law coincides with the demographic explosion of religious minorities, particularly of Protestantism (*latu* sensu). Although different agents had part in the claims for a revision of the legal system, the Protestant churches clearly were the most remarkable. They demand from the Government a law that guarantees both religious freedom and religious equality.

The Protestant churches, however, do not have a unified criterion as to what constitutes "religious equality." A number of churches aspire to obtain benefits similar to those that the Catholic Church has, while some others propose a model of separation of church and state, in which no church has such benefits. This has produced an inner tension in the Argentinean Protestantism. On the one hand, there is an attempt to create a strategy of unity that would allow a unified representation when dealing with the Government. On the other, there is no agreement on which should be the results of such negotiations.

In the following pages, we will analyze these tensions within the historical framework of Protestantism in Argentina. Later, we will analyze how these tensions have resumed as a consequence of the new Religious Freedom bill, drafted by the President Macri's government. The bill itself will not be analyzed here. Instead, the different reactions that said bill provoked among Argentinean Protestants that will be stressed here.

2 Attempts to Modify the Law

The system of relations between State and religious denominations is rooted in the National Constitution. In Section 2, it is stated that the State supports the Catholic Church financially. Section 14 guarantees religious freedom for all residents in Argentina. Based on this, a legal framework in the infraconstitutional scope has been crafted. This framework rules both the relationship between Church and State and the right to religious freedom, but also constitutes a system that generates disconformities and difficulties among religious minorities.

Considering these difficulties, the need to change the legal system has been pointed out. In the core of the legal system of relations between the State and the minority beliefs, there is the Decree-law 21745, named "Act of Cult". Any foreign spectator would be astonished by how long lasting this law is: dictated in 1980 by a de facto military government, through a procedure that violated the constitutional legislative procedures, it was conceived through the so-called national security doctrine. However, more than thirty years later, it is still in force. Regrettably, the recent passing of the Act 26939, known as "Digesto Jurídico Argentino" [Argentinean Law Digest], has not only failed to eliminate the Decree-law 21745 (unconstitutional, considering its origin), but has rather given it formal validity.

There have been many proposals to replace it. Truth be told, except for a few short periods (as, for example, at the end of President Menem's administration or during the short interregnum of President Duhalde), ever since 1983 the consecutive democratic governments have faced the challenge of replacing the Decree-law with a law that respects religious freedom (Padilla 2009). However, none of those projects has made its way through the parliamentary filters necessary to become an act (Esquivel 2009).

In any case, it is difficult to sustain that any of such drafts offered a complete solution to the difficulties minorities face. On the contrary: All these drafts posted a series of few but hard conditions to be inscribed in the Registry, which in practice equates to halving the religious field in organizations either capable of fulfilling these requisites or not.

Among the restrictions for inscribing in the so-called Registry of Cults, it has been proposed that the religious organizations prove they are the official church of a State with which Argentina keeps diplomatic relations or prove that they have been historically present in the national territory. Naturally, such conditions were to be requested to non-Catholic minorities, since in all drafts Catholicism would continue to enjoy the same privileges it has. This type of provisions would establish new inequalities among the religious communities, clearly favoring the national churches of European countries arising from Anglican and Oriental schisms. Other favored churches would be those arising from the first Protestant reform, Jewish, Muslim, and others which, in spite of not belonging to the aforementioned, were established in the country for several years (e.g., Methodist, Brethren of Plymouth, and Baptist).

In other drafts, conditions of demographic nature are requested to approve the inscription of a group as religious. That is, the request of an effective presence of the religious group in at least three provinces, or a minimum number of members equal to 10% of the population of the country, or 1% of the population of the provinces where they act. This would have benefited Pentecostal groups linked to major ecclesiastic networks of classic Pentecostalism. However, it would have greatly harmed independent groups called "new religious movements" (which have relatively few members in Argentina). Further, it would harm many historical churches whose numbers of members have severely diminished in comparison with the total population.

For some religious minorities, as those of African origin and Spiritualists, this type of draft could mean being completely excluded, with perhaps some exceptions linked to a greater chance of having sufficient financial resources, education, and lobbying.

In short, any of the modifications would have meant establishing a new breach between religious communities, more or less benefited by the legal system.

3 The Strategy of Protestantism

Some of the drafts initially seemed to be supported by the Catholic ecclesiastic leaders. However, the generality of the most conservative Catholic sectors objected to the proposals for being—in their opinion—too permissive with the non-Catholics (Navarro Floria 2003).

However, from our point of view, the most interesting reaction took place inside of the vast group of religious denominations reunited under the name "Protestantism". For the Evangelical field, the presence of requisites implied a division between the first and the second-class churches. For this reason, many Protestants systematically opposed to this type of drafts. Regardless, others valued the passing of a law that granted them similar benefits as to those the Catholic Church receives.

The first thing to take into account is that, in the last years, the Protestant demographic growth in Argentina has been decisively linked to the expansion of neo-Pentecostalism. It was this branch that contributed the critical mass—so to speak—necessary for Protestantism to play an important role in the civil society. However, for many times, the leaders of historical Protestantism were the ones that actually took the lead in demanding changes from the State.[1]

From 1990 onwards, the different federations representing Protestant denominations designed and applied the strategy of "church unity," which involved forming a unified front to defend their rights. This allowed them to compensate, up to a certain point, the negative effects that the Protestant tradition bears in this sense: its permanent tendency toward dispersion. This becomes clearer when contrasted, for example, with the Catholic Church, which—regardless of its inner dissents—generally presents a clear leadership and a defined official position.

Furthermore, this strategy meant closing the breach that had separated Protestantism in general and the Argentinean Protestantism in particular, causing a bipolar division.

Historically, Protestants have—as it occurs with other religious traditions—oscillated between two standpoints regarding reality. It is a bipolar system: One standpoint involves escaping from the world (denying secularity, standing apart from temporary things, rejecting or being indifferent to politics). The other one, quite the opposite, is trying to influence the State (if not directly controlling it), usually through political involvement. In the latter, religion tries to advance toward its aims by making use of the State machinery. These aims may involve transforming oppressive and unfair social structures (e.g., in the case of historical Protestants), or emancipating from sin and reaching personal salvation (as it is the case with conservative Protestants). These two extremes are in constant tension. In the context of Argentina, Protestantism suffered this polarization. The antagonisms "Capitalism vs. Socialism" and "political involvement vs. escapism" were the main factors of that tension since the 1960s.

[1] In order to outline this summary of the history of Protestant positions in Argentina regarding legislation and State political measures, we have followed (Wynarczyk 2009b, 2010), which originated from his Ph.D. thesis on the subject.

Historically, this tension increases when facing controversial matters and decreases when facing exterior threats to Protestantism, whether real or perceived.

For example, around the middle of the twentieth century, Argentinean Protestantism was united against Peronism that—linked to Catholic sectors—threatened the religious freedom of non-Catholic. Even though the confrontations of President Peron with the Catholic Church meant a brief period of approaching to religious minorities—thus obtaining, for example, sympathy from some Pentecostal sectors—it was a different circumstance that divided Argentinean Protestantism. During the post-war period, and especially during the Cold War, a polarizing segmentation phenomenon reached the whole Occident. Such division arose from the different religious lifestyles and, mainly, from the compromise with the social problems, giving place to a marked contradiction between the liberal and conservative Protestant denominations. In a way, a similar process to the one diving Protestantism took place in the USA regarding issues such as the Civil Rights of African–American minorities and the war in Vietnam.

Later, after receiving an external threat, the Protestant sector reunited. In the last decade of the twentieth century, a strong anti-cults movement began in Argentina, very likely as a reaction to the strong boost Evangelicals had been having since the middle of the 1980s. In these circumstances, the differences between sectors decreased, and together they undertook the defense of the Protestant sector. Within this context, the strategy of "church unity" aimed at reinforcing the coordination and reduction of differences between poles. As a consequence, Protestantism was drawn together through a movement known as "Argentinean Evangelistic Movement" (Maróstica 1997). This movement gathered, in some senses, the strengths of each fraction of Protestantism.

Within this merger, the conservative pole–especially its Pentecostal branch–provided the aforementioned critical mass, based on its significant growth since 1980. At the same time, the historical pole provided the academic prestige, the commitment of its leaders to Human Rights, and its links with sectors of the Argentinean politics. This, of course, did not imply that some leaders of the Evangelistic and Pentecostal sectors had this prestige as well.

As a token of this unity, in 1993, a team was formed ad hoc, to act in representation of the Protestant interests before the Secretary of Religious Affairs. This team, integrated by leaders of the main Protestant federations (FACIERA, FAIE, FECEP), was known as "Comisión Tripartita" [Tripartite Commission] and became the seed of a fourth-grade Protestant entity, a sort of "Protestant confederation."

In spite of this approach of the traditional poles, the Protestant intervention in the claims before the State caused a different kind of division between them. For example, when in 1991 the Secretary of Religious Affairs presented its bill regulating religious minorities (known as "Proyecto Centeno" ["Project Centeno"]), two tendencies became apparent within the Argentinean Protestant sphere. On one side, those who inclined toward developing a gradualist strategy, accepted the draft. They understood that the word "support" in Section 2 of the National Constitution ("the Federal Government supports the Roman Catholic Apostolic cult") was ambiguous enough to write—without modifying it—an act acceptable in practical terms. On the other side, those who rejected the draft considered that this was insufficient to solve the situation of the minority denominations. Two sectors can be identified within this last group: those who considered that Section 2 should be eliminated before passing any act, so that all religious beliefs could be in equal conditions before the law, and those who opposed to any type of registry system or inscription, in a fashion similar to that of the USA. In 1993, some religious leaders, members of this last group, organized the "Consejo Interdenominacional de Pastores de la República Argentina" (CIPRA) [Interdenominational Council of Argentinean Pastors]. This organization gathered mainly small autonomous Pentecostal churches (especially from Buenos Aires), which did not feel represented by the federations in the "Comisión Tripartita". Regardless, this organization did not have an influential role in the processes aimed at modifying the legislation. However, the very fact that they gathered proves, up to a point, the limits of the strategy of church unity promoted by the Protestant leaders.

As a sort of continuation of the process initiated by the "Comisión Tripartita", later expanded with the "Comisión Nacional Evangélica para la Reforma de la Constitución" [National Evangelical Commission for the Constitutional Reform], for their part, in 1996 the main Protestant federations formed the "Consejo Nacional Cristiano Evangélico" (CNCE) [National Christian Evangelical Council]. This organization was the main agent—among those arising from the religious minorities—to take part in debates and negotiations involving the reform of the Act of Cult, particularly in the period between 1996 and 2001.

It was the CNCE that called for a massive demonstration in Buenos Aires. The main goal was to protest against the existence of a legal framework that—in their opinion—put them as second-class citizens. In 1999, a crowd gathered to complain about the way the State distributed the benefits for the society. The speakers demanded the passing of an act that allowed churches to obtain religious legal personality, ensured equal treatment and non-discrimination, and created relation channels with the State. On July 3, 2001, the CNCE called for a second demonstration. The result was a larger mass than the previous one. Although the call appealed for the struggle for equality, from that moment, in the core of the social demonstration, it began to shift. It moved from the collective struggle in defense of rights to a prayer for the nation, perhaps following the serious socioeconomic troubles Argentina was undergoing (Wynarczyk 2009a). A third demonstration was called on November 1, 2003. However, its impact was smaller (Frigerio and Wynarczyk 2008), proving that the *momentum* of the claim for equality led by the CNCE had passed.

Henceforth, the tension between the two dominant poles in the Protestant sphere returned. In a way, the differences that have historically affected Protestantism since the Cold War have been re-edited, although perhaps with less intransigence. The core ideas in discussion were different: for example, the position regarding some progressive State politics. In 2005, this contradiction became visible in the response to initiatives the Government took regarding reproductive health (Wynarczyk 2003).

Concomitantly, a sector of Protestant leaders, which had led the movement to claim for religious equality, became lobbyists defending religious moral principles in the arena of the Parliamentary debate. This strategy, perceived by other Protestants as an inappropriate advance of religion on the State, became a cause of tension among Protestants as well.

Last but not the least, the tension arising between the different claims for the reform of the legal structure ruling the religious issues remains unsolved. Some sectors question the current system not only because it generates inequalities between the Catholic Church and the other religions, but because it is intrinsically an inadequate and unfair regime to rule the relationship between religious communities and State. Meanwhile, other sectors only share the first objection and thus aspire solely to obtain traditionally Catholic privileges from the State. In other words, there is, in the mind of many pastors and evangelical leaders, the idea of positioning their communities at the same level of the Catholic Church, thus extending their areas of influence to multiple spheres of society: education, health, armed forces, among others (Carbonelli 2009).

4 Protestants Before the New Bill on Religious Freedom

These tensions have been re-shaped due to the intention that president Macri's government has of presenting its own bill on religious freedom.[2] The bill, presented by the Secretary of Religious Affairs and expressly supported by the Conference of Catholic Bishops, caused the Protestants to take a stance.

The main federations and associations of Protestant churches formed an Evangelical Consulting Board. Regardless of their initial intention of assuming the representation for all the Argentinean Protestantism, the Board had to limit itself to act as coordinator of the different participating denominations. In any case, each church, association, or federation is free to adopt its own positions before the bill of the Government.

The Argentinean Government requested the opinion of the Evangelic Consulting Board and other religious minorities regarding the bill on religious freedom. In order to elaborate these proposals, the Evangelical Consulting Board went a long and productive path to obtain the necessary consensus. A group of experts in Law and Religion, representing the different federations and associations of Protestant churches, held periodic meetings for several months. This process showed the profound differences dividing Protestants in some topics related to religious freedom and the relation between the churches and the State. However, at the same time, it served to demonstrate that through respectful and productive dialogue, acceptable solutions for everyone regarding most of the topics can be achieved. As a result of this work, the Evangelical Consulting Board sent the Government a counter-proposal with various modifications to the bill.

Despite the suggestions made, the text of the bill essentially retains its original foundation. It is true that some suggestions have been accepted, for example, the recognition of the religiousness indigenous peoples, the express duty of reasonable

[2]Editor's note: See the Chapter "The 2017 Proposed Law on Religious Freedom for Argentina: Comparative Perspectives" by Navarro Floria in this book.

accommodation for religious practices in the workplace and schools, and the suppression of a list of phenomena a priori excluded from the religious category. But the main features of the system remain: a quasi-confessional State with the prominence of Catholicism over other religions, and a Government with the capacity of controlling religious minorities, which are implicitly still seen as suspicious. This regime results, for example, in the obligation for non-Catholic churches to be inscribed in the Cults Registry in order to obtain religious legal personality, and in that, the Government possesses extensive sanctioning faculties over the non-Catholic churches.

The text of the final bill, sent by the Government to the Congress in mid-June 2017, has once again opened the breach between Protestants. From the Government's viewpoint, this act should be approved by a general consensus, which is especially important in a moment of such political tension in Argentina. The exposition of the reasons for the act expresses this intention. It states that, in order to draft the bill, "the main religious entities were consulted, reaching a general consensus about the text."[3]

This alleged consensus was supposed to mean a quick and unproblematic approval of the Congress. However, reality seems to be different. Shortly after the bill was presented, the first voices of preoccupation—and even overt opposition—were raised.

Probably, the loudest of these voices among the first ones criticizing the bill was that of Amnesty International (AI). In an open letter addressed to President Macri,[4] the organization manifested its concern about the "use of language, principles and standards of Human Rights" when in fact the project "clearly undermines the rights and freedoms of individuals." From AI's point of view, the project fails to "strengthen a secular State that grants freedom to its individuals", while pretending to "favor a multi-confessional State, with a strong interference by religions in the exercise of the rights of individuals and in the public." The perspective from which AI makes these claims is clear: Preserving the right to follow a religion is just as important as preserving the right "not to follow one", the organization points out.

Similar to others, the critical evaluation made by AI seems to focus mainly on the secular sectors of the population. However, the important repercussion it had on the media (and, therefore, on the Congressmen and women who were to intervene in its debate) produced two effects on the Protestant sectors. The first effect was that the discussion of the bill became slower in the Congress, as a result of some Congressmen and women who were unwilling to support the bill before knowing the social consequences. This way, some churches and church federations had enough time to hold inner debates on what stance to take regarding the bill. Rapidity in the resolution of matters is not a typical feature of ecclesiastic structures, and many religious leaders lack experience in the political arena. Consequently, the extra time resulting from

---

[3]Proyecto 0010/PE/2017, de Ley de Libertad Religiosa [Bill for the Religious Freedom Act], exposition of reasons.

[4]Amnistía Internacional Argentina, "Carta abierta al Presidente Macri", available online at https://amnistia.org.ar/wp-content/uploads/delightful-downloads/2017/06/Carta-a-Macri-y-PEN-por-Proyecto-Libertad-religiosa-1.pdf.

the delay in the advancement of the bill in the Congress served Protestant churches to revise (i.e., establish, confirm, or modify) their positions on the matter.

The second effect was breaking the image of consensus some Protestant leaders had. It is fair to say that this occurred partly as a consequence of the first effect, that is, of the extra time to revise positions, but partly as well as a consequence of knowing about the criticism from other sectors. Even though the Argentine Episcopal Conference stated its support for the bill, the Metropolitan Archbishop of the Catholic Archdiocese of La Plata, Mons. Aguer, strongly challenged such decision.[5] According to Aguer, the bill "tends to make cults equal," something that, in his opinion, is unconstitutional and, further, "allows the number of uncontrollable sects to swarm." This Religious Freedom Act "harms the Catholic Church and thus harms the Argentinean society." The bill—Aguer stated—is a result of "the pressure of the numerous amounts of 'pastors' not conforming a specific church," clearly referencing Protestants.

In spite of Mons. Aguer not representing most Catholics, the message for many Protestants was clear: The unity of criteria demanded from Protestantism (which sometimes forces to give into reach consensus) is not complete within Catholicism. For some, this meant a "green light" to express their own criticism. For some others, the threat of a rupture in the consensus implied the need to reinforce their positions in favor of the bill.

Consequently, some Protestants support the bill. Among these are the more conservative, whose opinions are significantly close to those of the Catholic leaders (i.e., the Conference of Catholic Bishops) in many topics, such as sexual morality. Indeed, it was the opinion of the Catholic scholars that has inspired the first draft of the bill. But there are some others who support the bill as well, understanding that it is at least a step forward in the path to achieving more religious freedom and religious equality. Of course, another influencing factor is that, for many Protestants, the ideal model of State is not a non-confessional one, but a Christian multi-confessional one, with Catholicism and Protestantism as privileged religions.

This seems to be the position of, for example, the "Alianza Cristiana de Iglesias Evangélicas de la República Argentina" (ACIERA) [Christian Alliance of Argentina Evangelical Churches]. By the end of June 2017—that is, shortly after the bill was sent to the Congress—ACIERA published a note[6] signed by its President. The title of the note was "Before a New Act", and it highlighted the enormous satisfaction for the submission of the bill for the Religious Freedom Act to the Congress. The note stressed the virtues of the bill, among which it "will permit our churches to develop our mission more widely, granting the access of religious ministers to spheres such as health institutions, influential sectors and persons, prisons." It also emphasized that "through this bill, a national registry of religious entities will be created, which will

[5]Aguer made his statements in a television program. The transcription can be found in http://valoresreligiosos.com.ar/Noticias/durisima-critica-de-monsenor-aguer-al-proyecto-de-ley-de-libertad-religiosa-10371.

[6]Alianza Cristiana de Iglesias Evangélicas de la República Argentina, "A las puertas de una nueva ley", avaladleavailable online at http://aciera.org/a-las-puertas-de-una-nueva-ley.

allow going from obligation to willingness regarding registry, without this limiting the freedom of cult."

A few days later, another note circulated among the Evangelical leaders, expressly referring to the bill.[7] This note—signed by the President of the ACIERA as well—remarked the chance of occupying "with Evangelical presence the permitted places, especially decisive ones." According to the declaration, the work of ACIERA relating to this matter has "the ONLY aim of praising the name of Christ in our country, so that His word occupies a fundamental place in the Nation, and all this leads to the people inhabiting this land to FIND CHRIST and surrender to Him" [capital letters in the original]. The note urged Evangelical Christians to pray and intercede specifically for the debate and approval of the bill in the Congress.

Other Protestants, however, have a different viewpoint. The more traditional sectors of Protestantism oppose to the bill, many of which have a strong liberal tendency. For this branch, the Act only reinforces the differences between one religion—that is, the Catholic—and the others, reassuring the confessional State. For these Protestants, any law should move toward a greater separation between the churches and the State and toward a greater respect for the individual autonomy in life choices. Their informal motto is "we do not want any religion having privileges; neither want the privilege for ourselves."

Following this line, the Federación Argentina de Iglesias Evangélicas (FAIE) [Argentine Federation of Evangelical Churches] also issued a statement referring to the bill.[8] In it, FAIE recognizes being consulted during the drafting process and that some of its suggestions were considered. However, most suggestions were rejected or openly ignored. Furthermore, there had been last-moment modifications and additions to the text FAIE ignored until the filing of the bill.

The statement issued by FAIE points out some of the criticisms to the bill, among them the continuing inequality between the Catholic Church and the other religions. This inequality renders evident when the bill text expressly excludes the Catholic Church of the obligation of registering in the State. Therefore, Catholics and the Catholic Church will enjoy the benefits granted by the act but will not need to fulfill the obligations the same bill poses for the other religions. Even though the text sustains an atmosphere of dialogue and harmonic coexistence in our country's religious field, "a clear inequality remains, and as long as such inequality exists, freedom will not be complete."

The statement issued by FAIE manifests as well its concern about the controversy the conscientious objection clause provoked. FAIE seems to have a different position than that adopted by the bill. In any case, it proposes that the matter on conscientious objection be discussed later, within the framework of a specific act, so that the debate of other issues considered more urgent is not hindered.

---

[7] "Llamado a la oración por tratamiento y aprobación de la 'ley de libertad religiosa'", 06/30/2017, unpublished.

[8] Federación Argentina de Iglesias Evangélicas, "Sobre la ley de libertad religiosa", 07/14/2017, unpublished. The document was approved by the FAIE leaders and sent to the Mesa Evangélica Consultiva [Consultative Evangelic Board] (integrated by the other Evangelical entities) to be published. However, it never was.

These more urgent issues involve, for example, the previsions of the bill regarding the "Registro de Entidades Religiosas" (RENAER) [Registry of Religious Entities]. According to FAIE, these previsions—added or modified after the period of consulting churches—cause a limitation to broad rights enumerated in the first part of the bill. Particularly, the statement highlights the danger of excessive control power of the Secretariat of Religious Affairs. FAIE regrets as well that the bill does not recognize legal status to churches that do not register in the RENAER. The National Civil and Commercial Code, in its interpretation, recognizes this religious status without the necessity of registering in the RENAER, a "fundamental right won after several years of struggle in the social, religious, legal and political fields."

In the opinion of the FAIE, the "verticalization" promoted by the act is dangerous as well, since it demands the existence of an authorization from "the 'mother' entity so that an 'organic or hierarchically dependent' organization can be registered autonomously," which does not adapt well to the reality of many Protestant confessions.

Another issue about which the FAIE expressed its concern involves the amendment to the criminal law incorporated by this bill. Especially, the punishment provided for "those who, not being religious ministers, executes acts considered particular of such ministry" (Section 48 of the bill). FAIE sustains that given the fact that ministerial certifications are not uniform in the different churches and that there is no administrative authority external to the own religious organizations issuing them, "this clause may cause arbitrary issues."

In sum, FAIE's position on the bill is far from being as optimistic as ACIERA's. In spite of expressing a "willingness to collaborate" and to engage in "reasonable dialogue," FAIE's statement warns about the dangers faced if the bill is passed, since it could pose an "unconstitutional control" over religious entities, a restriction in obtaining religious legal status, and a deepening of the "already unfair inequality arising from the privileged statutes the Roman Catholic Apostolic Church enjoys."

5 Conclusions

Evidently, ACIERA's and FAIE's positions are not the only ones. They are, however, representative of the differences existing within Argentinean Protestantism, facing a hypothetical Religious Freedom Act.

This is due to the fact that, in spite of the unity strategy that from time to time gains strength, Protestantism cannot be considered a monolithic sector. It might perhaps be better to understand it as a *field*, in the sociological meaning of the term, where different sectors converge and coexist in tension.

Proposing a new legal framework for religion, with the resulting threats and opportunities this involves, has the potential of increasing to the maximum the old tensions among these sectors.

That for some sectors means accessing benefits granted by the State in similar conditions to those of the Catholic Church, for others it means giving into the historically sustained principle of Church and State separation. Where some see the opportunity to impose their own religious morality through civil power, so as to rescue the country from the inflicting loss of values, others see a threat to the respect of the most basic freedoms and rights. While some demand the State to establish order in society, and define which religions are "acceptable" and which are not, others refuse to grant the State authority in matters that correspond to the individual conscious of its citizens.

In any case, the attempt of the successive governments to obtain consensus between the different religious communities has done nothing but indefinitely postponing the replacement of the Act of Cults, that is currently short from an embarrassing for the Argentinean democracy. It would be adequate to enquire about this issue: Is it reasonable to require consensus between religious communities as a requisite *sine qua non* for the passing of a new act (or at least for abrogating the current act)? What is the acceptable degree of required consensus? And more importantly, is it not extortive to demand consensus of religious communities when the successive bills contain highly dividing provisions for them? The best example of this last issue is the persisting religious inequality, reinforced and even deepened by all bills and drafts.

Regardless of the bill becoming an act or not (a matter that will surely be resolved mostly because of political reasons, rather than academic or philosophic arguments), doubtlessly the challenge for Protestantism will be preserving—if not recovering—the inner harmony after going through a process that will surely leave deep marks.

References

Carbonelli M (2009) Campo Religioso Y Política: El Rol De Las Minorías Religiosas En El Proceso De Construcción De La Laicidad En Argentina. In: IV Curso Internacional "Fomentando el Conocimiento de las Libertades Laicas." Mexico

Esquivel JC (2009) Cultura Política Y Poder Eclesiástico: Encrucijadas Para La Construcción Del Estado Laico En Argentina. Arch des Sci Soc des Relig 41–59. https://doi.org/10.4000/assr.21217

Frigerio A, Wynarczyk H (2008) Diversidad No Es Lo Mismo Que Pluralismo: cambios en el campo religioso argentino (1985–2000) y luchas de los evangelicos por sus derechos religiosos. Soc e Estado 3:227–260

Maróstica MM (1997) Pentecostals and politics: the creation of the evangelical christian movement in Argentina, 1983–1993. University of California

Navarro Floria JG (2003) Una Nueva Ley De Cultos Para La Argentina. In: Bosca R (ed) La Libertad Religiosa En La Argentina: Aportes Para Una Legislación. Calir & Fundación Konrad Adenauer, Buenos Aires, pp 171–180

Padilla N (2009) Ley De Libertad Religiosa. La Historia Que He Vivido. In: Jornada del Consejo Argentino para la Libertad Religiosa. Calir, Buenos Aires

Wynarczyk H (2003) También En Argentina La Moral Sexual Divide a Los Evangélicos. Agencia Latinoam. y Caribeña Comun

Wynarczyk H (2009a) Los Que Salieron Del Templo. Le Monde Dipl. (Cono Sur)

Wynarczyk H (2009b) Ciudadanos De Dos Mundos: el Movimiento Evangélico En La Vida Pública Argentina 1980-2001. UNSAM, Buenos Aires

Wynarczyk H (2010) Sal y Luz a Las Naciones: Evangélicos Y Política En La Argentina (1980-2001). Instituto Di Tella & Siglo XXI, Buenos Aires

The 2017 Proposed Law on Religious Freedom for Argentina: Comparative Perspectives

Juan G. Navarro Floria

Abstract Once again, the Argentine Congress has under consideration a bill for a "Religious Freedom Law." This issue has been a pending assignment for the country since the return to democracy in 1983. This time, besides granting more effective protection to the right of religious freedom (which is guaranteed by international human rights treaties that have constitutional rank in Argentina), Congress needs to regulate the legal personality of churches, religious communities, and religious confessions, which was recognized by the new Civil and Commercial Code, in force since 2015. In this chapter, the content of the bill will be examined, comparing it with the current legislation in place in Spain, Portugal, Chile, Colombia, Peru, and Mexico. We consider certain novel aspects of this bill, such as the regulation of the right to conscientious objection and the mandate to employers to provide reasonable accommodation in the workplace for the employee´s religious needs. This bill creates a non-mandatory Registry of Churches and Religious Communities, dictates the transition from the current system (enacted by the military regime in the 1970s), and guarantees the internal autonomy of religious bodies. It also introduces reforms to the Argentine Penal Code to punish crimes against religious communities.

Keywords Religious freedom · Conscientious objection · Autonomy of religious organizations · Comparative law and religion · Religion in Argentina

1 Some Background

In December 1983, the Argentine Republic put an end to the last and bloodiest of its military dictatorships that alternated with some type of democratic governments for a good part of the twentieth century and began a new period of constitutional stability that, thankfully, continues until now. The approval and later ratification by the Nation of the main human rights treaties were among the first legislative measures of the reopened Congress, which the earlier military governments and the

J. G. Navarro Floria (✉)
Pontifical Catholic University of Argentina, Buenos Aires, Argentina
e-mail: JNavarro@nfla.com.ar

© Springer Nature Switzerland AG 2020

R. V. S. Alves (ed.), *Latin American Perspectives on Law and Religion*, Law and Religion in a Global Context 3,
https://doi.org/10.1007/978-3-030-46717-3_4

last Peronist government at the time (1973–1976) had failed to ratify. Law 23054 approved the American Convention on Human Rights "Pact of San Jose, Costa Rica," and Law 23313 approved the International Covenants on Civil and Political Rights, and on Economic, Social and Cultural Rights. In this way, the obligation to protect the fundamental right to religious freedom was fully and vigorously incorporated into the Argentine legal system, acting as a complement to the historic constitutional guarantee of freedom of worship (Articles 14 and 20 of the Constitution of 1853, still in force).

Additional international human rights treaties were approved and ratified during the following years until the national Constitution was reformed in 1994 and some of those treaties were given constitutional hierarchy (Article 75, Paragraph 22). That reform consolidated what had already been established by the jurisprudence of the Supreme Court of Justice, which is that international treaties approved by the Republic have a superior hierarchy to laws, especially human rights treaties. The same constitutional reform took the opportunity to remove some provisions from the constitutional text about the exercise of the right of patronage ("Patronato") over the Catholic Church, which had already lost their validity with the signing of the Agreement between Argentina and the Holy See in 1966.

These reforms to the highest legislative level called for the reform of domestic legislation inferior to the Constitution, especially the laws which came from the last military dictatorship and were issued to guarantee state control over religious groups other than the Catholic Church (Law 21745, on the creation and organization of the National Register of Religions—"Registro Nacional de Cultos").[1]

Thus, under the leadership of Dr. Angel Centeno (1989–1998), the National Secretariat for Religious Affairs made an intense effort to prepare a "religious freedom law," which effort included consultations with jurists, officials, and basically to all religious confessions. As an advisor to the Secretariat for Religious Affairs, it was my duty to actively participate in that process and draft the proposed law.[2] After an extensive stage of consultations, the draft was sent to Congress where it was reviewed by the Senate, which unanimously approved it in 1992. For various reasons, the Chamber of Deputies failed to take it up and the proposal expired. However, that first proposed law was the basis of all the other bills that continued through the last twenty-five years, and even the one that concerns us today.[3]

The extensive administration of the Kirchner government (2003–2015) had no real interest in this matter, and not only did the Executive Branch never send any legislative proposal to Congress, but it also managed to hinder another draft of good quality that had been presented by the legislators. The Argentine Legal Digest ("Digesto

[1] For background of this law, see Navarro Floria (1993).

[2] Strictly speaking, the tasks for that objective had begun during the government of President Alfonsín and during the administration by Dr. Juan Carlos Palmero in the Secretariat for Religious Affairs (1987–1989), with whom I also had the honor of collaborating.

[3] There have been several bills during that long period, some presented by legislators, others prepared by the Administration, and finally, others presented by civil society organizations, such as the Argentine Council for Religious Freedom (CALIR). For more information about these various bills, among other works, see (Navarro Floria 1997, 2001; Lo Prete 2013).

Jurídico Argentino")[4] was approved during that government, which gave legislative ratification to law 21745 of the military dictatorship (renamed Law ADM-1127), despite its widespread repudiation by religious communities.

In 2014, the Congress approved a new Civil and Commercial Code, replacing the historic Civil Code of 1870. The bill that the Executive Branch sent to Congress said nothing about religious confessions (except a provision to keep the recognition of the Roman Catholic Church as a public legal entity in Article 146, similar to the recognition that was already made in the old code). Due to the express request made by the Argentine Council for Religious Freedom ("CALIR") and by some religious confessions, including the Catholic Church itself, Congress included "churches, confessions, communities and religious entities" (Article 148) in the group of (private) legal persons, although Congress made no provisions in this regard. These entities became the only type of legal persons with such recognition, but without their own regulations in the Code or in any special law (Navarro Floria 2015a), which made and makes it more urgent to legislate on this matter.

This is why in 2017, and after numerous consultations with specialists and different religious groups, the Executive Branch sent a new bill to Congress, and hopefully, this will be a final proposed law on religious freedom. The following pages contain a brief review of this bill. At the very end of his term, in December 2019, President Macri sent a new version of that Project to Congress. It is very similar to the previous one, with just a couple of relevant changes, which will be indicated later.

To complete this introductory overview, it is worth remembering that there is legislation in this matter throughout Ibero-America. The pioneering law that has been in a certain way a model for the others (including the current Argentine proposed law) is Organic Law 7/1980 of Spain. Portugal enacted Law 16/2001 (June 22) on Religious Freedom, which is probably the most complete law in this subject.[5] In Latin America, we find Law 133 of 1994 of Colombia on Religious Freedom and Worship; Law 19638 on "Legal Constitution of Churches and Religious Organizations" of Chile; Law 29635 of Peru on Religious Freedom (the most recent); and, under a partially different model due to a particular historical situation, the Law of Religious Associations and Public Worship of Mexico.

2 The Structure of the Law

The proposed law is organized in four chapters.

The first one is "Fundamental Principles," and in eight articles, it develops the rights that derive from religious freedom and conscience in its individual and collective aspects. It is important to highlight that these rules are applicable to all people

[4] Law 26939, BO 16/6/2014. See (Navarro Floria 2014a).

[5] In Italy, like Argentina, there were several proposed laws that were not approved. The most recent and current one is the "Bill of freedom of conscience and religion" prepared by the Astrid Foundation, sent to the Senate on April 6, 2017.

and religious confessions. This is a necessary clarification because sometimes these laws are usually seen as intended exclusively for "non-Catholics," assuming that the Catholic Church has its own regime already in force. This is true about the recognition of their legal personality and their institutional aspects, but it is not true when thinking of the rights of individuals (obviously including Catholics) and the rights of institutions or related legal entities. Here, the state legal system is and should be uniform and equal for all.

The second chapter is about the National Registry of Religious Entities ("RENAER"). This is of main interest for churches and religious communities other than the Catholic Church, to which this chapter is directly applicable, but it is subsidiary for the Catholic Church (as clarified in Article 24 of the proposed law).[6] This National Registry (that replaces the existing National Register of Religions) is organized in seventeen articles, which establish rules regarding churches and religious communities as private legal entities.

The third chapter is focused on making some changes to the Civil and Commercial Code (one article) and to the Penal Code (four articles, three of those are modified, and the other one is repealed).

The fourth and last chapter of the proposed law has five normative articles and one that is a mere formality. This chapter is focused on transitory provisions, necessary for the transition between the current rules and the new rules.

3 Contents of the Proposed Law

3.1 Rights Derived from Freedom of Religion and Conscience

Freedom of religion and conscience includes a group of subjective rights, with the particularity that some of them correspond to individuals and others to collective subjects: religious communities. The definition of religious freedom itself makes reference to an exercise of that right that may be private or public, individual or collective. While freedom of conscience is personal to each person, religious freedom necessarily demands a collective exercise: There is no religion without it being an experience shared with others.

Surprisingly, the 2019 draft eliminates references to freedom of conscience. It is a painful claudication of the Government face to face the "pro abortion" groups. Precisely, the inclusion of the right to conscientious objection in the 2017 draft was the reason why it was not passed, because when it was ready to be approved, the legislative discussion of an abortion legalization began.

---

[6]This subsidiarity is explained because although the Catholic Church does not need to register in the Registry created by the law, and given that it has a public legal personality derived from its constitutional recognition and reaffirmed by the Civil and Commercial Code, the rights that the law recognizes to the other churches and religious communities should obviously be recognized also.

Article 2 of the proposed law establishes several rights of human beings ("*persona humana,*" according to the language adopted by the Civil and Commercial Code), while clarifying that it is a non-exhaustive list. Some of those are a restatement of rights that are already included in international treaties, while others are not. They are not presented in any particular order because some very specific rights, which are derived from the more generic religious freedom rights are mentioned before other more general rights. Also, they are not grouped in positive and negative freedoms, like the law in Portugal (Articles 8 and 9). The rights mentioned in the proposed law are:

(a) "*To profess beliefs of one's choice or refrain from doing so.*" This is the same language found in the international treaties and most laws on this matter.[7]
(b) "*To change or abandon religious beliefs,*" as expressly stated in Article 12 of the Pact of San José, Costa Rica and indirectly in Article 18 of the ICCPR. This terminology also coincides with comparative law.[8]
(c) "*To manifest beliefs or refrain from doing so,*" also coinciding with international treaties and some laws on the matter.[9]
(d) "*To impart and receive religious information through any lawful means, both publicly and privately.*" The language used to establish this right does not appear explicitly in the laws of other countries that have been mentioned, except for Colombia, in Article 6(g). The law of Portugal mentions it in a different way in Article 8(d).
(e) "*To not be forced to take an oath or make a promise, according to formulas that violate their religious beliefs or their convictions.*" This is a negative freedom that is assigned with an unusual relevance by placing it even before the freedom to practice one's religion. It is correct to make it explicit, because an oath (which is often compared wrongly to a type of promise) is always a religious act as it implies "placing God as a witness"; and such an oath should not be forced. Nevertheless, an oath is common practice imposed in various circumstances, such as the declaration of a witness in court, the appointment of public office

[7]Spain, Article 2(a); Chile, Article 6(a); Colombia, Article 6(a); Peru, Article 3(a). On the other hand, the laws of Portugal, in Article 8(a) and of Mexico, in Article 2(a), (b), speak of "having or not having religion" and of "having or adopting" a belief, respectively.

[8]Spain, Article 2.1(a); Chile, Article 6(a); Colombia, Article 6(a); Peru, Article 3(a); Portugal, Article 8(b). The law of Mexico does not include the right to change one's religion, but it does use the expression "to adopt" a religion just like the ICCPR that establishes such right. The law of Peru specifies that the right to abandon a belief is "*according to the proper procedure of each church, confession or religious community,*" which is problematic: What would happen if someone wants to leave a church but "their own procedure" does not allow it? Forcing him to stay would be a clear violation of his religious freedom.

[9]Spain, Article 2.1(a); Chile, Article 6(a); Colombia, Article 6(a). The laws of Portugal, Mexico and Peru do not expressly refer to the right to manifestation of religion.

or receiving a college degree. The freedom not to be forced to take an oath is also present in the law of Portugal, Article 9.1 and of Peru, Article 3(g).[10]

(f) "*To practice acts of worship, individually or collectively, publicly or privately.*" This is one of the basic manifestations of religious freedom, present in all international treaties, and also present in comparative legislation.[11] Naturally, the ways to practice religion are multiple and depend on the demands of each religion. The proposed law then mentions the corresponding negative freedom: the right to not be forced to practice acts of worship. This is also found in the laws of Portugal, Article 9—in a very detailed manner; Colombia, in Article 6(e); Spain, in Article 2.1(b); Chile, in Article 6(b); and Peru, in Article 9(c).[12]

(g) "*To receive religious or spiritual assistance from religious ministers of their own religious confession in places of confinement, detention or barracks.*" The right to religious assistance is correctly presented as a right for the people and not for religious confessions. Although it is particularly necessary to guarantee such assistance in the places indicated by this proposed law, it must be enjoyed in any circumstance, as specified in the laws of Chile, in Article 9(c), and Colombia, in Article 6(f). This right implies a correlative duty of the State to facilitate its enjoyment, according to the different possible modalities (which typically require appropriate regulations and, eventually, agreements with those confessions).[13] This proposed law in Argentina has not provided for any particular regulation or cooperation agreements in this matter.

(h) "*To receive proper burial according to their own beliefs or convictions.*" The wording of this right may be surprising because it seems to grant a right to a deceased person, who can no longer exercise it on his own. However, this should be read together with the rule found in the Civil and Commercial Code (Article 61) that makes reference to the personal right to arrange one's own funeral.[14] This is not a right that has been expressly recognized in international human rights treaties, although it is especially relevant for many religions, and it has

[10]In some ways, this is also found in the law of Mexico, which contains an unusual provision in Article 4: "*The mere promise to tell the truth and to fulfill obligations entered into, subjects the person making it to the sanctions established by law, in the event that such person fails to keep it.*".

[11]Spain, Article 2.1(b); Portugal, Article 8(c) and, in more detail, Article 10(a); Chile, Article 6(b); Colombia, Article 6(b), and Peru, Article 3(b). The law of Mexico, on the other hand, says nothing about it.

[12]The law of Mexico says nothing about this, but Mexican law does have a rule that is especially understood in relation to indigenous communities: no one may be "*obliged to provide personal services or contribute, with money or in kind, to the maintenance of an association, church or any other religious group, nor to participate or contribute in the same way in rites, ceremonies, festivities, services or acts of religious worship.*" (Article 2, Section d).

[13]This is provided by the laws of Spain (Article 2), Portugal (Article 13, quite extensively), Chile (Article 9(c)), Colombia (Article 8), and Peru (Article 3(c)).

[14]See (Navarro Floria 2016a, b).

been considered by some foreign legislations[15] as well as the jurisprudence of the Inter-American Court of Human Rights.[16]

(i) The proposed law also expressly includes the right of public assembly for religious purposes and the right of association with common religious purpose, which are provided for in human rights treaties and in comparative law.[17] These are basic rights that are self-explanatory.

(j) "*To impart and choose for themselves, or for minors, disabled people or people with restricted capacity who they legally represent, religious and moral education in accordance with their own beliefs or convictions, and to prevent them from receiving teachings or participating in practices contrary to such beliefs or convictions.*" This is a provision expressly stated in international human rights treaties. However, it has its own difficulties. In fact, while this proposed law is being analyzed, the Argentine Supreme Court has had to solve a case on the constitutionality of religious education in public schools in a specific province (Salta).[18] There are similar provisions to this one in the laws of Spain, in Article 2.1(c), Portugal, in Article 11 (which clarifies that minors may choose for themselves from the age of 16 on religious matters and regulates religious education in schools in Article 24), Chile, in Article 6(d), and Peru, in Articles 3(d) and 8. As one may expect, the law of Mexico is silent on this issue. In the 2019 Draft, the last phrase about prevention of receiving teachings against parent's believes inexplicably disappears.

(k) "*To commemorate religious festivities and to observe the days and hours dedicated to worship or observance according to their religion.*" Here, we are also facing a right explicitly established in international human rights treaties, also found in the 1981 UN Declaration on Religious Freedom. In order for this right to be effective, this proposed law includes an obligation of reasonable accommodation at work, which will be mentioned later. The laws of Portugal, in Article 10(c), Peru, in Article 3(f), and Spain (although not as clearly), in Article 2.1(a), contain a similar provision.

(l) "*To get married in accordance to the rites of their religion, without prejudice to compliance with civil laws.*" This is a provision that may be qualified as timid, since it does not say that religious marriages will have civil effects, as stated in the law of Chile, in Article 6(d), and the way it is organized in detail in the law of Portugal, in (Articles 10(b), 19, 59 and 60). In Argentina, it is difficult to have the possibility of granting civil effects to religious marriages due to the acceptance of marriage between people of the same sex and the adoption of

---

[15]Portugal, Article 10, and Peru, Article 3(h). The law of Colombia has paid special attention to this issue in a long provision, Article 6(c), to which it adds another one (Article 17) referring to municipal cemeteries.

[16]See (Navarro Floria 2017b).

[17]Spain, Article 2.1(d); Chile, Article 6); Portugal, Article 8(f); Mexico, Article 2(f); Colombia, Article 6(j); and Peru, Article 3(e).

[18]CSJ 1870/2014/CSI, "Castillo, Carina Viviana y otros el Provincia de Salta - Ministerio de Educación de la Prov. De Salta s/amparo", judgement of December 12, 2017.

legislation in matrimonial matters that departs completely from the traditional views on the family, which is supported by most religious confessions.

(m) "*To use symbols or clothing that shows affiliation to their own religious confession.*" It is well known that this is a burning issue in many places. There is no record of an express recognition of this right in the religious freedom laws that have been examined here.

Out of the laws that we have compared to the proposed law in Argentina, Portugal has the only law that establishes individual rights that have been omitted from the proposed law in Argentina (which does not mean that it negates them, since the list found in the proposed law is not limited), such as the right to act in accordance with the rules of each professed religion (which would be a "positive" wording of the right to conscientious objection), the right to choose children's names according to the tradition of each professed religion (indisputable in Argentina), and the right to "produce scientific, literary and artistic works on the subject of religion" (Article 10, subsections G, H, E and I).

After establishing these rights, the proposed law also recognizes a number of rights to "religious entities," in another non-exhaustive list. It is necessary to clarify that these rights do not depend on any registration or express recognition by the State, unlike the situation in Mexico, for example, as well as in Peru, and apparently also in Chile, where similar rights are only recognized to registered entities. We will review the concept of "religious entity" later, but for now, we will consider the rights that the proposed law recognizes to such entities, whether registered or not (Article 3):

(a) "*To define its doctrinal foundations, rites and public celebrations.*" This is a fundamental manifestation of the autonomy of religious communities, which, surprisingly, is not recognized in the laws of other countries within the cultural area that have enacted laws on the subject. This recognition has practical consequences because it makes clear that the State is incompetent to interfere in these matters.

(b) "*To determine its governing structure and function according to its own dogma.*" This also derives from the autonomy norm. The ways in which religious communities are organized follow their own principles, which are not necessarily subject to the rules of a republican democracy or civil society. The laws of Chile, in Article 7(b), and Colombia, in Article 7(c) recognize the right of religious entities to establish "their own hierarchy," which is only one aspect of the right as considered here.

(c) "*To enunciate, communicate, and disseminate its own creed, whether verbally, in writing or by any other means, and manifest its doctrine of faith and morals.*" This is collective religious freedom relating to freedom of expression. Both individuals and religious communities have the right to express their faith. The language used is similar to the one used in the laws of Chile, in Article 7(c), and Colombia, in Article 7(f); and the law of Peru, in Article 6(e), although the latter only recognizes the right of previously registered entities to disseminate their creed. The law of Portugal specifies that such guarantee includes the right to "*procure new believers*" (right to proselytize[19]).

(d) "*To establish temples or places dedicated to worship or religious activities.*" Having a temple or a place of worship is common to religion (to all of them, essentially), and clearly, the establishment, ownership, and management of temples or places of worship is the responsibility of the community and not of isolated individuals. The compared laws recognize it in different ways: as a right to "establish and maintain places" for worship and religious meetings in Chile, Article 7(a), and Colombia, Article 7(a), which adds the right to have respected "its religious purpose and its specific confessional character." Peru, in Article 6(d), grants this right to registered entities only.

(e) "*To have cemeteries in accordance with religious norms and in accordance with the applicable regulations*"; a corollary right to the one recognized for individuals. The other laws that have been analyzed do not include this topic, except for Colombia, as we have seen.

(f) "*To create and maintain, in accordance with current regulations, educational institutions, schools, homes, health centers, hospitals, publishing houses, media, service entities, and others that enable them to carry out their mission.*" This provides the possibility of creating derivative institutions or legal persons, generally recognized in comparative law (except as analyzed in some cases, in Mexico).[20]

(g) "*To communicate freely with its members and with other entities, inside or outside the country.*"[21] This right seems obvious but it is not. The Catholic Church used to be limited in this right by the Constitution, which required the "approval" or "*exequatur*" for the documents of the Pope or the councils. Such requirement existed at least as a formality until the 1966 Agreement.

(h) "*To own and use public media in accordance with the specific regulations in force.*" It is important to recognize this right in Argentina because for a long time churches and religious communities were denied the direct ownership of audiovisual media, a situation that today is superseded by the current law on the subject.[22] The conflict on this matter is noted in the fact that, in general, the laws of other countries are silent on this issue. The law of Colombia only makes reference to the right to publish books, in Article 7(e), while the law of Mexico (Article 21) is exceptionally restrictive.[23]

---

[19]On this sensitive issue, see (Navarro Floria and Lo Prete 2011).

[20]Spain, Article 6.2; Chile, Article 8; Peru, Article 7 (always limited to registered entities).

[21]In similar terms, the laws of Portugal, Colombia, in Article 7(b), and Peru, in Article 6(g), recognize the same right.

[22]Law 26,522 of 2009.

[23]"*Religious associations may only, in an extraordinary manner, transmit or disseminate acts of religious worship through non-print mass media, having been previously authorized by the Ministry of Interior. In no case may religious acts be disseminated during radio and television time assigned to the State. In the cases mentioned in the previous paragraph, the organizers, sponsors, concessionaires or owners of the media will be jointly and severally liable with the religious association in question to comply with the provisions regarding acts of public worship with extraordinary*

(i) "*To determine the requirements for admission, preparation, appointment, and removal of ministers of worship and to sustain them spiritually and economically.*" Everything that has to do with the ministerial regime is a central aspect of the autonomy of religious communities.

3.2 The Indigenous Peoples

The proposed law has an innovative rule, which did not exist in the previous bills reviewed by Congress, and is it not found in similar laws within the region: Article 4, referring to the "*spirituality of the indigenous peoples*." The text is carefully drafted and copies almost word for word the first two paragraphs of Article XVI of the "American Declaration on the Rights of Indigenous Peoples" of the OAS.[24] There is no talk of "indigenous religion" but "spirituality," which may be understood as a religious lifestyle applied both to indigenous religions and to foreign religions but adopted by indigenous peoples (specifically, Christianity in diverse aspects). The rule states:

> ARTICLE 4. Spirituality of the indigenous peoples. Indigenous peoples have the right to freely exercise their own spirituality and beliefs and, by virtue of that right, to practice, develop, transmit, and teach their traditions, customs, and ceremonies, and to carry them out in public and in private, individually and collectively. No indigenous people or person shall be subject to pressures or impositions, or any other type of coercive measures that impair or limit their right to freely exercise their spirituality and beliefs.

Given that members of indigenous peoples are also full citizens of the State, it is worth considering whether it is necessary to make reference to them separately, or whether their protections would be sufficient along with the application of the same rules to those who are not part of that group. However, it is also true that historically this is a discriminated minority that went through forced religious conversions.[25] These historical processes cannot be judged anachronistically, and they also seem irreversible. However, in light of the current sensitivity in terms of religious freedom, this reference made by the proposed law seems reasonable, especially because of its limited, specific terms.

---

character." Notice the restriction is on the very act of religious transmission: not to mention media ownership.

[24] AG/RES. 2888 (XLVI-O/ 16), Approved on June 14, 2016. However, the Proposed Law has omitted the other two paragraphs of the same article from the statement: "*3. Indigenous Peoples have the right to preserve, protect, and access their sacred sites, including their burial grounds; to use and control their sacred objects relics, and to recover their human remains. 4. States, in conjunction with indigenous peoples, shall adopt effective measures, to promote respect for indigenous spirituality and beliefs, and to protect the integrity of the symbols, practices, ceremonies, expressions, and spiritual protocols of indigenous peoples, in accordance with international law.*".

[25] It is worth remembering that even the Constitution of Argentina of 1853 contained a clause, eliminated in 1994, which entrusted Congress with the "conversion of the Indians to Catholicism" (former Article 67, paragraph 15). In 1994, it was the Catholic Church that asked for its elimination.

3.3 *Equality and Non-discrimination. Restrictions to Religious Freedom*

Articles 5 and 6 of the proposed law are dedicated, respectively, to the prohibition of religious discrimination and to limitations to the exercise of rights derived from religious freedom.

The principle of non-discrimination is already established in the declarations and international treaties on human rights: In all of those and from the outset, religion or "creed" are mentioned among the categories that cannot justify unequal treatment or a disproportionate allocation of rights (discrimination); that is, they are part of the "suspect classifications." In Argentine domestic law, at both the federal and provincial levels, there are many rules that prohibit and sanction religious discrimination, in addition to the very broad "Anti-discrimination law" (Law 23562) in force.

Article 5 of the proposed law ratifies the prohibition of discrimination based on religious beliefs, and it especially applies to access to public office.

The obligation not to discriminate based on religion governs both individuals and the State and its agencies. This is why the proposed law includes an important exception in Article 5:

> This law preserves the right of religious entities or institutions with a confessional ideology to demand their members, volunteers or employees to adjust their behavior to their doctrine, to the religious or moral principles of the institution, and to reasonably exercise the right of admission and exclusion.

This is a logical exception. The prohibition of discrimination based on religion is not absolute. The fact that religion is a "suspect classification" when it comes to establishing a disproportionate allocation of rights does not mean that such a distinction can never be made, but that it is subject to strict scrutiny and must be reasonably justified. And the case contemplated by this rule is precisely one of those reasonable exceptions: A religious entity (or a confessional institution) has the right to demand from its members, managers, employees, and volunteers a certain religious affiliation (if it can be considered a requirement of suitability for such position) and to also comply with the religious and moral standards of the confession involved. Those who violate said code of conduct may be legitimately excluded, or not admitted, to perform those functions.

Regarding the admissible limitations to the exercise of the rights derived from religious freedom, Article 6 of the proposed law repeats what is already established in international human rights treaties on the matter (e.g., Article 12 of the Pact of San José, Costa Rica), including the requirement that such limitations be imposed by law. The innovative element, worthy of support, is that the proposed law recognizes "respect for human dignity" as a possible foundation for these limitations.

3.4 Right to Conscientious Objection

The most remarkable innovation of the proposed law and the one that has provoked the most intense controversy was the article intended to regulate the exercise of the right to conscientious objection, both in its individual and institutional aspects, or "ideological objection." The article, which is unprecedented in previous drafts, stated:

> ARTICLE 7. Right to conscientious, institutional or ideological objection. The right to raise the objections provided in this article may be exercised by those holding such rights according to what is established in the following sections:
>
> (I) Everyone has the right to invoke a relevant religious duty or a substantial religious or moral conviction as a reason to refuse to fulfill a legal obligation. Whenever possible, the objector must offer the performance of a substitute performance that could, as far as possible, satisfy the public charge.
>
> Compliance with the objected obligation is only required if:
>
> (a) the public authority that has imposed the obligation considers that it is due to a compelling public interest, which is impossible to achieve without effective compliance to the rule, and it is not possible to make a reasonable accommodation that would avoid the violation of the freedom of conscience of the objector; or
> (b) The exercise of conscientious objection there would produce direct damage to the rights of a third-party that could be avoided through the objected conduct.
>
> The good faith of the objector is presumed by the willingness to comply with a reasonable alternative performance, or by the existence of an express mandatory rule imposed by the religious entity to which the objector belongs as established by evidence.
>
> The objector cannot be sanctioned or suffer any discrimination for the exercise of his right.
>
> The right to conscientious objection may be exercised, among other circumstances, in the following cases: military service, fulfillment of professional tasks in the healthcare sector, submission to medical treatment, active tribute to national symbols, oaths, work or school activity on holidays or religious rest days; the preceding without prejudice to the provisions of Article 8 on reasonable accommodation in the relevant areas.
>
> (II) Legal entities may similarly raise institutional or ideological objections, in any of the following:
>
> (a) In the case of religious entities or legal entities constituted by religious entities for the fulfillment of their purposes, or
> (b) In the case of private legal entities, for-profit and nonprofit, that establish in their bylaws the religious or ethical principles on which the objection is based, or
> (c) In the case of legal entities, for-profit and nonprofit, constituted for the exercise of any lawful activity by clearly identified individual persons and the obligation objected to violate the freedom of conscience of those persons.

The recognition of conscientious objection as a subjective right rooted in the freedom of conscience protected by the National Constitution and by international human rights treaties is a very healthy and significant advance, even if the proposed clause could be improved. Its background consists of the recognition made by the Supreme

Court of this right in several cases related to compulsory military service,[26] blood transfusions,[27] and even to abortion[28] and to situations related to euthanasia,[29] as well as a good number of laws and regulations, at both national and provincial levels, that have established and regulated conscientious objection in different cases.[30]

The article seems to establish a substitute action as a condition to the exercise of this right. This is correct in some cases where it is possible (for example, military service), but not in others, or at least not as clearly. This should be improved on the drafting.[31] The two scenarios that limit the possibility of raising a conscientious objection are an echo of the USA jurisprudence in the matter, and are presented in an alternative way ("or"), when it would be better that it be cumulative ("and"). In addition, the second clause is worded inadequately: The objected-to conduct should not be imposed if its omission could be followed by harm to a third-party, but instead only in the case that such direct harm could not be avoided in any way other than by forcing the objector to act or stop doing what his conscience prevents him to do. It is not the same.

With these adjustments, the rule has great relevance, and it is praiseworthy.

The law of Portugal (Article 6) has general guidelines on matters of conscientious objection, but it is limited to certain provisions of specific rules. But it mentions the subject again with greater precision and broadness in Article 12.

The law of Peru (Article 4) dedicates an article specifically to this issue, but introduces an incorrect restriction: The objection would only be admissible if there is a contradiction between the behavior governed by the law and an imperative duty "recognized by the religious entity to which [the objector] belongs." This would work well, for example, in the case of the Sabbath rest for the Adventists or the Jews. But it would not allow objection to military service to a Catholic or an Evangelical (because the confessions to which they belong do not prohibit compliance with such service) not even in the case of a deeply rooted and strong pacifist conviction.[32] That is wrong, because conscience is still personal, although it can be formed or determined by the ethical norms of the religious confession to which one belongs.

The law of Mexico, on the other hand, directly prohibits conscientious objection, and does so in Article 1, which demonstrates Mexico's current situation and frames

---

[26]"Portillo" (ED 133-365). Today, mandatory military service is not required, but in the case of it re-introduction the law itself (No. 24,429) provides for and regulates the exercise of conscientious objection.

[27]"Bahamondez" (ED 153-249).

[28]"F., A. L. s/Medida autosatisfactiva", decision F. 259. XLVI., of March 13, 2012.

[29]"Diez", of July 7, 2015.

[30]See (Navarro Floria 2004, 2014b). On the general issue of conscientious objection, see (Navarro-Valls and Martínez-Torron 2012).

[31]For example, there is no substitute performance, in a strict sense, for conscientious objection to performing an abortion, although it is reasonable to expect the objecting doctor or health worker to work in the hospital for the same amount of time, performing other tasks that are not linked directly or indirectly to the objected task.

[32]With this criterion, in Argentina, conscientious objection in the "Portillo" case would not have been admitted.

the debate on this issue. The laws of Spain, Chile, and Colombia say nothing on the matter.

The provision about the "institutional objection" or ideological objection, which is found in the second part of Article 7 of the Argentine proposed law, does not have any equivalents in the other laws that have been analyzed, and it is an important advance.

But as stated above, in the 2019 version of the bill, this section, referring to conscientious objection, disappears completely. It is hoped that during the legislative discussion it will be possible to return to it, although the simultaneous discussion about the legalization of abortion makes it difficult. It is a shame, because obviously the right to conscientious objection goes beyond the case of abortion.

3.5 Right to Reasonable Accommodation

Another relevant innovation of this proposed law, which has no parallel in previous drafts or in most of the laws already in force in other countries,[33] is the obligation imposed on employers to seek "reasonable accommodation" of working conditions to enable their employees to comply with their religious duties. The proposed law establishes this right in these terms:

> ARTICLE 8. Duty of reasonable accommodation. Employers, both State and private, have a duty to reasonably accommodate their activities to the religious practices of their workers and potential workers. The same duty applies to educational institutions with regard to their students and potential students.
>
> To require reasonable accommodation, the person, offering his or her collaboration with the employer or the educational institution, must prove:
>
> (a) That the practice that requires accommodation is based on a relevant religious or moral belief;
> (b) That such belief is sincere, for which it will be sufficient–if it be the case– the verification of the existence of a rule or precept within the religious entity to which the person belongs; and
> (c) That the inconsistency between the required behavior and the religious practice is of sufficient relevance to affect the person's freedom of religion and conscience.
>
> Once these conditions are met, the private employer or the institution may only be exempted from carrying out the accommodation if they show the following:
>
> (a) That there is a compelling state interest or a substantial need for the activity of the private employer that justifies the required conduct;
> (b) That there has been an attempt to accommodate such activities; and
> (c) That it is not possible to accommodate the religious practice without suffering an excessive burden.

[33] A similar rule, but somewhat more restrictive and less detailed, is found in Article 14 of the Law on Religious Freedom of Portugal.

As noted, the provision includes both work and educational aspects, including school activities. The obligation to attend class or take exams is a recurring issue, especially on a Saturday, which affects the religious obligation of day of rest of religious confessions such as Jewish or Adventist.

It is worth noting that the 1981 United Nations Declaration on the Elimination of All Forms of Intolerance and of Discrimination Based on Religion or Belief proclaims that the right to religious freedom includes the freedom "To observe days of rest and to celebrate holidays and ceremonies in accordance with the precepts of one's religion or belief." (Article 6, Section h).[34]

Up until now, these problems are resolved within the framework of conscientious objection. In Argentina, judicial rulings protect Adventist employees in conflict with their employers who try to impose work on a Saturday.[35] There are rules in the education system that grant an exemption from Saturday activities for Jewish and Adventist students.[36]

This proposed law is even broader, because it does not make reference to a particular religious group, and it certainly deserves to be approved. It is unprecedented in the laws of the region, except for the law of Portugal, in Article 14, and in the law of Peru, in its Article 3(f) but that provision refers to a subsequent regulation. The 2019 text is somewhat more restrictive than the 2017 one, because it does not apply at the time of hiring employees.

4 Churches and Religious Communities as Legal Persons

When introducing this question, which is presented as the central topic of the proposed law, it is necessary to clarify its language.

The proposed law defines it as follows, in its Article 3:

> 'Religious entities' in this law are defined as churches, confessions or religious communities that bring together those who share the same faith in order to enable, facilitate or promote the rights set forth in Article 2 and perform activities related to the exercise of such rights, whatever the name or the organizational model they adopt.

This is an attempt to clarify what the Civil and Commercial Code states in Article 148(e) when it recognizes "*churches, communities, confessions and religious entities*" as legal persons: This proposed law assigns a generic meaning to the term

[34]ILO Convention 14 of 1921 on Weekly Rest (Industry), and ratified by Argentina (Law 12232, BO 18/10/1935), states that "Rest shall coincide, wherever possible, with the days established by the tradition or customs of the country or region" (Article 2.3). Convention 106, of 1957, on Weekly Rest (Commerce and offices)—which has not been ratified by Argentina—reproduces the same rule but clarifies that "the traditions and customs of religious minorities will be respected, wherever possible" (Article 6.4).

[35]CNTrab, sala X, 26/04/2004, "S., M. R. c/ Longseller S.A. s/ despido", ED 28/7/2004, annotated by Navarro Floria (2015b).

[36]I.e. in the national order: resolutions 650/68, 1047/68 and 1325/87 of the Ministry of Education.

"entities" in order to define "churches, communities and religious confessions," as they are stated in the law of Spain (Article 2.2), as well as Portugal (Article 20), although the latter does not include confessions. It is the same method used by the law of Peru (Article 5),[37] and of Chile (Article 4) which replaces "confessions" with "institutions."

The recognition of the legal personality of churches and religious communities is an exceptionally complex problem (Navarro Floria 2006). These are bodies that have their own characteristics, which distinguish them from other legal persons, and, in addition, there are big differences among them in terms of structure, size, constitution, and internal operating rules. This makes it practically impossible for the legislator to establish general or common rules for these entities but, at the same time, the State feels under the obligation to try.

One of the characteristics of these institutions is that they often differ from any other associative group (associations, societies, labor unions, political parties, cooperatives) not only because of their purpose and activity (religious), but even in the way human persons form or join them. The affiliation or association to a society, party, mutual, or similar entity, is a voluntary act, normally reserved for persons of legal age or with sufficient capacity to do so. Conversely, there are religious communities into which one is directly "born." While it is possible to convert to Judaism or Islam, for example, the vast majority of its followers were born Jews or Muslims by blood.[38] In other cases, members join by the decision of their parents or other persons at an early age (as is normally the case in the Catholic Church, Orthodox churches, or Protestant churches that allow the baptism of children).

The second problem is establishing who should be recognized as a legal entity or person, and this is linked to the internal structure of religious organizations. There are churches that are the same worldwide, with local communities subject to a single central authority. It is possible that this authority resides abroad and has a form of legal organization already recognized in its country of origin or establishment. While in other religions, there is a certain spiritual communion and faith among the believers, but each community is perfectly autonomous with respect to the others. Which entity will be given legal recognition? Will it be the "religion" even if it does not have its own legal structure? Or will it be the individual community?

The third problem is that some religious communities have their own "right" (or legal status) already established and known to some extent (albeit not necessarily written or codified) while others do not have such rules. This alerts State bureaucrats who are eager to register (and, if possible, to review and amend) a charter as if it were a foundation or a corporation.

One could continue to add more questions: Should the State keep a registry of churches and religious communities? Could the State do it without imposing changes to the autonomy and uniqueness of each church or religious community? Could or

[37] The law of Peru, however, includes the requirement that "entities" have "*creed, sacred writings, moral doctrine, worship, organization and ministry of their own*," which will be difficult for some to prove.

[38] In relation to this topic, see (Navarro Floria and Lo Prete 2011).

should the State force them to constitute some form of institution or entity in order for them to participate in legal affairs? If there is a registration, should it be compulsory or merely optional? In either case, what happens to a religious community that decides not to register, but exists in fact? Should that be sanctioned, ignored, allowed?

4.1 The Registration and Control Regime

The proposed law in Argentina, due to its history and background, decided to create a Registry of religious entities (we have already seen that churches, communities, and confessions are included under that name) and assigns it a "voluntary" character.

Registration in such Registry, according to Article 10, is "*voluntary and free and implies the recognition of the legal personality provided for in article 148, paragraph e), of the Civil and Commercial Code of the Nation, without the need for any other registration or authorization.*" And then it is clarified that:

> Religious entities that decide not to register may exercise, as well as their members, the rights of association and religious freedom in accordance with the National Constitution and international human rights treaties.

This rule is confusing. It is clear that the entities that choose to register are recognized as legal persons. It seems that it is precisely such registration that gives them a legal person character in the terms of the CCC and that therefore, the churches, confessions, and religious communities are private legal entities that need state authorization in order to function. This does not contradict the second paragraph transcribed above, because it is one thing to be able to exercise individual rights, including the right of association (for example, forming civil associations, or simple associations with religious purposes) and a different one is the right of a church or community to be recognized as a legal entity. Ultimately, it seems that according to the proposed law, unregistered churches or communities would not be legal entities under the terms of the CCC. The 2019 text improves and clarifies this point, because it expressly says that the registration in the Registry is only to publicize the religious entities that already exist without the need for any registration.

The Registry is unique and depends on the Federal Government. It is an exception (and not the only one) to the rule that states that the registration and authorization (when appropriate) of private legal entities is the responsibility of the Provinces. The law could have laid the foundation for that registration or authorization without encroaching on provincial jurisdiction in matters of law enforcement, but it has opted for centralization instead.

There are several requirements to access this registry (and if these views are shared, they are requirements to access to legal personality):

(a) "*certify its constitution or establishment in the Argentine territory, its length of time in the country, as well as the effective exercise of religious activities*": the proposed law provides both the possibility of entities created in Argentina, as well as abroad. The determining factor is the "effective exercise of religious activities," which means that they have certain background or history, although there is no minimum period of activity, like there is in Mexico (five years, Article 7), Peru (seven years, Article 14), or Portugal (thirty years, Article 37).

(b) *"accurately prove the number of followers according to the parameters provided by the respective regulations*": as is the case of Peru, in Article 14(a), there will be regulations that determine the minimum number of followers. Such number should be low, so as not to de-legitimize the regime.

(c) *"Communicate their religious principles, the most important sources of their doctrine, and their dogmas or doctrinal body*": This is only an informative obligation; the state authority has no jurisdiction to judge the contents of their religious beliefs.[39]

(d) *"Describe its domestic and international organization, if there is one*": This is also just an informative obligation.

(e) *"together with its statutory regulations, provide a public deed or a private document with a signature certified by a public notary, which contains, at least: I. its name, which should not be confused with other entities already registered, legal address, and other data that allows recognition of the entity; II. A clear and exact expression of their religious purposes; III. Internal rules of operation and government of the entity; IV. Decision-making bodies of the entity, their powers, and requirements for the appointment of authorities; V. ministerial structure and the way to get access to the ministry, and the form of entry and exit of the followers; VI. Rules of administration and disposition of goods, as well as their destination in case of dissolution*": It may be difficult to comply with this obligation. What are the statutory rules of the Orthodox Church, or of Judaism, or of Islam? There is an unresolved tension between the possibilities of registering churches or religious confessions as such and registering representative entities that can have a charter. The requirements for the organization's charter, as required by these rules, are reasonable and match the requirements found in several parallel laws.[40]

(f) *"Indicate the location of their temples or places of worship and places dedicated to religious activity*": This assumes that the entity already has temples or places of worship at the time of registration. But if this were not the case, because it is an entity in the process of being established in the country (and wishes to do so), the lack of such places should not be an obstacle to registration.

(g) *"Briefly describe the main rites, worship services, and celebrations, which should not affect security, order, health, public morals and respect for human dignity*": Once again, the obligation is informative. Presumably, no church or community would report the performance of rites that do not meet these requirements.

---

[39]This coincides with Article 35 of the Law of Portugal. There is no equivalent requirement in the other laws of the region.

[40]México, Articles 6 and 7; Chile, Article 12; Peru, Article 14.

(h) *"Identify its administrative and religious authorities; in case they do not coincide, describe the relationship between them"*: This refers to those entities that are in exercise or functioning at the time of applying for the registration. Article 18 of the proposed law requires that, after the initial registration, this information be kept updated through reports showing the changes that are made.

The authorities of the Registry will have the ability to sanction those registered entities that deviate from the law, even to the canceling of the registration (Article 19). There was an excess here that had to be corrected, because a cancellation should be reserved for judges, after a process in which the right to be heard is guaranteed, as foreseen by the laws of Spain (Article 5) and Peru (Article 14). An administrative cancellation is only provided for in Law of Mexico, which at least establishes a detailed procedure (Article 30). The proposed law in Argentina only provides judicial recourse from decisions already made by the Ministry of Religion (Article 23).[41] The correction was made in the 2019 text.

Registrations and cancellations must be published in the Official Gazette (which is not the case now), according to Article 20.[42] This is correct. This allows third parties who are affected to intervene and be heard (Article 21).

4.2 *Particular Cases*

The proposed law refers to some special cases in particular.

Article 12 refers to second-degree entities (federations or confederations of churches) that can also obtain their registration and recognition, explaining what type of representation they exercise with respect to their affiliated entities.

Article 13 refers to churches or religious communities established abroad, which are many, and that perform or intend to carry out activity in Argentina. It is correctly established that they are governed by the statutory and legal rules of their place of incorporation, and by the applicable public order rules of Argentina. By doing so, this corrects an error found in the Civil and Commercial Code on the applicable law to foreign legal persons (Navarro Floria 2017a).

Article 14 introduced an original rule, which was not present in the previous drafts or in the laws of other countries. It provides that when registering an entity that "*has hierarchical or organic dependency*" with respect to another (for example, a parish that is part of a diocese, or a branch that integrates a larger church), there must be an authorization by the authority of the parent entity. This is a reasonable and useful rule to prevent conflicts. However, this article disappeared in the 2019 text.

[41] Similar resources are provided for in the laws of Mexico (Article 33–35) and Chile (Article 11).

[42] Coincidentally, present in the laws of Mexico (Article 7) and Colombia (Article 10).

4.3 *Situation of the Catholic Church*

Article 24 of the proposed law exempts the Catholic Church from registration in the Registry and makes reference to the regime already in force that recognizes its legal personality. This is done in the following way:

> ARTICLE 24. - Scope of application. The Roman Catholic Apostolic Church maintains the recognition of its current public legal personality, without having to register in the Registry created by this law. Its relations with the National State are governed by the National Constitution, by the Agreements signed between the Argentine Republic and the Holy See, by the norms of the Civil and Commercial Code of the Nation and by the special laws applicable and ancillary to the present Law.

The recognition of the public legal personality of the Catholic Church, pre-existent to the National State itself, is confirmed in Argentina and was ratified by the new Civil and Commercial Code, though not without some debate.[43] The solution offered by the proposed law coincides with that of the laws of Portugal (Article 58), Peru (Second complementary provision), Colombia (Article 11), and Chile (Article 20).[44]

The proposed law still applies to the Catholic Church: some provisions clearly apply, such as the first chapter, the third, and, in a subsidiary way, some rules of the second chapter (such as Articles 14, 16, and 17 that recognize the autonomy of churches and some specific rights, which the Catholic Church definitely must also enjoy).

The difference in treatment is justified by the fact that not only does the Catholic Church have a constitutional recognition in Argentina, but it also has the possibility of entering into agreements with the State, governed by international law, due to the international legal personality of the Holy See, which is universally recognized. It is not, therefore, an undue privilege, but rather the verification of a reality, both legal and de facto.

4.4 *Rights of the Registered Entities*

What are the consequences of registration?

First, the recognition of legal capacity (Article 15),[45] limited by the principle of specialty that governs generally for all legal persons: that capacity is "*to perform legal acts and hold rights and duties that are necessary for the fulfillment of their purposes*," which, in principle, excludes lucrative activities.

[43] See (Navarro Floria 2015a).

[44] The law of Chile avoided mentioning the Catholic Church by name, making reference only to churches that had their legal status already recognized "at the date of publication of this law," although jurists unanimously understood that it was a reference to the Catholic Church (and the Orthodox Church of Antioch).

[45] This reinforces the interpretation that non-registered churches or communities are not recognized as legal persons.

It is expressly provided that to perform activities related to religion (educational, publishing, etc.) they may constitute other legal entities subject to the corresponding regulations.[46]

Second, the recognition of their ministers of worship, as well as the right these ministers hold to facilitate their ministry and the provision of religious assistance, and the protection granted to religious secrecy, in Articles 16(a) and (g). The law does not define what is understood by "ministers of worship" (it will depend on the statutory rules of each religious denomination). These rules deserved a more specific and clear development, like the one found in other parallel laws.[47] Ministers of worship are exempted from military service in Article 16(b), as is the case in the law of Portugal (Article 17) and what was already found in the Argentine regulations dedicated to this matter (Law 17,531).

Third, registered entities have the tax exemptions provided by the laws for religious entities, in Article 16(d).[48] This suggests that unregistered entities will not be exempt.

Moreover, temples, places of worship, and objects intended for worship are declared a type of property that cannot be attached or seized in Article 16(e). This was already a rule, but it was poorly drafted in the Civil and Commercial Code. This proposed law modifies the relevant article in the Code (Article 744), creating two standards with equal content. The one in the proposed law refers to registered entities in the Registry, while the one in force in the Civil Code seems to apply to entities that are not registered (therefore, the protection in the new law is more limited).

An innovative and much-appreciated provision, which is not present in the laws of other countries, is the right recognized to churches and religious communities to actively and passively represent their members in defense of their religious freedom rights, in Article 16(f).

Article 17 outlines the fundamental right of the recognition of the internal autonomy of these entities. However, Article 3 of the proposed law also recognizes this right to unregistered entities as a fundamental element of their right to religious freedom. This autonomy is also generally recognized in comparative law: Spain (Article 6.1), Portugal (Article 22), Colombia (Article 13), and Peru (Article 6).

---

[46]Similarly, the laws of Peru (Article 6), Colombia (Article 14), and Portugal (Article 27). In Chile, the rules of derivative legal entities (Article 9) has been quite complex.

[47]Especially, the law of Portugal, in Articles 15.2, 3, and 16, but also Chile (Article 13), Colombia (Article 16), and Peru (Articles 6 and 9). The law of Mexico deals extensively with ministers but restricts their rights, according to their long-standing constitutional tradition (Articles 9 and 15).

[48]Similarly, the law of Chile (Article 17), and more generically, the law of Peru (Article 11).

5 Legislative Amendments

5.1 *Civil and Commercial Code*

The previous "religious freedom law" proposals included the proposal to modify several articles of the existing Civil Code. Most of those modifications are unnecessary today, due to the validity of a new Civil and Commercial Code passed in 2014. However, an article in that code has a defect in its wording and the new proposed law intends to correct it. That is Subsection (d) of Article 744, which makes reference to goods that are not in the market and therefore cannot be attached or seized.

The wording of the new proposed law limits this condition to "*the temples and places of worship and their dependencies, as well as sacred objects or objects destined for worship owned by religious entities that are recognized by the State, except for debts incurred during their acquisition, construction or repair.*"

The rule is correct, but it also has two surprising differences with another one included in the same proposed law, which is Article 16(e), with almost the same content, but limits this protection to objects destined "exclusively" to worship (an adverb that is not proposed to be included in the Code), and that only admits the foreclosure or enforcement of payment of debts derived from the acquisition or construction of property, but not from its repairs, as is stated in the proposed modification to the Code. The repetition of rules, with almost the same content (although not entirely identical), seems unnecessary: the Code would be sufficient.[49]

5.2 *Penal Code*

Also following the pattern of previous drafts, the 2017 proposed law intended to modify three articles of the Penal Code, and repeal another.

Two of the modifications consist in establishing a type of aggravated theft (Article 163 of the Penal Code, an aggravating circumstance that also applies to the crime of robbery according to Article 167 of the same code), as well as regarding the crime of damage to property (Article 184), when the act affects an "*object considered to be sacred or destined exclusively to worship by a religious entity,*" or a "*building considered to be sacred or destined exclusively to worship by a religious entity.*" This proposed modification is plausible, although unnecessarily limited by the adverb "exclusively" that is used in both cases. Why would the intentional damage of a church destined just for worship is aggravated but not if there are concerts held periodically in the same premises?

[49]Although there is also a confusing expression here, given that it speaks of "*religious entities recognized by the State.*" The Catholic Church should undoubtedly be included in this concept, and surely, if this proposed law is approved, it should also include the churches and religious communities that register before the RENAER; even if that registration does not exactly create "recognition.".

Another timely proposed modification is the one made with respect to Article 247 of the Penal Code, which punishes the misappropriation or misrepresentation of titles and honors, or the illegal exercise of a profession. This modification intends to include the punishment of someone who "*without turning out to be a minister of worship, performs acts considered that is unique to that ministry*."[50]

Finally, the proposed law intends to repeal Article 228 of the Criminal Code, a rule that inexplicably retains formal validity but is not applicable because it refers to acts committed in violation of the right of Patronage, which is not in force now. This modification is correct.

Unlike previous proposed bills, it is a pity that this time religious freedom has not been included as a protected legal interest, and it did not criminalize actions in direct violation of that freedom, such as forcing someone to participate in an act of worship against his will or preventing him from doing so.[51] The laws of other countries do not include such modification in criminal law. However, this does not mean that a religious factor may not exist in criminal law.[52]

However, this whole section is absent in the 2019 text. Surely, this is due to the fact that there is already a draft new Criminal Code, which includes several of these reforms.

6 Transition Rules

Given that the proposed regulation replaces a previous one, it is essential to include rules that regulate such transition.[53] Chapter IV establishes those rules in Articles 30–33.

Basically, those entities that have operated with a non-religious structure (civil association, foundation or other) before the new law are allowed to transform into what they really are, with a moderate cost (being able to make the necessary adjustments in their property records without cost), and retaining the tax exemptions they had before.[54]

---

[50] In this language, the words "turning out to" ("resulte" in Spanish) are not necessary.

[51] In 1989, President Alfonsín sent a proposed law to Congress to introduce specific protection of religious freedom into the Penal Code. Because it was not examined, the same proposed law was sent again with some additions by President Menem (Message 1991/92). It was unanimously approved by the Senate on June 16, 1993, and it received commendable comments by jurists [for example, (Frías 1994)]. The approved text may be read in "Trámite Parlamentario" 1993, nº 37 (21/6/93). For another draft of the Criminal Code that considered the topic, see (Navarro Floria).

[52] The law of Peru contains a generic rule in this matter, the First Final Complementary Disposition, which is limited to make reference to "current criminal or administrative regulations.".

[53] The laws of Spain (transitory and final provisions), Portugal (Articles 62, 63 and 69), Chile (Article 18), Colombia (Article 18), and Peru (transitory complementary provision) did the same thing.

[54] Regarding taxation, the proposed law only refers to laws on this matter that are already in force. This was different from the law of Portugal, which included a regulation of the subject (Articles 31 and 32, very detailed).

As expected, the legislator assigns the making of the regulations to the Executive Power, and appoints the Secretariat of Religious Affairs as the application authority, which operates in Argentina within the scope of the Ministry of Foreign Affairs and Religious Affairs (Article 33); and Law 21745 is repealed (Article 34), which created the National Registry of Religions.

7 The Subjects Omitted

After comparing this proposed law with its national background and with some of the laws already in force in Ibero-America, the conclusion is that some provisions present in those foreign laws are missing here.

First of all, the proposed bill fails to establish a mechanism of agreements between the State and religious confessions, to regulate subjects of common interest or of particular interest to any of them. Agreements with religious confessions have been a useful tool in practice, though not exempt from criticism, i.e., in Spain (established by the law in Article 7), as well as in Italy, although there is no law that regulates such agreements since they originate directly from the Constitution. In Latin America, they have been established by the law of Colombia (Article 15), where a public legal agreement was signed with the evangelical churches; and in Peru (Article 15), but not in Chile or Mexico. They are also established by the law of Portugal, which allocates a whole chapter (Articles 45–51) and includes a proclamation of the principle of cooperation between the State and religious confessions (Article 5), which is ultimately the foundation for this type of agreement.

Domestic legal agreements with religious confessions are a sort of imitation of the concordats and agreements (of public international law) that the State can sign and in fact signs with the Catholic Church, represented by the Holy See. This possibility does not exist for other religious confessions that lack international legal personality. Significantly, the countries that have established the signing of these agreements in their laws or have such practices are those that have concordats in force with the Holy See, while those who do not have concordats have omitted this provision.[55] That being the case, it was expected that the law in Argentina would establish them. They are not established due to a poorly justified opposition from the evangelical churches, a situation that deprives the country of a useful tool for the development of Ecclesiastical Law.

Another institution present in both comparative law (in the laws of Spain, in Article 8, and the laws of Portugal, in Articles 52–57) and in previous Argentine drafts, which has now been omitted, is the creation of a commission or advisory council on matters of religious freedom. It is true that this commission may have some practical difficulties with its implementation, and specifically when it comes to the selection of its members in order to satisfy the different religious trends. But

[55]See (Navarro Floria 2011).

it is also true that even in Argentina there is valuable and successful background in this area, which could have been institutionalized.[56]

Of course, the proposed law could also include other rules that have not been provided, probably in a deliberate manner due to the complexities inherent to these topics. I think, for example, of the recognition of civil effects to the celebration of religious marriages,[57] the issue of religious education in public schools,[58] or religious assistance in the armed or security forces. Nothing prevents them from being part of subsequent legislation.

8 Conclusion

The new proposed law in Argentina, both the 2017 version and the almost equal version of 2019, should be well received, and the hope is that this time it will obtain legislative approval. The overall assessment of it is clearly positive, although it could be improved, as has been explained in the previous pages.

References

Frías PJ (1994) Academie internationale de droit compare: la liberte religieuse, freedom of religion: informe nacional de la Republica Argentina. In: Sanchez AM (ed) El Derecho Público actual. Depalma, Buenos Aires, pp 87–98

Lo Prete O (2013) Una ley de libertad religiosa en la Argentina: asignatura pendiente. Derecho y Reli VIII

Navarro Floria JG (1993) Las confesiones religiosas distintas de la Iglesia Católica en el derecho argentino. El Derecho 151–897

Navarro Floria JG (1997) El nuevo proyecto de ley de cultos de libertad religiosa. El Derecho Legis Argentina 2

Navarro Floria JG (2001) Un nuevo proyecto de ley de libertad religiosa. El Derecho Legis Argentina 19

Navarro Floria JG (2004) El derecho a la objeción de conciencia. Ábaco, Buenos Aires

Navarro Floria JG (2006) El reconocimiento jurídico de las iglesias, comunidades y entidades religiosas. In: Actas del V Coloquio del Consorcio Latinoamericano de Libertad Religiosa: Actualidad y retos del Derecho Eclesiástico del Estado en Latinoamérica. Consorcio Latinoamericano de Libertad Religiosa, Ciudad del Mexico

Navarro Floria JG (ed) (2011) Acuerdos y concordatos entre la Santa Sede y los países americanos. Universidad Catolica Argentina, Buenos Aires

[56]In the years 2000 and 2001, being the Secretary of Religious Affairs Norberto Padilla, I was the coordinator of an Advisory Council on Religious Freedom, which was the seed for the later Argentine Council for Religious Freedom (CALIR), currently operating in the non-governmental sector.

[57]This issue has been regulated in the law of Portugal, in its extensive Article 19. In contrast, the law of Mexico ratifies the exclusive jurisdiction of the State over acts regarding the civil status of persons (Article 4).

[58]Also, in this case, the law of Portugal includes a detailed regulation, in Article 24.

Navarro Floria JG (2014a) El Derecho Eclesiástico en el Digesto Jurídico Argentino, ED 260-615 y EDLA 2014-B-951. El Derecho Legis, Argentina
Navarro Floria JG (2014b) Objeción de conciencia. In: Rivera JC, Elias JS, Grosman LS, Legarre S (eds) Tratado de los Derechos Constitucionales. Abeledo Perrot, Buenos Aires
Navarro Floria JG (2015a) La personalidad jurídica de iglesias, confesiones y comunidades religiosas. Rev Derecho Priv y Comunitario 113–141
Navarro Floria JG (2015b) El derecho a la objeción de consciencia a partir de una oportuna sentencia en materia laboral. Rev Latinoam Derecho y Reli I:1–17. doi:10.7764/RLDR.1.12
Navarro Floria JG (2016a) Los derechos personalísimos. El Derecho, Buenos Aires
Navarro Floria JG (2016b) Disposición de un cadáver: problemas jurídicos y religiosos, ED 251-407. El Derecho
Navarro Floria JG (2017a) El inadecuado régimen de las personas jurídicas privadas extranjeras en el Código Civil y Comercial, ED 275. El Derecho D Doctrin y Jurisprud
Navarro Floria JG (2017b) La (relativamente ausente) libertad religiosa y de conciencia en la jurisprudencia de la Corte Interamericana de Derechos Humanos. In: Antón MM (ed) Sociedad, Derecho y factor religioso: estudios en honor del professor Isidoro Martín Sánchez. Granada, Comares, pp 465–478
Navarro Floria JG, Lo Prete O (2011) Proselitismo y libertad religiosa: una visión desde América Latina. Anu Derecho Eclesiástico del Estado XXVII:59–96
Navarro-Valls R, Martínez-Torron J (2012) Conflictos entre consciencia y ley. Las objeciones de consciencia, Iustel, Madrid

Secular State and Religious Education in Public Schools: The Brazilian Case

Jayme Weingartner Neto

Abstract The present work is about religion classes in the elementary schools of the Brazilian public education system, a controversial topic since the 1988 Federal Constitution first enlists it in Article 210. Even though the enrollment in the religious education class is optional, the classes are conducted on regular school hours, according to what the constitutional text determines, as an expression of the fundamental right to freedom of religion. Apart from the Constitution, there are also statutes that regulate religion teaching. That is precisely the case of the National Education Guidelines Act (federal statute n. 9394/1996), which ensures respect for religious and cultural diversity and prohibits any form of proselytism. Article 33 of such statute establishes that each State should determine the content of the religious education classes, as well as set the rules for the admission of teachers. The treaty signed by Brazil and the Holy See in 2008 also deals with religious education. Article 11 of the treaty allows for both catholic and other religions education classes. The Attorney General challenged all these statutes in the Supreme Court. In 2010, it filed an Action of Unconstitutionality, alleging that the statutes in regard to religious education classes in public schools violate Article 19 of the 1988 Federal Constitution, which defines Brazil as a secular State. In 2017, the Supreme Court of Justice, by a majority, dismissed the case, deeming the Action of Unconstitutionality devoid of legal grounds, and ruled that the government, observing the binomial State secularity (CF, Section 19,I)/acknowledgment of religious freedom (CF, Section 5th, VI), shall act in full regulation of compliance with the constitutional provision set forth in Section 210, §1st, authorizing the public school system, under equal conditions (CF, Article 5th, caput), to offer religious education of various beliefs by means of formal requirements previously set by the Brazilian Ministry of Education. The anxiety generated by the case depicts the dynamic religious pluralism that exists in Brazil, and exposes the dispute for the public arena, in a polarized environment in which fundamentalism speeches are not uncommon. The text concludes that as long as the Government is not excessively involved, neither confessional nor nonconfessional religious classes violate the Constitution.

J. Weingartner Neto (✉)
Rio Grande do Sul Court of Justice, LaSalle University, Porto Alegre, Brazil
e-mail: jwneto@tj.rs.gov.br

© Springer Nature Switzerland AG 2020

R. V. S. Alves (ed.), *Latin American Perspectives on Law and Religion*, Law and Religion in a Global Context 3,
https://doi.org/10.1007/978-3-030-46717-3_5

Keywords Religious education in public schools · Secular state · Freedom of religion or belief · Equality · Religion in Brazil

1 Introduction

The religious issue has been increasingly present on the international agenda and in the everyday life of people (even of atheists and agnostics). However, confluences and conflicts between religion and education deserve more attention. Brazil experiences an increase in social disputes regarding the religious matter. Regarding the governmental restrictions and constraints, the legal and institutional framework is currently at a low level, in comparison with 198 countries observed by the Pew Research Center in a series between 2007 and 2013. However, social hostilities, practiced by individuals, organizations, or private groups (which can go from armed conflicts to harassment and intimidation, vandalism, and outrage) are ranked at a high level and the bias is of an increase in risk despite such indicator (sum of high and very high levels), in a world average, has fallen from 33% (2012) to 27% (2013).[1]

The Brazilian religious experience, although very ambiguous, is very rich, having a great majority of Christians and an important minority composed of African descent religions, introduced at the time of slavery. According to the Brazilian Institute of Geography and Statistics—IBGE Census of 2000/2010, umbanda and candomblé (the major Afro-Brazilian religions) represent 0.3% of Brazilian religious diversity, with around 600,000 devotees. In a substantially Christian country, in which "the pastor is ascending and the priest is descending" (that were 123.2 million Catholics, a fall [of unprecedent numbers] in absolute figures in the period of a decade [a decrease of 9% points, from 73.6 to 64.6%]; 42.2 million of Protestants have reached 22.2% from the previous 15.4% [most of them Pentecostals and Neo-pentecostals]—which would currently mean 45 million), the African descent religions have remained unchanged well below the Spiritualists (3.8 million) and of those with no declared religion (15.3 million).[2]

This text discusses the intersection of religion and education, focusing on the tension of the secular State with religious education in public schools, as provided for in the Federal Constitution (CF, in the Portuguese abbreviation). To do so, upon the presentation of a brief general framework on the right to religious freedom as the one presented in Brazil (2), the impact of infra-constitutional legislation on the matter

[1]Thus, among the 25 most populous countries in the world, taking into consideration both indicators, Brazil, along with the Democratic Republic of the Congo, Japan, Philippines, and South Africa, are at the lower threshold, while Egypt, Indonesia, Pakistan, Russia, and Turkey lead the troubling rankings. Cf. Pew Research Center Religion and Public Life (www.pewforum.org/2015/02/26/religious-hostilities/).

[2]"On average, the Catholic Church lost 465 devotees a day between 2000 and 2010. Protestants have attracted 4383 new believers per day in the same period," with the Pentecostal denominations presenting the fastest growing number of devotees, according to the magazine Valor Econômico, Eu & Fim de Semana, 10/9/2015, p. 5.

is analyzed (3). Finally, the controversy brought to the Supreme Court is explored (4), and the final considerations are presented (5).

2 General Framework

In Brazil, the Federal Constitution of 1988 establishes a general right to religious freedom. In the constitutional text, starting from Sections 5, subsections VI, VII, and VIII; 19, subsection I; 143, §§ 1st and 2nd; 150, subsection VI, "b"; 210, § 1st [the religious education, which is of optional enrollment, shall constitute a subject of the regular schedule of public schools for elementary school]; 213, Caput, and subsection II; and 226, § 2nd (in addition to the reference, in the preamble: "Under the Protection of God").

The three items of Section 5 grant, strictly speaking, two fundamental rights, very much related: freedom of conscience and freedom of religion. The first part of subsection VI generically ensures the freedom of conscience that, further on, in subsection VIII, shall present the right to objection (or excuse) of conscience in a much broader sense. Such freedom, in short, reflects on the practical moral autonomy of the individual, the ability of self-determination with regard to ethical and existential standards, whether related to one's conduct or to the conduct of others—in the total freedom of self-perception, being either on a rational level, a symbolic-mythical level or even of mystery. As for *freedom of religion* as a *complex right*, it encompasses, in its *core, the freedom to have, not to have or to stop having a religion* and it unfolds in *several other rights*: *freedom of belief* (2nd part of subsection VI), freedom of expression and information on religious matters, *freedom of worship* (3rd part of subsection VI) and a specification, the *right to religious assistance* (subsection VII) and other related fundamental rights, such as of assembly, association and privacy, with the peculiarities that the religious dimension entails.

Regarding the *normative scope,* religious freedom comprises two large dimensions, being presented as *subjective right* (1) and *objective vector* (2). When examined in terms of subjective law, it includes two other categories, depending on the individual: *individual subjective rights* (1.1), which belong to Brazilians and foreigners (natural people), including minors and the disabled (with particularities in their exercise); and *subjective rights of legal entities* (1.2) entitled by churches and religious denominations. From an objective point of view, religious freedom has at least three aspects: *principles* (2.1), *duties of protection* (2.2), and *institutional guarantees* (2.3).[3]

Regarding the objective dimension (2), it is a structural problem, related to the organization of the State, which is part of the political–administrative organization of

[3]In another work, I have presented a *Jusfundamental positions catalog* (CPJ, in the Portuguese abbreviation; over eighty) which encapsulates the content and scope of religious freedom. For a wide and detailed discussion, including historical aspects, with full bibliographic indication, see Weingartner Neto (2007).

democratic State of law that declares that *religious denominations must be separated from the State*—an idea of separation of religious denominations from the State, the principle of Church–State separation, enshrined in subsection I of Section 19 of the Brazilian Constitution. Brazilian doctrine usually deals with the subject under the scope of freedom of religious organization, identifying the principle of separation (also of neutrality and/or nondenominationalism), sparingly referring to cooperation.

In the constitutional jurisprudence,[4] there is an important precedent of the Brazilian Supreme Federal Court (STF, in the Portuguese abbreviation) that settled controversy opposing the right to education and religious freedom. It refers to the Regulatory Appeal in the Suspension of Injunctive Relief 389, 2009 (STA AgR 389, in the Portuguese abbreviation), in which the Federal Court—*by rejecting a regulatory appeal entered against a decision (from an Appeals Court Judge from Brazilian Regional Federal Courts of the 3rd Region), which had suspended the determination that it would be appropriate for authors of an ordinary lawsuit from the Brazilian state of Minas Gerais [secondary school students professing the Jewish faith] to participate in the Brazilian government National High School Exam [ENEM, in the Portuguese abbreviation] on a date compatible with the exercise of faith professed by them (which would be set by the authorities responsible for the administration of the tests and would have the same degree of difficulty as the tests carried out by all other students), maintained the basis of the decision challenged (risk to public order, in terms of legal and administrative order).*[5]

The Court has stated that the fundamental right to religious freedom imposes, on the State, the *duty of neutrality in view of religious phenomena,* forbidden to privilege a certain denomination to the detriment of others—which *does not mean* "*state indifference*, being necessary that the State, in certain situations, adopt *positive behaviors* in order to avoid barriers or overloads that may impede or hinder some options in terms of faith." It was emphasized that it is not unconstitutional for the State to relate to religious denominations, even in view of social benefits that they are capable of generating, not allowing themselves to take on certain religious conceptions as the official or right ones, which benefit a religious group or grant it privileges to the detriment of others. Therefore, it should promote free competition in the "market of religious ideas."

It was asserted that the designation of an *alternative date* for carrying out the ENEM tests by the religious group in question, although it could be, *in principle, considered an "accommodation" measure, designed to eliminate the undesirable overloads mentioned*, would not be in line with the principle of isonomy, becoming a privilege for that group. It was observed then that the *Brazilian Ministry of Education offers the applicants, who by virtue of religious options cannot do the tests on Saturdays, the possibility of doing them after sunset, an option that has been applied*

[4] A more systematic jurisprudential perspective of the Federal Supreme Court (STF) can be found in Weingartner Neto (2011). Latest and detailed comments on freedom of religion, through the constitutional perspective, including foreign constitutions and international law, see Weingartner Neto (2014).

[5] STF, STA/389, Suspension of Injunction, Full Court, Chief Justice of the Brazilian Supreme Federal Court Gilmar Ferreira Mendes, sentence on December 3, 2009, *DJE* 11/12/2009.

for some time, in relation to the Seventh-day Adventist Church, a religious group that also has the Sabbath, which should be observed on the seventh day of the week, specifically, from Friday sunset to Saturday sunset. However, not being insensitive to the argument that the measure adopted by the Brazilian Ministry of Education could harm the applicants practicing of such religious denomination—who *would have to be confined* so that only at the end of the day the tests would begin—it was considered that such measure would be, in view of the problems arising from the *designation of an alternative date*, more consistent with the State's duty to be neutral in view of religious phenomena and with the need to treat all religious denominations in an isonomic manner.

Chief Justice of the Brazilian Supreme Federal Court Gilmar Ferreira Mendes finally stated that *one would not take into account a definitive position* on the matter given the existence of two direct unconstitutional actions pending judgment, in which it shall be possible to deepen the subject, in order to define more precisely the scopes of protection and of the fundamental right to religious freedom (CF, Section 5th, VIII). Defeating Brazilian justice of the Supreme Federal Court Marco Aurélio Mendes de Farias Mello, who would give judicial relief to the appeal, reinstating the decision of the Brazilian Regional Federal Courts of the 3rd Region which determined that the final clause of subsection VIII of Section 5th of the Federal Constitution should be observed, showing that one should always present an alternative provision as, in this case, the administration of the examination on a business day.

This is another case of the "tests and examinations" series [pending also ADI 3714/SP (2006) and 3901/PA (2007)—*according to state laws, university and government public servant entrance tests and examinations, carried out by public or private schools, must present alternative timetables for Sabbatarians and others.*[6]]. The Court, in an objective dimension, recognized the principle of nondenominationalism (called "duty of neutrality"), which does not mean indifference nor rules out positive behavior by the State. It seems that the Supreme Court recognizes the constitutionality of "accommodation" of religions by the government—in the scope of avoiding overloads for minorities—something that, in this case, was reasonably achieved by the Ministry of Education (despite the confinement). The subjective right to exemption from work and from classes/tests for religious reasons, affirmed "a priori," shall only become a definite position when considered with other circumstances (reasonable accommodation of the situation by the Administration, non-violation of isonomy with adherents of other religions and even non-believers, etc.). The topic

[6]STF, ADI 3714, distributed on April 26, 2006, last operation: process forwarded to the replacement of the Justice Rapporteur of the decision Justice Alexandre de Moraes on March 22, 2017; and STF, ADI 3.901, former Justice of the Supreme Federal Court in Brazil Joaquim Barbosa, filed on June 8, 2007, last operation: process forwarded to the Justice Rapporteur on October 19, 2015, respectively.

of accommodating religion at work is dealt with here, without much development,[7] reflecting on leave of absence from work and from classes/tests for religious reasons.[8]

The infra-constitutional legislator, on the specific subject of religious education in public schools, has regulated the issue in two legislative acts, which shall be examined below.

3 The Education Act and the Concordat

In relation to education, reflections of religious freedom are listed: freedom to learn and teach religion; the right to the education of children consistent with their religious convictions in religious matters; the right to exemption from classes/tests for religious reasons; the right to religious education in public elementary schools; the right of the churches to teach the doctrine of the professed religion; the creation, by the churches, of private schools or cooperatives; the principle of separation; the principle of "nondenominationalism" in the course schedule; public education cannot be religious; the principle of cooperation, whereby the State assures religious education, of optional enrollment, in public elementary schools; the State shall assist parents in the exercise of family autonomy so that they can educate their children according to their religious beliefs; the principle of tolerance.

The constitutional starting point is the aforementioned § 1st of Section 210 of 1988 CF, inserted in Title VII of the Brazilian Constitution (*social order*), in its Chapter III, Section I (*Education*)—guided by the principles set forth in Section 206 and specifies what is provided for in the *caput* of Section 210 (minimum syllabi shall be set for primary education in order to ensure common basic training and respect for cultural and artistic, national and regional values).

In its task of democratic conformation and reduction of complexity, the infra-constitutional legislator regulated the matter through Law no. 9.394 of December 20, 1996, which establishes the Brazilian National Educational Bases and Guidelines Law (LDB, in the Portuguese abbreviation). In dealing with elementary education (second stage of basic education), Section 33 provided for the provision of religious education, initially scheduled (in the original wording of the LDB) without charge to government coffers and in two modalities: (a) *denominational*, according to the religious option of the student/legal guardians from the respective churches/religious denominations; (b) *interdenominational*, by an agreement among the various religious entities.[9]

---

[7]There is an interesting decision by the European Court of Human Rights, curiously applying the duty of accommodation to a Christian [Nadia Eweida x UK (ECHR, 1/15/2013)].

[8]The full discussion, starting from the linking of fundamental rights in relationships among individuals, including topics on a "special equality right" and religious harassment, is found in Weingartner Neto (2007). In the labor context, the excellent book of dos Santos Junior (2013) has to be acknowledged.

[9]Section 33 [original wording of the Brazilian National Educational Bases and Guidelines Law (LDB)]: *Religious education, with optional enrollment, shall be a school subject at the regular hours*

According to Brazilian politician Marcelo Castro, *it was intended that expenses arising from the offer of religious education would not be funded by the government* (de Castro 1998). Therefore, Brazilian government National Education Council (CNE, in the Portuguese abbreviation), in position paper no. 05/97, would present three reasons for such: (a) To avoid violation of Section 19 of the Federal Constitution, which prohibits grant to religious practices and churches; (b) The creation of an unequal treatment from the State in relation to the various churches because the subsidy would be disproportionate to the demand—since the teacher would be paid per hour of work, one or two students of a certain religion would demand the same State expenditure that could account for thirty or forty others, because the law guarantees denominationalism and students choice; (c) There could be an absurdity of religious education for dozens of differentiated denominations, in case of demand, to be more expensive than the teaching of other subjects with higher working hours. Under this interpretation, the religious choice of a student could only be met if an entity of his devotion would be willing to send an accredited teacher to school, and to be responsible for any costs with educational materials. As for the interdenominational form, it would require an agreement among religious entities—if it were not obtained, or were only partially, the school should open its doors to representatives of the various religious practices or churches requested by the students and their legal guardians.

Castro informs about the discontentment at the National Conference of Bishops of Brazil (CNBB, in the Portuguese abbreviation) and the political pressure that almost led the President of the Republic to veto such section. The Executive has sent a new bill to the National Congress on the subject. Thus, Law no. 9475 of July 23, 1997, promoted the first amendment of the LDB and provided new wording to Section 33, ensuring compliance to the cultural diversity of religions in Brazil and prohibiting any form of proselytism. It now refers to education systems, regulation of the religious education syllabi and rules for qualification and employment of teachers.[10]

Later, CNE, in Resolution no. 2 of April 7, 1998, of the Brazilian government Basic Education Chamber (CEB, in the Portuguese abbreviation), which instituted the national curriculum guidelines for elementary education, inserted *religious education* in the areas of common national base knowledge.[11]

---

of public elementary schools, being offered free of charge to public coffers, according to preferences expressed by the students or by their legal guardians, being: I—denominational, according to the religious option of the student or their legal guardians, taught by teachers or religious advisers prepared and accredited by the respective churches or religious entities; II—interdenominational, resulting from an agreement among the different religious entities that shall be responsible for the preparation of the respective program.

[10]Section 33 (wording by law No. 9.475, dated 7/23/1997) *Religious education, with optional enrollment, is an integral part of the citizens' basic education and it is a school subject at the regular hours of public elementary schools, ensuring compliance with the cultural diversity of religions in Brazil, prohibiting any form of proselytism.* § 1st Education systems shall regulate procedures for definition of the religious education syllabi and shall establish the rules for the qualification and employment of teachers. § 2nd Education systems shall listen to a civil entity constituted by different religious denominations for definition of the religious teaching syllabi.

[11]It refers to one of the ten "branches of knowledge."

Observing the legislative operations, the doctrine was gradually manifested. Alexandre de Moraes would mention that Section 210, § 1st, must conform to other public freedoms, such as religious worship and provision for a secular State. He emphasizes, in the provision, a double constitutional guarantee: (1st) The teaching of a single religion or the instruction of students in particular beliefs cannot be instituted in public schools; (2nd) The freedom of people to enroll or not (full religious freedom "also consists in freedom for atheism") (Moraes 2003, 2005). Brazilian jurist José Afonso da Silva emphasizes that, "it is the right of the religious student to be able to enroll in the subject, but it is not his duty to do so. Nor is it a subject that requires tests or examination which implies failing or succeeding for school achievement purposes."(da Silva 2005)[12]

Celso Ribeiro Bastos and Ives Gandra da Silva Martins connect the provision with subsections II, IV, VI, and VII of Section 5th of the 1988 Federal Constitution and cite the "stabilizing effectiveness of religious education" mentioned by Brazilian jurist Francisco Cavalcanti Pontes de Miranda. The 1988 Federal Constitution, in particular, "reveres the democratic spirit and the principle of equality, by *allowing* those who wish to attend religious classes, offering those who do not wish to do so the negative right." Students then have "the right to obtain religious instruction and the right to choose between learning about one religion or another according to their personal convictions."[13] § 1st of Section 210 could be seen as an *attenuation* of the principle of separation. They affirm that students' individual right (of requesting access to religious education) has the counterpart in the State duty to allow it to take place in public schools, but it should not be confused with "subjective public law," since "the State is not obliged to offer religious education itself" but rather "to provide periods at regular hours" because "offering religious education is provided by religious entities" (Bastos and Martins 1989).[14]

Writing in 1997 (before the amendment promoted by Law no. 9.475), Anna Candida da Cunha Ferraz pointed out that the exegesis of the precept must be made in light of the right to education, freedom of religion, and the constitutional subject of the Public Administration (da Ferraz 1997). She recalls the objectives of the initial precept of the social order (*well-being* and *social justice*, Section 193, 1988 CF), as well as the objectives of education and its principles (Sections 205 and 206, respectively, 1988 CF). After presenting the "mitigation of the State–Church separation"

[12]Only public schools are obliged and only in elementary school, since the private ones "can adopt it as it seems fit to them, as long as they do not impose certain religious denominations to those who do not want them."

[13]They also have the right not to attend religious classes, if so desired (Bastos and Martins 1989). In reviewing the previous constitutional law, it is observed that "religious education has always been present," endowed either with a compulsory nature or with an optional one (in the latter case, an authorization from the very separation of State and religion takes place). The first written instrument to provide over the matter was the 1891 CF, when saying that teaching provided in public establishments would be a lay one (Section 72, § 6th).

[14]Private schools, which may be denominational (Section 20, III, LDB), are free to offer religious education or not, and it is up to the learner/legal guardian "to choose in these cases the denominational school that best suits their personal beliefs and convictions." On this topic, see also Martins (1995).

in the 1988 Federal Constitution, she considers religious education a projection of freedom of religion, as "a formula for the realization of freedom of religion." The rule has an "exceptional dispositional character": it opens in public school some room for teaching religion. It commands the State to insert religious education into the minimum basic education curricula (which should occur independently of law), but "the applicability of the rule is not immediate," because it demands regulation "that establishes conditions for its inclusion at regular hours." This is an individual right: "One cannot deny to elementary school students in public schools the right to religious education" (the individual would be the student, when parents or legal guardians express their religious denominations)—but it could not be exercised against the State, which could not be the passive addressee of the rule, since it cannot interfere in religious matters (the State cannot be "compelled 'to provide religious education'"). Only religious denominations could provide such teaching and it would be impossible for the State to compel churches to do so. Therefore, what can the student require from the State? Simply assure that, at regular hours, the "religious education of any religion can be taught, if requested by the student."[15] Religious education "is not some regular and compulsory elementary school curriculum subject," it is only a "school subject." Being optional, it cannot be conditioned to any constraint (da Ferraz 1997).[16]

As for the syllabi, Ferraz understands that it is a matter of *teaching religion*, where the constituent's good intentions are permissible (to contribute to the elimination of religious conflicts in the world), but that she has not perceived that it could serve *improper purposes*, as "to bring conflict to schools (…) with the difficulty of establishing, in public schools, the teaching of all religions of the country and the modus vivendi among them." It is up to the denominational entity the task of teaching, some necessary infra-constitutional subject, which should consider: (a) in view of the principle of separation, "it shall not be for the State to provide material resources for the accompaniment of education (notebooks, books etc.)"; (b) the necessary compatibility, so that such teaching "is not embarrassed by anyone, but also does not embarrass anyone"; (c) the need to reconcile it with constitutional requirements of education and basic education; (d) the State positive performance, in order to effectively open room and "enable conditions for it to be administered"; (e) the State negative performance, so that it does not interfere in religious matters (da Ferraz 1997).

Still according to Anna Ferraz, the problem of religious education teachers' remuneration remains to be seen. Pontes de Miranda would admit State hiring and the resulting remuneration. The author, however, in view of the State/Church separation and the constitutional system of education, considers it impracticable for the State to appoint, hire and/or remunerate the respective teachers. She relies on her reading of

[15] The State must "provide sites by designating classrooms and setting day and time and shift so that, if requested, such teaching may be taught by the respective religious denominations" (da Ferraz 1997).

[16] Such as, e.g., presence check, measuring results, impossibility of changing options, requesting students to remain in the classroom. José Afonso da Silva is mentioned, for whom there can be no tests showing failing or passing grades.

an exception to the parameter-rule and in the absence of an express authorization for "remuneration." She thinks, with Brazilian jurist Manoel Gonçalves Ferreira Filho, that *collaboration* "can not take place in a fundamentally religious field, such as that of catechesis" (in addition, favoring each student's freedom of religion would not fit into "public interest collaboration"). Hence, the conclusion that "the State cannot directly provide, through teachers named and linked to it, religious education," just as the State cannot hire a teacher for this purpose (in particular, resulting from Section 206, V, 1988 CF, teachers as public servants, working for the government, with all the consequences) (da Ferraz 1997).[17] The author reiterates that it is not for the State to set syllabi and rules of learning or attendance, but it shall have to "exercise at least the supervision," so that religious education does not violate the order of the establishment or may lead to practices that are inadmissible under the constitutional order, as well as violate rights of freedom or discriminate—and, "what is more important, disrupting the basic education whose essentiality and quality the State has to ensure."[18]

In this line of *distrust*, Garcia (2009), thus concludes her comment: "Ideally there would simply be an exclusion of this possibility of religious education in public schools," because there would be no other way to defend the coherence and secularity of the constitutional system.

Recognizing that the constitutional text, in adopting the generic formula, has left many questions open, Leite (2014) points to "a discretion conferred by the Constitution on infra-constitutional legislation to respond to such inquiries." It is noted that the constitutional provision has not expressly opted for the denominational model (as have the 1934 and 1946 Brazilian Constitutions). However, the regulatory legislation autonomy is not so "broad" and exemplifies: when the respective religious institutions adopt the denominational model, and designate the teachers without public bid, the legislator shall not be able to determine remuneration from public coffers. He also highlights "the difficulty to understand religious education as a category from which denominational and interdenominational approaches would be varied." By alluding to Ferraz's observations, it is mentioned that "they lack argumentative force in the

[17] In addition to the fact that the subject is optional (which plays against permanent teachers' employment), "there is no officially qualified training" (nor is there any provision for higher level courses for such modality [theology college courses are not recognized by the Brazilian Ministry of Education] which makes unfeasible "public servant entrance examination" by the State, which could not even establish the "syllabi" of the course). It is not admissible that teachers who have been hired for other areas may teach religious education—which would be impeded by the principles of neutrality and secularity. Nor is Section 37, IX, 1988 of the Federal Constitution (CF) applicable (temporary hiring would clash with the permanence of religious teaching). In short, the question must be *settled within religious denominations*. Nor does Section 213 of 1988 CF helps in the matter, which authorizes public resources for "denominational schools." Neither could religious associations hire the services, by means of *agreements*, by what was said and by the "demand of public bid or the legal budgetary provision."

[18] It is about establishing "appropriate limits" to reconcile the various interests of groups and individuals. These aspects must be used to control the exercise of policing power by the government—it is for the State "to prevent and repress violations of the right to freedom of thought and religion, including in relations among persons" (da Ferraz 1997).

light of an interdenominational teaching," not preventing a teacher of this modality from integrating a teaching career and "applying for a public servant entrance examination promoted by the State and being remunerated for this." There is some inclination toward a nondenominational teaching, so that religious education ceases to be "a foreign body at school—or the ugly duckling of public education." Finally, he mentions the different experiences of State education systems, with the Brazilian city of São Paulo opting for nondenominational education (and understanding what is denominational as a mere assignment of physical space within public schools so that volunteers of various religious denominations provide their teachings, without being linked to the State and without remuneration); while the Brazilian state of Rio de Janeiro adopted an exclusively religious denominational education, creating a peculiar system in which religion teachers are selected by state sponsored public servant entrance examination but subordinated to their respective religious authorities, which can legally remove them from the job.[19]

Just over ten years after the LDB amendment, new legislative data disrupt the scenario. On November 13, 2008, an *Agreement* (Concordat) was signed between the Federative Republic of Brazil and the Holy See (the See of Rome) regarding the *Legal Statute of the Catholic Church in Brazil*. The text, consisting of 20 sections, was approved by Executive Order no. 698/2009 and enacted by the President of Brazil by Ruling no. 7107/2010. Negotiations go back to September 2006, at the initiative of the Holy See.

Brazilian government's considerations emphasize that "Brazil is the country that houses the largest Catholic population in the world and was the only one that did not have an agreement on the presence of the Catholic Church in its territory." Although it has had diplomatic relations with the Holy See since 1826, there are only two agreements in force.[20] The purpose of the agreement is to consolidate several aspects of this more than secular relationship with the Holy See and also stemming from the presence of the Catholic Church in Brazil. Let us look at the central guidelines of the agreement: preservation of the Constitution and ordinary legislation on the secular character of the Brazilian State, religious freedom and the equitable treatment of the rights and duties of religious institutions legally established in Brazil.

It is a structural problem related to the organization of the State, essential to the notion that religious denominations must be separated from the State building—an idea of separation of religious denominations from the State, the principle of

---

[19]The municipality of Rio de Janeiro created in the Executive Branch Permanent Staff the functional category of "religious teaching teacher, whose entrance shall be by state sponsored public servant entrance examination and with accreditation by the competent religious authorities," which shall require religious training obtained in an institution maintained or recognized by them" (Section 4th of Municipal Law no. 5303 of October 19, 2011). ADI no. 3268/2004 questions the denominationalism adopted in Law no. 3459/2000. With an opinion by lacking grounds from the Prosecutor General of the Republic, it is a process forwarded to the Justice Rapporteur and Dean of the Court Celso de Mello since April 9, 2013.

[20]An Administrative Agreement for exchange of diplomatic correspondence (1935) and an Agreement on the establishment of Military Ordinance and appointment of military Chaplain ministers (1989).

Church/State separation, enshrined in subsection I of Section 19 of the Brazilian Federal Constitution. I differentiate between the principle of separation and the principle of nondenominationalism; I also identify the principles of cooperation from the solidarity of tolerance.

The principle of separation of religious denominations from the State is a product of liberal constitutionalism and precisely represents the overcoming of models of political–religious union. However, it does not mean a strongly secular conception. One adopts, as does Jónatas Machado, the distinction that is usual in the European doctrine, which distinguishes "laicism" from "laicity," the latter seen as "an attitude of benevolent neutrality on the part of the government, which respects what is religious," in which the State refrains from "taking a position on the problem of religious truth," while the first one can be defined as a global philosophy of an exasperated anthropological rationalism that "excludes any reference to a transcendent truth grounded in revelation." The "truth that sets you free" is now anti-metaphysical and positivist and revolves around an "almost metaphysical principle of verification," in an attitude of "relative hostility towards religion," confined from public spaces, being aware of the deliberate promotion of a "secularized and indifferent mentality" regarding religion (Machado 1996).[21]

Pontes de Miranda has adopted a successful expression on the subject when comparing the Brazilian Constitutions in this particular subject. He would say that, in the one from 1967, "no aggression against religions is observed," as was also the case with the one from 1946. There remained the points where the 1934 Constitution revealed "the most open sympathy, without the State ceasing to be secular. Laicity that remained neutral, since it was no longer indifferent, nor hostile" (the one from 1937 would be again, as the one from 1891, indifferent)—"and the one from 1967, as the ones from 1934 and 1946, attentive" (de Miranda 1967). Neither indifferent, nor even less hostile, is the 1988 Federal Constitution, an attentive, separate but cooperative, nondenominational but with solidarity, tolerant one.

The principle of separation, in which there is no hostility or substitutive scope in relation to the religious phenomenon, is thus demarcated. The aim is to "construct an open space for religion that is free from coercion or discrimination," anchored in the vision of free citizens who are equal in rights. In the Legal and Democratic State,[22] religion is not "a matter for public authorities, but for the citizens"—except for the State task of ensuring a normative program. Freedom and secularism are seen as expression and content of the democratic rule of law. The State renouncing to any competence in matters of religious truth, remains faithful to a "principle of denominational non-identification"—by remaining silent when questioned about the meaning of life, it can be the "common house of all citizens." The way by which it

[21]For the *sons of Voltaire* (free masons), clericalism was the "enemy to slaughter" (*Le cléricalisme, voilà l'ennemi!*), all in the radical climate in which the religious denominations, in turn, would cling to the defense of traditional privileges.

[22]With no accurate translation to the English language, this concept, according to the Continental European and Brazilian contexts, encompasses, at least, the ideas of Rule of Law, Democracy and Constitutionalism. In German, *Rechtsstaat*. Also referred to as Constitutional Democratic State.

is welcomed signals the degree of importance given by constitutional order on the "principle of equal religious freedom" (Machado 1996).

On the other hand, the principle of nondenominationalism, in another line of thought, separates the State from religious questions (matters) and subjects—the State does not adopt any religion (it does not join them nor does it obstruct them); official acts and State protocol submit to nondenominationalism; education and culture cannot be scheduled by religious guidelines; public education cannot be denominational and commands an impartial State action. In line with Machado (2013), the Constitutional State must be neutral in relation to different worldviews, not because they are ethical or axiologically indifferent, but because they evaluate them all on the basis of the same constitutional principles (dignity, freedom, equality and justice) and, as they are more or less close to them, they may take advantage, "to a greater or lesser extent, of constitutional protection guarantees. (…) The principle of neutrality arises, above all, as a diversity management stratagem." Said otherwise, the Constitutional State is socially and culturally contextualized, based on ethical presuppositions, cultural postulates, which is the reason why total neutrality is, "ultimately, impossible to sustain, to the extent that this [free and democratic constitutional order] is based on a positive affirmation of certain values and principles."

Concerning the Concordat, religious education deserves special attention in its Section 11, verbis: The *Federal Republic of Brazil, respecting the right of religious freedom, cultural diversity and denominational plurality of the country, acknowledges the importance of religious education in view of people's integral formation. §1st. Religious education, whether being it Catholic or another religious denominations, under optional enrollment, is a subject at regular hours in public elementary schools, ensuring respect for the cultural diversity of religions in Brazil, in accordance with the Constitution and other laws in force, without any discrimination.*

Despite some controversy, I believe that the concordat system agreed does not suffer from constitutionality vices. On the contrary, it encapsulates a series of juridical positions that have already resulted from a systematic interpretation of the Federal Constitution, having the merit of making them explicit and consistent with the fundamental principle of a secular State, of non-identification with separation, which is not compliant with hostility or opposition to religious phenomena. The Agreement therefore embodies the principles of cooperation and solidarity. In addition, the State fulfills its duties as regards the duties of protection, of creating conditions for religious denominations to carry out their missions (duty to improve). Finally, collective religious freedom is protected as a constitutional guarantee, that is, churches as institutions.

However, doctrinal positions differ. de Mazzuoli (2009), in a text prior to the concordat in question, considers that international concordat law itself is unconstitutional in Brazil, since such treaties would create distinctions-privileges among Brazilians in terms of religious freedom—although it seems to be possible to establish an international agreement in which there is no difference of any kind (a hypothesis that would not conceptually configure a "concordat"). Leite (2014) considers that the Agreement was "unnecessary, discussed without considerable media coverage, hastily approved, without a debate with society and of uncertain convenience," but does not appear to conclude that it is unconstitutional.

The main criticism would be of eventual privilege of the Catholic Church in relation to other religious institutions. At this point, however, instead of a restrictive reading of the catalog of fundamental rights, a more generous position would be better, giving shelter to the principle of equality and the institutional guarantee of diversity and religious pluralism, which play in favor of greater openness and pluralism of public spaces. Therefore, the principle of equality, rather than an insurmountable obstacle, can be realized "without law, against the law and instead of the law" (Canotilho 1999), so that, given the unequal political weight of different religious denominations, it is reasonable to automatically extend the level of some more favorable protection obtained by the Catholic Church to minorities.[23] Leite (2014), when commenting Section 11, paragraph 1st of the Agreement, interprets that the provision acknowledges the denominational teaching of religious nature and that it is not included among those, considering that this modality of religious education contravenes the Constitution. He warns, however, that such an option "cannot generate an involvement between the government and religious authorities, and it is incumbent on the latter to freely appoint teachers (or even remove them) without any interference on the part of the State, and without any burden to public coffers in the cost of that teaching."

The political–educational–religious debate would be made judicial shortly after the Concordat was promulgated by a Presidential Ordinance.[24]

4 A Controversy at STF

By means of Direct Action of Unconstitutionality (ADI, in the Portuguese abbreviation) 4.439 (2010), the Office of the Prosecutor General of the Republic postulates an interpretation according to the Constitution to the LDB and the Agreement with the Holy See to state that *religious education in public schools can only be nondenominational and hiring teachers representing religious denominations is prohibited; secondarily, it contests the partial unconstitutionality of the Concordat rule to suppress from the text of Section 11, § 1st, the expression "Catholic and other religious denominations."*[25]

---

[23]In any case, shortly after voting on the text of the Agreement, the Chamber of Deputies approved a bill called the *general law of religions*, which has the same base as the Agreement. Leite (2014) sees the act as some kind of response to the Agreement, some "cry of the minorities" that reproduces two vices: vague terms, "that escape the approach of concrete topics," and a concern to protect religion exclusively, "leaving aside other issues of constitutional value."

[24]For an analysis of the Brazilian secularity and the agreements between the Holy See and Brazil, see (Souza Alves 2016).

[25]Direct Action of Unconstitutionality No. 4439, DF. Justice Rapporteur Roberto Barroso Begun on August 30, 2017, the judgment proceeded on August 31, September 21 and finished on September 27, 2017, when this text was already finished. The Court, by a majority, deemed devoid of legal

The Public Prosecutor's Office wants the STF to carry out an interpretation according to the Constitution of Section 33, *caput*, and §§ 1 and 2 of Law no. 9.394/96, as well as it attacks the Concordat rule mentioned. The injunction was denied on August 3, 2010. Since then, a number of entities have been admitted to the proceedings as amicus curiae (National Conference of Bishops of Brazil, National Permanent Forum of Religious Education, National Association of Catholic Education of Brazil, Conference of Religious People of Brazil, Masonic Grand Lodge of the Brazilian State of Rio de Janeiro, Latin American and Caribbean Committee on Women's Rights, Brazilian Association of Atheists and Agnostics, among others). On June 15, 2015, there was a public hearing when 31 religious or educational entities or people interested in the subject, in addition to specialists, were heard. The majority of the participants advocated for the practical impossibility of reconciling denominational and interdenominational models of education with the State secularity (32, among the 31, defended the rightfulness of the action).

In a different way, CNBB advocated for the *recognition of the constitutionality of the understanding that religious education in public schools of basic education under optional enrollment (CF, Section 210, paragraph 1) can and ought to be taught in a denominational way insofar as the secular State's neutrality in relation to religions cannot be understood as intolerance to faith, since only in this way shall effectiveness be given to freedom of belief (CF, Section 5, VI), which includes assistance and education provided by those who profess the same religion, while the Brazilian Constitution acknowledges that public funds should be allocated to denominational schools (Section 213), therefore avoiding discrimination of students in the public education system.*

The action seeks to establish that religious education in public schools should be of nondenominational nature, prohibiting the hiring of teachers as representatives of religious denominations, which would be the only way to reconcile religious education with the Brazilian State's secular character. The content of the subject in the model proposed is some kind of history and sociology of religions and of nondenominational positions, without educators taking sides, who should be teachers of the public education system and not people linked to churches or religious denominations. The initial one, therefore, rejects the denominational and interdenominational models (or an ecumenical one that would promote consensual values of "dominant" religions and could be taught by representatives of religious communities or by public school teachers).

The Justice Rapporteur's vote is based on two premises: (a) The constitutional principle of secularism (CF, Section 19, I) that presents three contents: (i) Formal separation between the State and churches; (ii) State neutrality in religious matters; and (iii) Guarantee of religious freedom; (b) religious education in public schools, in theory, can be taught in one of three models: (i) Denominational, which has as

---

grounds the direct action of unconstitutionality, defeating Ministers Roberto Barroso (Rapporteur), Rosa Weber, Luiz Fux, Marco Aurélio and Celso de Mello. The Supreme Court decision can be found at http://redir.stf.jus.br/paginadorpub/paginador.jsp?docTP=TP&docID=15085915.

its object the promotion of one or more religious denominations; (ii) Interdenominational, which corresponds to the teaching of religious values and practices based on elements common to dominant creeds in society; and (iii) Nondenominational, which is unrelated to specific religions.

He argues that "Only the nondenominational model of religious education in public schools is capable of reconciling with the principle of State secularism. In this modality, the subject consists of a neutral and objective exposition of doctrines, practices, history and social dimensions of different religions (including nondenominational positions), and is taught by regular teachers of the public school system and not by people linked to religious denominations." He concludes with the validity of the application, with the hypothesis: "Religious education provided in public schools must be effectively optional and nondenominational in nature, and hiring teachers as representatives of religions to be taught is prohibited."[26]

The Justice Rapporteur notes that secularism does not imply disrespect to religion or religiosity and that the modernity and transformations of the last 500 years have not led to the decline of religions. Since the State must ensure religious freedom and maintain neutrality in relation to different religions, religious education of Brazilian children and adolescents is at stake. It is urgent "to establish how to best prepare them, with values and information, so that they can make their own choices in life." Reconciling State secularism and religious education makes it possible for the State to opt for the denominational or interdenominational modality, incompatible with the requirement of a formal separation between the State and religions, since allowing students to receive religious instruction within public schools makes "institutional identification inevitable," especially if the teachers are representatives or accredited by the churches and remunerated by the State. It also breaks the neutrality, because it is impossible to accommodate the more than 140 religious denominations that make up the Brazilian plurality, which would favor the major ones. He notes that children and adolescents are especially influenceable by teachers and colleagues and therefore lack the State's duty of protection.

Thus, only nondenominational, plural, objective and neutral teaching is in harmony with secularity. And even in this theoretically compatible one, there is no way to ignore the practical complexities of "bringing religion into the classroom," the first of which is due to the lack of national school curriculum guidelines, which makes

[26]Justice Rosa Weber followed the Justice Rapporteur ("Religion and faith relate to the private domain and not to the public one. The State must be neutral.") and also Justice Luiz Fux (he questioned whether it is reasonable for public schools to be a site for giving lessons of faith to children and adolescents; "Universal and nondenominational religious public education is the only one able to promote tolerant generations which can live in harmony with different beliefs in plural, ethical and religious societies"). Justice Marco Aurélio proceeded in the same line when considering that denominational education in public schools damages the situation of balance between State and religion, required by the principle of secularity. Justice Celso de Mello affirmed the nondenominationalism in comparing the current Federal Constitution and what was prescribed by the 1946 Constitution, as well as in the counter-majoritarian role of the STF in advocating or not for religious minorities, all of this to keep the State in a position of strict axiological neutrality.

it difficult to prevent proselytism and makes the picture confusing.[27] The second problem is the financial support of the school subject by the government, indicating Rio de Janeiro's system as a violation of the secular principles governing public servant entrance examination, making the position of teachers depend on credentials for denominations. Finally, in order to implement the nondenominational model, it is convenient for the Brazilian Ministry of Education to define national curricular parameters and ensure the optionality of religious education.[28]

Justice Alexandre de Moraes started the divergence, which prevailed in the end, broadening the discussion to the field of freedom of expression, in the light of tolerance and diversity of opinions, even in classrooms. He wonders that such a program, valid for all other manifestations of thought, turns into "prior censorship to free manifestation of religious conceptions in classrooms, even in subjects with optional enrollment, turning religious education into a neutral subject with syllabi imposed by the State in disrespect for religious freedom," which limits the legitimate and subjective right of the student (or parent/legal guardian) who already has a religion, to enroll in religious education of their own religious denomination, restricting religious freedom of 92% of the Brazilian population that has certain religious beliefs (Brazilian IBGE Census, 2010). He notes that the implementation of religious education is an original constitutive text and voluntary enrollment protects 8% (who do not profess religious faith) and those who do not have an interest in enrolling. Paradoxical: "Groups that have helped minorities to legitimately and correctly gain the right to freedom of expression of their ideas and beliefs, even in classrooms and curricula of compulsory enrollment, intend to impose remarkable prior restraint to diverse religious opinions, while pleading for neutral and merely descriptive syllabi of religions, in an unthinkable 'official religious doctrines', artificially created by the government, even in subjects of optional enrollment."

Thus, he sums up his position by dismissing the action: *The government, observing the binomial State secularity (CF, Section 19, I)/acknowledgment of religious freedom (CF, Section 5th, VI), shall act in full regulation of compliance with the constitutional provision set forth in Section 210, §1st, authorizing the public school system, under equal conditions (CF, Article 5th, caput), to offer religious education of various beliefs by means of formal requirements previously set by the Brazilian Ministry of Education.* In this way, students who expressly and voluntarily enroll shall be allowed the full exercise of their subjective right to religious education as a subject

[27]Currently, 4 geographical states adopt the denominational model (Acre, Bahia, Ceará and Rio de Janeiro); the majority (20 plus the Brazilian Federal District) work with interdenominational teaching; only São Paulo adopted the "teaching religions." In addition, the syllabi, the form of enrollment, the verification of results and the requirements for hiring teachers vary. The Justice Rapporteur endorses Brazilian anthropologist and law professor Debora Diniz's opinion at the public hearing of subjecting religious teaching to the national system for assessing the quality of teaching material by the Ministry of Education to ensure nondenominationalism.

[28]The Justice Rapporteur recommends: public servant teachers cannot depend on an act of will of any religious denominations; enrollment cannot be automatic; those who do not opt for it must have pedagogical alternatives to reach the minimum annual workload; teaching must take place in a specific class (barring transversality); students can drop out at any time.

at regular hours in public elementary schools, taught according to the principles of their religious denomination by its members duly accredited by public servant entrance exams and preferably without any financial burden for the government.

Justice Alexandre de Moraes emphasizes the uniqueness of the constitutional provision of religious education based on dogmas of faith as individuals' subjective right and not some duty imposed by the government. He cites: "Neutrality does not exist in religious education of any religious denomination, which is fundamentally based on dogmas of faith, fully protected by the freedom of belief, according to the decision of the First Senate of the German Federal Constitutional Court of October 19, 1971" (1 BvR 387/65. Fifty years of jurisprudence by the German Constitutional Court. Konrad Adenauer Stiftung. Original collection: Jürgen Schwabe). It is not proselytism, "which has the purpose of converting a certain person to a religion, since the primary constitutional requirement is the optional enrollment of the student who already professes the belief which is the topic of the subject."

The divergence rejects that the Court "replaced the legitimate choice that the original constituent legislator made by religious education of optional enrollment by teachings of philosophy, history or science of religions," and it is prohibited to the government, when teaching the syllabus of religious education, to adopt any of the two aspects of State dirigisme, whether in favor of a single belief or in the development of a single official syllabus, a sum of descriptive, historical, and philosophical aspects, rejecting the various dogmas and obliging students of certain faith to have contact with other people's dogmas. In the interests of equality, it is committed to general administrative rules allowing voluntary partnerships (Law 13,204/2015) without transfer of funds, a system of mutual cooperation with all religious denominations, as it is already the case, for example, with religious assistance in prisons.

Justice Edson Fachin also disagreed, even if supported by other fundamentals. He noted that the Justice Rapporteur's vote was in accordance with the precedents of the STF and the international human rights entities, quoting General Comment No. 22/1993 of the Human Rights Committee under the United Nations General Assembly International Covenant on Civil and Political Rights (ICCPR) and decisions of the European Court of Justice (ECJ) and the Inter-American Commission on Human Rights (IACHR). If the appeal [by American moral and political philosopher John Rawls] to "common sense" can ground the Church/State separation to withdraw the religious motivation (by definition, private) of public spaces, nevertheless, "it is necessary to warn that the definition of these limits must take into account the exact content of the right to religious freedom, as expressed in the Union's Charter itself."

In this context, Section 5th, VI, of the CF is integrated by the provisions in Articles 12 of the Pact of San Jose, Costa Rica (freedom to profess and disclose a religion, individually or collectively, both in public and in private) and 18 of the International Covenant on Civil and Political Rights (ICCPR) (teaching as a scope of freedom to profess religion). Hence, the public dimension of religious freedom, since democratic pluralism does not exempt "private religious convictions." It is stated: "It is incorrect, therefore, to assert that the religious dimension coincides only with private spatiality. This does not mean, however, that public spaces can be founded on religious grounds. (…) The separation between Church and State cannot, therefore, imply the isolation of those who keep a religion in their private sphere. The principle of laicity is not confused with laicism." Citing German sociologist and philosopher Habermas, the "ethics of democratic citizenship," with reciprocal onus for religious and nonreligious ones to consider all the contributions made to public debate. The Minister connects pluralism to learning from differences and the neutrality of the State itself is subject to dialogue and the learning process seen as an integral part of the right to education. Therefore, "schools must mirror Brazilian society's pluralism. They must be a microcosm of the participation of all religions and also of those who freely choose to have none." Moreover, it is part of ensuring democratic management of public education (CF, Section 206, VI) the possibility that federated entities may deliberate on the way in which religious education shall be provided.

It is concluded: "We cannot fail to recognize that, although it may be denominational, religious education cannot be compulsory (Section 210, § 1st, of the Constitution of the Federative Republic of Brazil). In addition, because it is based on its own democratic plurality, denominational, interdenominational or nondenominational teaching cannot become proselytizing or disrespect the cultural diversity of religions in Brazil, which also includes denominational religions that assert themselves only by uses, costumes and traditions." This interpretation does not diverge from the aforementioned General Commentary 22, since "religious education is only incompatible with the Covenant if dispensations or 'alternatives harmonizing teaching with the wishes of parents and legal guardians' are not ensured". In the strict limits of the constitutional text, optionality and emphasis on respect to plurality do not exclude, therefore, the possibility of other forms of religious education.[29]

[29]Votes by Justices Gilmar Mendes, Dias Toffoli, and Ricardo Lewandowski were also for the dismissing the action, and the tiebreaker, in the same sense of dismissal, was up to the Court President, Justice Carmen Lúcia. Dias Toffoli stated that there was an express and conscious authorization from the constituent legislator for the historical model of denominational teaching, whose optionality makes it compatible with the laicity of the State, while safeguarding the person's individuality and their freedom of belief. The difficulties of practical implementation (risks for minorities) cannot result in annihilation of the right for all, as the law prohibits proselytizing and expected consultation with civil society, in harmony with the education system decentralization (CF, Article 211) and the principle of democratic management (CF, Section 206, VI). Citing precedents of the European Court of Human Rights, Justice Ricardo Lewandowski emphasized that optionality is sufficiently safeguarded for compliance with democratic pluralism and freedom of belief (for which it is necessary to ensure the right to dismissal at any time and no grades should be assigned) since the separation between State and Church does not constitute a wall separating incommunicable worldviews. And the fact that there is a majority denomination (due to the country's historical formation) does not imply religious proselytism or violation of equality.

5 Final Remarks

The debate continues in the public sphere. It is argued that the State cannot support religiosity at the expense of non-religiosity. However, the Federal Constitution decided, axiologically, that there shall be religious education, under voluntary enrollment (preserving the freedom and autonomy of others) in public schools.

With such a premise, more harmonious with the Federation, in which the Brazilian Republic is structured, the forwarding of syllabi/teacher's regulation to the education systems within the federated entities takes place. The prohibition of proselytism has traditionally been accepted in comparative law when it comes from legislative intervention and considering the safeguarding of the educational process and the very self-development of the personality of the students in development. Votes by the Justice Rapporteur and by Justice Alexandre seem to reveal an *implicit* normative intention, paradoxically of inverse signs: either religious education must be denominational or nondenominational, with no room for accomplishment, according to the LDB, in the educational systems. Minister Fachin's vote is preferable, preserving spaces of legislative compliance.

From Portugal, Professor Paulo Ferreira da Cunha warns about the need for multiple sensitivities and to weigh situations and values in each case: "It is not always that the offer of a thousand and one *à la carte* creeds for a religion class shall be the best way. Either the teaching of all (and none) by a teacher of one, or, more commonly, by a sociologist, historian, or other social scientist as religiously aseptic as ignorant of the depth of the phenomenon" (da Cunha 2007).

Students' right is to learn—the guarantee of fundamental education (Section 208, I, CF 88) encompasses, in combination with Section 210, *caput*, and § 1st, religious education—while the right *to teach the doctrine of a professed religious denomination* is incumbent upon religious denominations, including as a safeguard of their right to self-understanding and self-definition. The principle of collaboration would allow for harmonization, including proportionate public expenditures and compatible with State tasks (at least, taking religious education seriously in public schools). The interdenominational model is not unconstitutional. Even the denominational one, save for avoiding excessive involvement of the State (which also applies to the nondenominational) can coexist in a constitutional system.

Is there any possibility of improper effects? Yes, there are, but they can be prevented and must be tackled in concrete terms. It is to refuse a negative pre-understanding of the constitutional decision itself (not taking religious education seriously enough in public schools); it is urgent to break some basic misunderstanding, as if religious education, despite the constitutional precept, were not part of elementary school.

It is also said that it would be disproportionate to exercise the option of refusal for children or adolescents. However, based on this burden not empirically demonstrated (sounding more as a rhetorical argument, surmountable with specific and commissive enrollment), it is not considered disproportionate the alternative imposed on children and adolescents who wish to enjoy the constitutional right of interdenominational religious education, which would be, tout court, deprived of the possibility. Paradoxically, item 46 of the petition states that the option of interdenominational teaching "fails to promote learners' autonomy." I think, alternatively, that removing such an option constitutes State paternalism.

In this sense, the Supreme Court's decision took into consideration the broader range of interests and values involved. It seems that the initial reduction of complexity operated by infra-constitutional legislators offers some reasonable level for the right accomplishments in the educational system of different federative entities involved.

By reaffirming the constitutionality of Article. 33 and its paragraphs 1 and 2 of the Brazilian National Educational Bases and Guidelines Law (LDB) as well as Decree 7.107/2010, the majority of the Supreme Court indicated, in the wake of the "republican tradition" that religious freedom is carried out in two dimensions: protection of the individual and various religious denominations from any state intervention or command; and secularism of the State. These are basic premises for the interpretation of religious education with optional registration, which also reaches freedom of religious expression, in the prism of pluralism, essential foundation of democratic societies, to even include subjects that can "cause upheavals, resistance, disquiet people," in the dialogic horizon of tolerance. Both "**implies full regulation of compliance with the constitutional provision provided for in article 210, paragraph 1, authorizing the public education schools to offer, on equal terms (CF, Article 5, caput), confessional teaching of the various beliefs**" and means the guarantee for those students that voluntarily enroll themselves of the full exercise of their "**subjective right to religious education as a discipline of the normal schedule of public elementary schools, taught in accordance with the principles of their religious confession**" (according to the dogmas of faith—the Court rejects, by majority, a secular substitute of religious teaching, such as history, philosophy or science of religions). The binomial secularity of the state/religious freedom as a subjective right implies: voluntary enrollment for religious education (and correlate and strict state respect for agnostics and atheists); and prevents the public powers from creating a kind of official religious education (prohibits a certain state content for the discipline), and prohibits "favoring or hierarchizing biblical and religious interpretations of one or more groups to the detriment of others."

In short, what was established by the original Constituent Power and was regulated by the Legislative Branch (LDB) was preserved by the judicial system, which also guaranteed, in the paradigm, the agglutinating constitutional values (equal in freedom and dignity and political, expressive and religious pluralism). Of course, we must remain vigilant so that the practice does not detract from abuses against minorities or progressive, albeit indirect, violation of the laicity of the State.

References

Bastos CR, Martins IG (1989) Comentários à Constituição do Brasil. Saraiva, São Paulo

Canotilho JJG (1999) Direito Constitucional e Teoria da Constituição, 3 edn. Livraria Almedina, Coimbra

Cunha PF (2007) A Constituição Viva: cidadania e direitos humanos. Livraria do Advogado, Porto Alegre

Ferraz AC (1997) O ensino religioso nas escolas públicas: exegese do §1º do artigo 210 de da CF 05.10.1988. Rev dos Trib Cad Direito Const e Ciência Política 5:19–47

Silva JA (2005) Curso de Direito Constitucional, 24th edn. Malheiros, São Paulo

Castro MLO (1998) A educação na Constituição de 1988 e a LDB. André Quicé, Brasília

Mazzuoli VO (2009) O Direito Internacional Concordatário na ordem jurídica brasileira. In: de Mazzuoli VO, Soriano AG (eds) Direito à liberdade religiosa: desafios e perspectivas para o século XXI. Forum, Belo Horizonte, pp 251–270

Miranda P (1967) Comentários à Constituição de 1967 - Tomo IV. Revista dos Tribunais, São Paulo

Moraes A (2003) Direito constitucional, 13th edn. Atlas, São Paulo

Moraes A (2005) Direitos humanos fundamentais: teoria geral, comentários aos art. 1º a 5º da Constituição da República Federativa do Brasil, doutrina e jurisprudência. Atlas, São Paulo

Santos Junior AC (2013) A liberdade religiosa e contrato de trabalho – a dogmática dos direitos fundamentais e a construção de respostas constitucionalmente adequadas aos conflitos religiosos no ambiente de trabalho. Impetus, Niterói

Garcia M (2009) A Constituição e ensino religioso nas escolas públicas. In: de Mazzuoli VO, Soriano AG (eds) Direito à liberdade religiosa: desafios e perspectivas para o século XXI. Fórum, Belo Horizonte, pp 235–249

Leite FC (2014) Estado e Religião: A Liberdade Religiosa no Brasil. Juruá, Curitiba

Machado JEM (1996) Liberdade religiosa numa comunidade constitucional inclusiva: dos direitos da verdade aos direitos dos cidadãos. Coimbra Editora, Coimbra

Machado JEM (2013) Estado Constitucional e Neutralidade Religiosa: Entre o Teísmo e o (Neo)Ateísmo. Livraria do Advogado, Porto Alegre

Martins IG (1995) Educação religiosa nas escolas públicas – inteligência do art. 210 da CF. Rev dos Trib 84

Souza Alves RV (2016) Separation, cooperation and freedom of religion or belief: analyzing the constitutionality of the agreements between the Federal Republic of Brazil and the Holy See. Rev Latinoam Derecho y Reli 2:1–18

Weingartner Neto J (2007) Liberdade Religiosa na Constituição: Fundamentalismo, Pluralismo, Crenças, Cultos. Livraria do Advogado, Porto Alegre

Weingartner Neto J (2011) Liberdade Religiosa na jurisprudência do STF. In: Sarmento D, Sarlet IW (eds) Direitos fundamentais no Supremo Tribunal federal: balanço e crítica. Lúmen Juris, Rio de Janeiro, pp 481–530

Weingartner Neto J (2014) Comentários ao artigo 5º, incisos VI a VIII e artigo 19, incisos I a III. In: Canotilho JJG, Mendes GF, Sarlet IW, Streck LL (eds) Comentários à Constituição do Brasil. Saraiva/Almedina, São Paulo, pp 264,706

Religious Intolerance in Brazil: An Analysis of the Social Reality

Alexandre Brasil Fonseca

Abstract Brazil has an increasingly varied society in which religious diversity is inherent. Processes that occurred in the context of the proclamation of the Republic of Brazil at the end of the nineteenth century were referred to as the first wave of Brazilian secularism, having in the separation of Church and State and religious freedom some of the elements that characterised that moment and suffered resistance in different fields. The start of the twentieth century sees a situation in which religious freedom and pluralism coexist with the rise of cases of religious intolerance. There is today, early in the twenty-first century, a diversity of beliefs and non-beliefs, often combined, that require the State to have awareness and reflect, with civil society, with public bodies, religious organisations and universities, aiming to produce knowledge for the development of actions that promote respect for religious diversity. Available official data has been incapable of capturing this diversity and unable to produce information which permits understanding of the complexity of religion in the Brazilian context. This work, after a brief historical contextualisation, discusses national-level data gathered through the production of the Report on Religious Intolerance and Violence in Brazil (2011–2015) by the Secretariat for Human Rights from data collected by ombudsmen, judicial processes and the media. An increase in cases of religious intolerance was identified, with one episode occurring on average every two days in the five years studied, a total of 965 cases. Victims were most commonly from Afro-Brazilian religions followed by Evangelical Christians and Roman Catholics. Significant rates of psychological attacks and attacks against property have been seen in different areas of the country. The home was the primary location of attacks, demonstrating proximity between victims and their attackers. Though there is little information about the aggressors, it is possible to identify that, among other religions, there are a large number identified as Evangelicals and to a lesser extent Catholics. Atheists also appear as aggressors in various groups, while each religious group has some followers that promote intolerance. Importantly, a

Translated by Jonathan Nunn.

A. B. Fonseca (✉)
Federal University of Rio de Janeiro, Rio de Janeiro, Brazil
e-mail: abrasil@ufrj.br

© Springer Nature Switzerland AG 2020
R. V. S. Alves (ed.), *Latin American Perspectives on Law and Religion*, Law and Religion in a Global Context 3,
https://doi.org/10.1007/978-3-030-46717-3_6

significant number of cases occur within the school environment, this being a situation that requires a rapid resolution and represents a fundamental step in overcoming religious intolerance in Brazilian society.

Keywords Religious pluralism · Secular state · Human rights · Religious intolerance · Religion in Brazil

1 Introduction

The end of the twentieth century saw an unexpected spread of religion. Wars and disputes of global dimensions became apparent, and a "Clash of Civilisations" (Huntington 1996) was announced while the influential presence of "public religion" grew consistently within society (Casanova 1994). There is consensus that the "Secular Era" no longer represents denial of the presence of religion, and discussions of its decline have been substituted by the search to understand the terms and conditions of its continuation (Taylor 2007) or its reconfiguration (Casanova 1994).

Only in this period in Brazil, the "largest Catholic country" in the world, comes to experience religious plurality (da Fonseca 2011), a situation in which the issue of freedom of religion and belief gains even greater importance. Conceptualising the presence of the sacred, religion and the religious in the contemporary Brazilian State and society is a challenge. The discussion that follows initially presents a brief consideration of the historical process of the separation of Church and State in Brazil, to subsequently present data collected for the Report on Religious Intolerance and Violence in Brazil (RIVIR), developed under my coordination by the Secretariat for Human Rights of the Presidency of the Republic between the end of 2015 and May 2016.[1] In conclusion, is noted the importance of Brazilian society confronting the challenge of promotion of respect of religious diversity as one of the constituent elements, not just of democracy, but of promotion of a culture of peace in Brazil.

[1]The development of this report was supported by the Higher School of Theology (EST) and the Organization of Ibero-American States (OEI). The team was composed of the researchers: Alexandre Brasil Fonseca (general coordinator), André Meireles Oliveira, Andréa Letícia Carvalho Guimaraes, Christiane Falcão, Clara Jane Costa Adad (executive coordinator), Felipe Augusto Carvalho, Graziela Freitas, José Farias dos Santos, Juliana Cíntia Lima e Silva, Juliana dos Anjos de Souza, Palloma Cavalcanti and Rosana Carvalho Paiva. An additional support team was formed of: Ana Luíza Gonçalves Costa da Luz, Jéssica Paula de Melo, Laís Fonseca and Maria da Conceição Diniz Lopes. An Advisory Council was formed of: Ana Paula Miranda (UFF), Joanildo de Albuquerque Burity (FUNDAJ), Oneide Bobsin (EST), Rafael Soares de Oliveira (KOINONIA) and Regina Reyes Novaes (UFRJ). For further details, see da Fonseca and Adad (2016).

2 Origins of the Separation of Church and State and of Religious Pluralism in Brazil

> Now, liberty and religion are partners, not enemies. There is no religion without liberty. There is no liberty without religion.
>
> Rui Barbosa—Speech to Anchieta College, 1903

Rui Barbosa, Brazilian jurist, intellectual and politician, played an important role in the separation of Church and State in Brazil at the end of the nineteenth century. As minister of the recently created republican government, he was responsible for the text of the Decree 119-A of 1890 that introduced to the Brazilian legislation a new perspective on the presence and status of religion, in a period in which the presence of the Catholic Church reached practically the whole population.

> **Marshal Manoel Deodoro da Fonseca, Head of the Provisional Government of the Republic of the United States of Brazil,** constituted by the Army and Navy, in name of the Nation,
>
> **DECREES:**
>
> Art. 1: It is prohibited for the federal authority, as well as the federated states, to issue laws, regulations or administrative acts, establishing or prohibiting any religion, or creating differences between inhabitants of the country, in services provided through the treasury, on the basis of belief, or philosophical or religious opinions.
>
> Art. 2: All religious denominations are equally entitled to practice their worship, according to their beliefs and not to be contradicted in private or public acts, which may concern the exercise of this decree.
>
> Art. 3: The freedom instituted herein includes not only individuals in individual acts, but also churches, associations and institutes in which they are members; and all individuals have the full right to form and live collectively, according to his creed and discipline, without the intervention of the public power.
>
> Art. 4: The patronage is made extinct including all its institutions, resources and prerogatives.
>
> Art. 5: All churches and religious denominations are recognized as juridical persons, in order to acquire and administer assets, under the limits established by the laws concerning mortmain property, while maintaining control of their existing assets, and of their houses of meeting.
>
> Art. 6: The Federal Government will continue to provide for the sustenance of present servants of Catholic worship, and will subsidize for each year the chairs of the seminaries; leaving each state free to retain future ministers of this or other denomination, without contravention of the provisions of the preceding articles.
>
> Art. 7: Provisions to the contrary are repealed.
>
> Chamber of sessions of the Provisional Government, 7th January 1890

In assuming leadership of the process of Brazilian secularisation, Barbosa creates enemies within the Catholic clergy and some attribute his subsequent failure as a presidential candidate to this role. Particularly interesting here is the affirmation of Cunha (2017) that Brazil's slow and bitter experience of separation of Church and State is not reproduced in that of either France or the USA. The formulations and proposals of Rui Barbosa and his contemporaries represent a "secularism à la Brazil", and understanding this first movement is fundamental to understanding the current state of religious pluralism and increasing religious intolerance. If the disputes and tensions confronted by Rui Barbosa were limited to Christianity, today it is recognised and affirmed that in the current context of promotion of respect of religious diversity Afro-Brazilian religions are the ones most suffering situations of religious intolerance.

Central to democracy and foundational to the principals of human rights, religious freedom can even be understood as a central element in the establishment of new social rights such as for the LGBT population. The central point to be highlighted is the affirmation that the secular State and the defence of freedom of beliefs and convictions are effective examples of the possibility of groups living together in society that share distinct understandings and views of the world and that assume different practices and habits. Religious freedom is the materialisation of the possibility of the coexistence of diversity, not only in religious choices but also through a plethora of other differences.

In this sense, the "first wave of Brazilian secularism" represents a fundamental element both for better understanding the current context and for reflection on the possible bases that support, following Cunha's hypothesis, the establishment of a "second wave of secularism" at the beginning of the twenty-first century (Cunha 2017).

Themes that have warranted the dedication of various Brazilian intellectuals at the end of the nineteenth and beginning of the twentieth centuries remain. Issues related to religious education that warranted significant attention from Rui Barbosa remain current, having had regressions and disputes since the establishment of the separation of Church and State in the Constitution of 1891 until the alterations introduced in its 1934 version, retention of religious teaching in public schools in later constitutions and the recent decision of the Brazilian Supreme Court to permit religious and confessional teaching, issues that afflict and threaten both the concepts of liberty and of secularism.

In the field of religion, the tensions felt and confronted by Rui Barbosa were concentrated in the issues involving the differences at the heart of Catholicism, especially its opposition to ultramontanism, a situation that at the same time placed it as an ally of Protestant groups in the defence of liberty and of initiatives for change in education through the New School Movement inspired by Adolphe Ferrière and John Dewey.

A question that arose in this process is: How much have theories that founded initiatives such as New School created problems for religion? What possible roles that this could play in a modern and secular society? Would religion disappear? Blossom anew? What can be identified in studies about secularisation is that there has been a decline in the meaning of religion in Brazilian society following the experience of modernisation. In the process of differentiation, religion lost the privileged space it held, becoming one among various available spheres.

The attempt to avoid ecclesiastical domination in the recently formed republican government permitted the Constitution of 1891 to clearly mark a distance between the Church and the State, ratifying the Decree of 1890. Secularisation demarcated its spaces in the emergent nation with the presence of liberty of belief and worship; civil marriage; lay teaching in public schools; secularisation of cemeteries; and the prohibition of State subsidy of churches, that is, the separation of Church and State. For their part, the Catholic clergy avoided the confiscation of their goods and the orders and congregations had permission to continue functioning (Moura and Almeida 1978).

If implementation of the secular State was less traumatic in the Brazilian case than in some other countries of the continent, we can also see that the anticlerical forces failed to undo the Catholic tradition present in the national culture. We have not here experienced the first and important step of the Protestant Reformation, which had the role of removing Catholic values embedded in the culture. Similar to what Hervieu-Lerger (2001) finds for France—noting the paradox of secularisation—we have here a society in which Catholicism continues to influence social processes through the continued preservation of its symbolic structure within society and in institutions, leading some years later to the formation of a "moral concordat" (Serbin 1996) between Church and State.

The nineteenth century bore witness to a series of groups formed with the objective of confronting the existing monarchic system. The Catholic Church, deeply entwined with the regime, also becomes a target of these discontented groups and was consequently opposed. The Latin American Plenary Council was organised in Rome in 1899 with the objective of developing strategies to regain the political space lost by the institution in the continent. The formation of the Liberal States in Latin America was accompanied by changes in the constitutional legislation of the majority of countries towards the separation of Church and State.

Beyond the link with the monarchy, the Catholic Church, under the direction of Pius IX, required that the temporal power—the State–to be subordinated to the spiritual power—the Church. Motivated by supporters of ultramontanism and through an anti-liberal mentality which opposed the "notion of autonomy of the human conscience, the sovereignty of reason and the secularisation of moral life" (Oliveira 1986) Catholicism saw itself excluded from the process of formation of the Republic, and the union of Freemasons, liberals and the newly arrived Protestants around the secularisation of the State was read as an "anti-Catholic front", which was consolidated through an important ideological contribution from Positivism. Liberals and Positivists saw Catholicism as reactionary and contrary to progress.

It is in this religious context that the Republic began, almost totally populated by Catholics (98.9% in the 1890 Census) against the 1% of Protestants of a Church which was, ethnically and geographically, significantly localised and the remaining 0.1% from other religious denominations, probably in their majority followers of Judaism as the religion of the indigenous or African slaves was not considered. The defence of religious freedom was the first option for early Protestant missionaries for penetration of their beliefs. The work of Fletcher—opting to invest in personal contacts—stands out. He sought the support of Freemasons, liberals and those he considered "friends of progress" and took up the role of Acting Secretary to the United States Legation in Rio de Janeiro.

For the missionaries, the "progress" sought would only be achieved with adoption of a liberal posture, and economic and commercial improvements. The religious issue was certainly a minor point in this process, but the separation between the State and the Church and religious freedom were central details for Brazil to the select group of prosperous and modern nations. Fletcher's work was carried out through actions by his influential friends, small interventions in the public sphere and among the elites, seeking to support the implementation of Protestantism in Brazil, for example the proposal of the civil marriage law; regular speeches and anticlerical positions in the Chamber of Deputies; actions supporting the immigration of Protestants; and provision of space for publication of anti-Catholic articles in important periodicals of the era.

The Scottish missionary Robert Kalley also opted to establish his missionary work through proximity with the public sphere. He chose to rent the American Ambassador's house in Petrópolis, certainly facilitating his contact with Dom Pedro II who, besides not being a fan of Catholicism, considered the exclusive dedication of the priests to religious issues a waste of time, having been described by Gilberto Freyre as having a "Protestant soul" (Schwarcz 1998). Rui Barbosa merited special mention, having been called the "oracle" among the Baptists and having gained the post of "greatest Brazilian commander" among Protestant groups (Fonseca 2004).

Ecclesia est in Respublica, non Respublica in Ecclesia. Considering the diversity present in Brazil and with a strengthening anticlerical front led by a handful of Freemasons and liberals, Brazilian society sought to follow first world standards. However, as a Catholic nation, there were certainly many differences (Martin 1978), especially in an extremely unequal society with a large mass of outcasts formed of ex-slaves and far from experiencing the process of industrialisation on the scale of the old continent. Only from the 1930s can you speak here of machines being protagonists alongside the expansion of an organised proletariat.

That said, despite these limitations, a "secularisation à la Brazil" begins with the formation of a State free of religious ties and in defence of religious freedom, which half a century later would be considered as one of the human rights. While significant, the removal of the Catholic Church from public life was not complete. Some subsidies remained (Serbin 1996), and in some areas of the country it was only possible to gain documents or make claims through religious institutions. The division between the community and the religious world view became effective among the incipient Positivist elite, but with little effect in the expansive rural Brazil that still had religious festivities as its main references. The overthrow of yesterday's society required the hard task of removing four centuries of "social cement" so embedded in our structures, both in beliefs but also our personal, social, cultural, political and institutional relations.

Bruce argues that, as a consequence of socio-structural differentiation, countries with a Catholic monopoly tend to witness strong anticlerical movements that end up dividing society between those who favour religious tradition and those opposed, leading, as in French and Spanish cases, to the creation of strong communist parties. This was not the case in Brazil. The coalition with the Positivists and the experiences confronted by the Catholic Church in Europe and in the USA were assimilated, and under the leadership of a more able Pope, Catholicism was able to find the right tone, to first survive and to later increase its social importance in the face of subsequent social upheavals such as the 1930 Revolution.

With the Republic proclaimed and the separation between Church and State decreed, a new phase for the religions begins. Curiously, it is the Catholic Church that, without the direct tutelage of the imperial power, invests most in growing the number of parishes and priests and in implementation of improved institutional structures. It is under Pope Leon XIII (*Rerum Novarum*) that the Church moves from opposition to the Republic to a "policy of good neighbourliness". The final document of the Plenary Council promoted the political participation of lay Catholics "to introduce into the veins of the State, in the guise of blood … the wisdom and virtue of the Catholic religion" (Deiros 1994). Some of the problems faced by Catholicism in the continent discussed in the document are: paganism, superstition, religious ignorance, socialism, Freemasonry, lay teaching, relations with the State and with society, and the confiscation of the Church's goods.

As observed by Della Cava, the subsistence of Catholicism in the midst of adversity was fruit of its "position of de facto official State religion, the nation and the dominant elites" (Della Cava 1975), defined by Bruneau (1974) as "neocristandade". However, it must be noted that in the period between 1889 and 1930, in Brazil, this reality was not maintained, removing from the Catholic Church various privileges previously provided by the State.

An important part of this movement was the regionalisation of Catholicism within each State, consistent with the spirit of the times, losing the understanding of the existence of a national church. Each bishop sought to guarantee their subsistence through their contacts within the local elite. Investment in education was part of this strategy seeking to provide school places for the middle classes and elites. The Old Republic saw the creation of 56 new dioceses (previously only 13), extending the Catholic Church's network of action.

All this involvement of clergy in the management of businesses and struggling to survive in the early years of the Republic brought some negative images and accusations. A "minimum programme of action" for each diocese defined as obligations the construction of an episcopal palace, creation of seminaries, cathedral refurbishments and the foundation of teaching establishments and media outlets. Accusations soon surfaced that some religious figures were "self-interested, slandered as practitioners of simony, materialistic, denounced for being only interested in taking personal advantage of fund-raising campaigns". Miceli (1988) continues affirming that "certain accusations [had] some ground", though the majority resulted from "growing institutional visibility of the ecclesiastical corporation, or else, originated from those sectors that most had their political interests hurt through alignment of the Church with other oligarchical factions".

These first years of the Republic represent a time of "institutional construction" for the Catholic Church (Miceli 1988), with economic and administrative adaptations alongside with processes of regionalisation (greater proximity with local elites and investment in education) and Romanisation (organisation and moralisation of the clergy). These initiatives provided the basis for more intense recuperation of space and prestige lost nationally from the 1920s. In 1921, Dom Sebastião Leme is named Auxiliary Archbishop of Rio de Janeiro, and the capital of the Republic begins to centralise initiatives of the country's clergy, strengthening its visibility and effectiveness. He was the leader the Church required at that moment (de Lustosa 1990), to unite and give voice to the demands and desires of the bishops dispersed around Brazil.

The political position of the Church towards the establishment of a "Catholic Republic" comes to be promoted in public events and any relation with the monarchy denied. Firstly, the Eucharistic Congress is organised in Rio de Janeiro in 1922. At this event, belief and patriotism are defended through "The Christian restoration of Brazil through Eucharistic life, primarily in the family, in childhood and youth" (Dias 1996). It is at this event that Dom Leme confirms his prominence within the Catholic Church, emerging through his Pastoral Letter of 1916 as the ambassador of choice to the State. In the same year, the foundation stone of the Christ the Redeemer statue was laid, followed by a series of campaigns in the successive years to raise funds for its completion which would occur in 1931.

The vision of the clergy emphasised that Brazilian society was in crisis due to the religious ignorance of the people and the divorce between the (Catholic) nation and the government. An approximation was necessary, and to achieve this, it was necessary to return to religious marriage and Catholic education in public schools. Brazilian representation in the Holy See and introduction of military chaplains were other solutions proposed. This movement was part of new Vatican guidance, as Oliveira (1986) writes:

> From the 20th Century the church changed strategy, passing from a distant postulant to a close collaborator, that offered its support in defence of order against those movements that began to question the prevailing status quo.

The magazine "The Order" (1921) was one such example that intended to be the "organ of catholicisation of Brazilian laws and intellectuality". Arthur Bernardes' government enshrines the approximation of the Church and State, initiated during that of Epitácio Pessoa. Bernardes was the first president to visit the ecclesiastical hierarchy in the republican history, thus affirming the role of the Church in the maintenance of order. In 1924, on the golden jubilee of Cardinal Arcoverde, the government gave a banquet in the Itamaraty Palace following the participation of the president, and all the ministers, in the religious solemnities marking the event. During the dinner, the "fervent Catholic" and Minister of Foreign Relations Félix Pacheco (de Lustosa 1990) congratulated the Cardinal on behalf of the government, receiving in response the following words from the Archbishop (de Lustosa 1990):

> The communion of views between the temporal heads and the spiritual heads; our always well accepted collaboration, so often requested, for the strengthening of the common Homeland; the union of feelings, passing from the surface of the courtesies to a more intimate and deeper layer, are favourable signs for the future.

In the clergy's view, this event represented the "true baptism of the Republic of Brazil" (Farias 1998). Animated by the possibilities, Dom Leme proposed in 1926 a "constitutional amendment that officially recognised the Catholic religion as the faith of the people" (Casali 1985). Even with the small subtlety that the proposal linked the religion to society and not the State, a different situation to that of the Empire, but with the maintenance of a differentiated status for Catholicism, the amendment was vetoed. Perceiving that the political route would be insufficient to achieve his objectives, Dom Leme opts to affect his actions more within civil society.

The Catholic elites who defended the "recatholicisation of the State" were of fundamental importance in this process. Figures such as Julio Maria, Farias Brito, Jackson de Figueiredo, Eduardo Prado, Alceu de Amoroso Lima and Dom Sebastião Leme himself, representatives of Catholic elites, played a fundamental role in this process to the "recatholicisation of the State". The Dom Vital Centre (1922), the Catholic Student Action (1929), the Catholic Electoral League (1932), that would have its role substituted by Brazilian Catholic Action (1935), and the Catholic Institute of Advanced Studies (1932), that would give rise to the Catholic Pontifical University in 1941, were bodies that boosted the strategy that promoted the re-approximation of the Church with the State "from on high".

In these early years of the Republic, the other religions with some presence in Brazil failed to take advantage of this moment of retraction and reorganisation of the Catholic Church to advance in new spheres. The main mobilisation is of the Kardecist Spiritists against the 1890 Penal Code in which the "practice of spiritism, magic and its sorcery" is considered a crime (Maggie 1992), alongside the prohibition of practising medicine without training.

The newly created Brazilian Spiritist Federation (FEB) sought on various fronts—representations to the president and the National Congress—to alter the terms of this law that criminalised its religion, an item only removed in the Code's 1942 version, continuing to criminalise adherents of Umbanda and Candomblé. Even categorised as a crime, "it was difficult to charge some leading members of the FEB: these were deputies, senators, ex-provincial presidents, renowned liberal professionals and members of the military" (Damazio 1994). The notion of "low spiritism" already came into use in the 1910s to safeguard yet further the middle classes and elites that participated in Kardecism which would conversely represent "high spiritism".

The Protestants went through a series of crises and schisms in this period, a phase Pierson (1971) notes as a moment of seeking maturity in the Brazilian Presbyterian Church, while Léornard (1963) suggests the existence of a crisis in the majority of Protestantism. There were recurrent internal disputes and conflicts with the American bases that sent missionaries. Significant energy was spent on these issues alongside internal disputes around the presence of Freemasons and how teaching institutions would be managed. Divisions occurred and situations of conflict were reported in various States between 1898 and 1922. In relation to the State, the main plea—religious freedom—was already constitutionally guaranteed.

The Pentecostal Movement began timidly in the 1910s directly related to the periphery of Brazilian society. The State of Pará experienced, from the final decades of the nineteenth century, the prosperity of the Rubber Cycle caused by migration from the North-East resulting from the drought of 1877–1879, being 1912 seen as the peak of this process with high volumes of exports. From 1910, we see the decline of Brazil's share of the international market against competitors in the East, with English and Dutch support, taking the Amazon region into a period of decline that would extend to the 1950s. The city of Belém, which through rubber had strong trade with the USA, was chosen in 1910 as the port of entry for the Swedish–American missionaries Vingren and Berg. In the first 13 years of activities, churches were opened only in the North and North-East, arriving at the capital of the Republic only in 1924. A reading of the book of Conde (1960), the denomination's official historian, is interesting in respect of the cities chosen as pioneering fronts of the Assemblies of God, marking out its peripheral position in the society in formation.

It was in the "senzalas" (slave quarters) that the Afro-Brazilian religions were forged. There, it was fermenting, fed by the slave trafficking that brought priests, fortune-tellers and witch doctors on the slave ships promoting a constant meeting of the new and old of different nations. This led to a "chaotic proliferation of sects, or fragments of sects, which were born only to be extinguished, replaced by others as new Africans arrived" (Bastide 1971). Considering this religiosity in the context of the slaves' suffering is fundamental to a better understanding of the Brazilian reality. Slavery in Brazil would receive special attention, understood as it was by Rui Barbosa, according to Silva (2000), as "theft in all senses, direct, positive, material and pecuniary theft".

The religions of the Afro-descendants came to receive the majority of public bodies' attention in application of the Penal Code's articles related to shamanism. Kardecism came to defend itself using the argument that its practices were restricted to charity founded on a "religion–science", predominantly formed of whites and led by "respected" professionals, thus gaining legitimacy. On the other hand, we have Umbanda and other religions which were the expression of the "magic–superstition" binary, with leadership and affluence composed of blacks and *mestiços* (mixed), warranting repression and complete suspicion (Negrão 1996).

Negrão (1996) presents an extensive survey of how the Afro-Brazilian sects were treated in the press. In 1931, the police creates a specific division for the "practice of magic and sorceries", also responsible for gambling, drugs and prostitution. Between 1929 and 1944 occurred the most repressive period when, under the New State, these religions were combated in the name of "defence of rationality" and through arguments that classified magic and curative practices as elements of backwardness and ignorance.

The different religions dedicated themselves in the first years of the secular State mostly to internal problems, to institutional strengthening and surviving when persecuted, while Catholicism went through a process of organisation and institutionalisation. This movement explains the strong Catholic presence until the mid-twentieth century and it only being possible to speak of religious pluralism in Brazil from the 1990s. The separation of Church and State only saw an environment of religious pluralism a century after its decree. The guarantee of freedom and exercise of religion alongside the separation of Church and State describe important characteristics for Brazilian religious freedom, which took time to be genuinely experienced, and can now be seen in the midst of a reality of increasing religious intolerance.

In recent times, Brazil and various Latin American countries have experienced a greater conservative presence that questions and places in check exactly some of the fundamental values of this liberal paradigm. Mirroring the similarity of experience across the content in the processes of separation of Church and State (da Fonseca 2011), again this theme sees similar repercussions: the questioning of foundational assumptions of human rights and conservative causes related to gender identity and orientation and plurality of thought in society come to be questioned, while positions in defence of censorship and groups that defend the return to military government become strengthened.

Understanding the disputes between the liberal and anti-liberal forces that saw the separation of Church and State is an important element that occurred in parallel to establishing the foundations of Brazilian democracy. The Republic was born in the midst of crises, disputes and issues involving the originating denominations of Catholicism and Protestantism, at the same time that the presence of other religious options—while still marginal—became apparent, particularly the Afro-Brazilian religions, spiritism and Pentecostalism.

If today religious pluralism is a fact, the growth of religiously motivated intolerance is also a reality and it becomes fundamental to overcome it to strengthen both the democracy but also a process of confronting regressions and possible exclusionary postures with fascist tones that appear to proliferate among some sectors that as well as not accepting diversity have assumed aggressive postures against groups that do not share the same beliefs or world view. For this reason, data is presented below which helps dissect some of the characteristics of religious intolerance in Brazil.

3 Statistics on Religious Intolerance and Violence in Brazil Today

> Genuine tolerance does not require me to agree with him or her that I tolerate nor that I esteem him or her. What authentic tolerance demands of me is that I respect the different, their dreams, their ideas, their choices, their tastes, that I do not deny them simply for being different. What legitimate tolerance teaches me is that, in their experience, I learn from the different.
>
> Paulo Freire

Through the data compiled for the Religious Intolerance and Violence in Brazil (RIVIR), 965 cases of religious intolerance were identified in the country between 2011 and 2015. Most cases were obtained through newspapers with 409 articles (42% of the total). Further 394 cases (41%) were gathered from ombudsmen and 162 (17%) from judicial processes. The first issue to consider from these statistics is that it was possible to identify a religiously motivated human rights violation in Brazil every two days during the studied period.

The statistics compiled in the RIVIR come from three sources: (1) periodical magazines (two from each State) and a selection of national periodicals , magazines and Internet portals, representing 65 communication outlets; (2) judicial processes: the judgements of 61 tribunals were considered; and (3) institutional statistics: data from ombudsmen, municipal, State and federal public institutions as well as police departments specialised in intolerance and racism.

Each researcher consulted online databases, from both media outlets and judicial tribunals using keywords defined through bibliographic review and team discussion. Information requested from the ombudsmen and other institutions was supplied as per the classification adopted by each body.

In addition to these documents, interviews were conducted with a total of 20 individuals from the ten States where the researchers operated, namely: Rio Grande do Sul, São Paulo, Rio de Janeiro, Espírito Santo, Minas Gerais, Brasília, Paraíba, Bahia, Recife and Amazonas. The choice of interviews in each State, after the media outlet research, selected actors of particular prominence or who were involved in emblematic cases. The ten States were defined using data from the Human Rights Ombudsman, selecting those with the highest numbers of reported cases of intolerance, both in absolute and in relative terms to the population size.

The States with the highest absolute numbers of cases are practically the same as where field research was undertaken. Among the ten greatest, two were identified—Paraná and Ceará—that were not considered from the initial data. Of the ten selected, two States included on the basis of relative number—Amazonas and Espírito Santo—fell quantitatively in low positions. Rio de Janeiro takes on prominence as a result of the case of the girl Kaylane, aged 13 years, who was stoned in the street simply for wearing the religious dress of Candomblé, a case that received significant press coverage. São Paulo, the most populous State, the Federal District and Bahia follow.

The data demonstrates that religious intolerance increases over time in number of cases: doubled between 2012 (154 cases) and 2015 (313 cases). The same increase can be seen in other statistics available on religious intolerance in Brazil, as much as its quantification is difficult, also conscious that obviously this data represents only a portion of the situations of religious intolerance and violence that occur in people's daily reality. What appears to be confirmed by the RIVIR, as well as other sources, is the increase of cases of religious intolerance in Brazil.

In discussing religious intolerance, it is notable that this subject still provokes resistance from segments of the population that affirm that it is an "invention". One example of this resulted from the written entry examination for public universities (ENEM) in 2016 that took the subject as its theme, requesting candidates to write a text about religious intolerance. A good number of the discussions in the press around the theme included the affirmation that it related to something non-existent in Brazil, a country marked by "cordiality and the coexistence of difference".

These sorts of reactions provide a highly symptomatic statistic of the importance of the deep need to discuss the theme of religious intolerance. In the process of the report elaboration and in a prior document of the SDH (Sydow 2015), a typology was developed that identified eight different types of violence present in Brazil, which were described according to the existing Brazilian legislation, particularly Law 11.340/2006, specifically:

1. **RELIGIOUSLY MOTIVATED PSYCHOLOGICAL ABUSE:**

Characterised as any conduct that causes emotional harm and diminishes self-esteem or that harms and disrupts full development or that seeks to degrade or control their beliefs and behaviours through threats, embarrassment, humiliation, manipulation, isolation, constant surveillance, persistent persecution, insult, blackmail, ridicule, exploitation and limitation of the right to come and go or any other means that causes harm to psychological health and self-determination, motivated by the religious belief of the victim.

2. **RELIGIOUSLY MOTIVATED PHYSICAL ABUSE:**

Characterised by any conduct that harms bodily integrity or health, motivated by the religious belief of the victim.

3. **ABUSE RELATED TO THE PRACTICE OF RELIGIOUS ACTS/RITES:**

Characterised by the prohibition of rites, prayers and offerings; by the misuse and disrespect of religious images, through the impediment of renewal of the rent of properties; through expulsion from home or its threat, due to religious belief. That is, any act that restricts or prevents the practice of religious acts or rites.

4. **RELIGIOUSLY MOTIVATED PSYCHOLOGICAL HARASSMENT:**

Under this topic, will be included behaviours described as crimes against dignity by articles 138, 139 and 140 of the National Penal Code (Brazil, 1940), with the intention of disrespecting the religious belief or position. These behaviours must be religiously motivated and are defined as follows:

(A) Slander: "slander someone, falsely accusing them of an act defined as criminal" (Art 138 of the NPC). Defined as the statement of a criminal act of one person accusing another, containing the supposed location of the crime's perpetration and the time of its execution, which they know to be false with the specific intention of offending the individual's honour.

(B) Defamation: "defame someone, accusing them of an act offensive to their reputation" (Art 139 of the NPC). Defined as the statement of a fact, true or false, not typified in penal law, by the active subject accusing the passive subject, containing concretely or fictitiously the location of the act's perpetration and the time of its execution, with the object of violating the individual's honour.

(C) Defame, to besmirch means to publically discredit a person. The intention of the legislator was to underline that defamation consists of the affirmation of an act, true or not, not considered by Penal Law detailing the individuals involved, the location, the time of perpetration as well as other elements which are offensive to the reputation of the other.

(D) Revile: "Revile someone, offending their dignity or decorum" (Art 140 of the NPC). Occurs when someone, through gestures, words, images or outrageous actions offends the dignity or decorum of another.

5. **RELIGIOUSLY MOTIVATED INSTITUTIONAL ABUSES:**

Abuse motivated by divergence of beliefs or (religious) convictions predominantly in different societies, in the formalisation and institutionalisation of different public and private organisations.

In this category, the word institution should be understood in the broad sense, as any organisation or social structure established through law of through customs.

6. **RELIGIOUSLY MOTIVATED OFFENCES AGAINST PROPERTY:**

Characterised as any conduct that involves the retention, removal, partial or total destruction of religious objects, physical spaces which house religious temples or individuals' homes, due to their religious belief, other than in the case of trespassing.

7. **RELIGIOUSLY MOTIVATED SEXUAL ABUSE:**

Characterised by acts that force an individual to observe or participate in sexual acts under intimidation, threat, coercion or use of force or power relations, motivated by their religious belief. Examples of power relations include teacher-student and priest-follower. Lustful acts and use of obscene gestures or terms are included in this category.

8. **RELIGIOUSLY MOTIVATED NEGLIGENCE:**

Characterised by abandonment, carelessness, helplessness, lack of responsibility and failure to provide care and affection, motivated by the victim's religious belief. Situations in which an individual acts with indifference to another that requires their care and attention are included in this category.

The largest number of cases (40%) involves those considered psychological abuse. This is followed by psychological harassment—which is very close to psychological abuse; institutional abuse, frequently situations linked to education and work; and the unacceptable and frequent identification of cases of physical abuse. The RIVIR even identified eight cases of homicide which either the civil police or the Public Ministry determined had been religiously motivated. During the five years, four victims were identified from Afro-Brazilian religions and four from Evangelical Christians. All these murders were committed with knives, and of the eight victims, three were children. In these cases, there is a significant component of passion and the victims and their aggressors were closely related, underlining the importance of looking at this issue and how something present in the daily reality leads to death.

After physical abuse follow offences against property (15% of the total) ranging from the desecration of religious spaces as well as vandalism of sacred images and books. This type of attack is the most common type against Catholicism, representing 29% of cases, while Afro-Brazilian religions suffer the highest number of such cases. Of 144 cases identified, 82 distributed across 11 cities involved these groups, against 31 cases across 13 cities towards Catholics. Attacks that involved Islamic and Evangelical spaces and objects were also encountered.

The concentration of attacks appears to be associated with organised actions—to greater and lesser extents—that demanded an official response which saw the creation, in Cuiabá and Brasília, of police departments specialised in crimes of religious intolerance. These cases demonstrate the existence of a serious problem nationally. One that is extremely serious, both in terms of offences against property, but also for what it represents when individuals vandalise buildings and objects used by others to express their religion.

Each case was classified with up to three types of abuse, leading to 1488 abuses being identified in the 965 cases as it cannot be ignored that an offence against property or a physical abuse also carries a psychological element. Table 1 summarises

Table 1 Types of violence—total and by religion (*n*)

Types of religiously motivated abuse	Total	Afro-Brazilian religions	Evangelicals	Catholics	Other
Psychological abuse	582	221	70	33	258
Psychological harassment	235	120	24	16	75
Institutional	244	48	77	9	110
Physical	148	84	13	3	48
Property	144	82	9	31	22
Related to the practice of religious acts/rites	109	54	11	15	29
Negligence	17	2	1	1	13
Sexual	9	0	2	0	7
Total	1488	611	207	108	562

$N = 1488$; *Source* RIVIR, SDH, 2016

the violations by religion highlighting the three with the largest number of followers in the research database.

Different types of abuse predominated between the sources surveyed. The ombudsmen received significantly more complaints linked to psychological abuse; judicial processes related mostly to institutional abuses by the State, teaching institutions or companies—employment issues. Newspapers, however, reflected greater interest in episodes involving physical abuse or psychological harassment. In the case of Evangelicals, institutional abuses predominated, cases in which organisations are the authors of religious intolerance and violence; in the case of religions of African origin, physical violence and psychological harassment are more present than average in this sector. In relation to Catholics, there is an increased presence of offences against property, such as vandalism of images and churches, which are not small in number.

It is possible to make several observations about the locations in which religious intolerance or violence occur, with interesting differences between the sources and the locations. In complaints to ombudsmen, the primary location of the violation is an individual's home—be it of the victim, of the aggressor or of a shared acquaintance. In judicial processes, the primary location is the educational or working environment, while in newspapers, various locations appear, but most often the place of worship or public space, the street, locations typical of the violations most covered by newspapers: vandalism, attacks on property and physical aggressions.

The identity of aggressors and victims is a central issue in relation to violations of human rights related to religious intolerance. Victims of cases identified through ombudsmen, newspapers and judicial processes demonstrate that around 35% relate to religions of African origin followed by Evangelicals and Catholics with 19% and

Table 2 Religion of victims—total (*n* and %)

Religion	*n*	%
Afro-Brazilian	334	34.61
Evangelical	187	19.38
Catholic	78	8.08
Spiritist	37	3.83
Islamic	24	2.49
Other	88	9.12
Not specified	217	22.49
Total	965	100

Source RIVIR, SDH, 2016

8%, respectively. Spiritists appear with 4% and Muslims with 2.5%. The remaining 9% are accounted for by 15 different religions. As Table 2 shows, there is no information for 22.5% of victims.

Across the different sources, it was possible to identify that in judicial processes there is a higher representation of Evangelicals—primarily Seventh-day Adventists. It was noted that in 45% of cases the originator, that is the victim, was an Adventist and another 10% Evangelicals of other denominations. In newspapers, 53% of victims were individuals from religions of African origin. Members of Afro-Brazilian religions were also most represented in cases from ombudsmen (23% of victims), followed by Evangelicals (16%).

The ombudsmen data permits further analysis, and a finding which draws attention is the recurrence of violations between individuals known to each other that are closely related (Table 3). This is the issue of religious intolerance and violence in the home, in which there is proximity between victim and aggressor. Consequently, relations, neighbours and spouses significantly make up 53% of aggressors in the ombudsmen data. Another prominent and extremely concerning point is the fact 11% of offenders are teachers or school directors.

Table 3 Relationship between victim and aggressors—complaints to ombudsmen (*n* and %)

Relationship	*n*	%
Neighbours	72	27
Relations	60	23
Public agents	32	12
Teachers	28	11
Media	25	9
Spouses	8	3
Strangers	18	7
Other	21	8
Total	264	100

Source RIVIR, SDH, 2016 $N = 264$, missing 130

Table 4 Religious affiliation of victims and aggressors by religious segment in occurrences with information (%)

Religious affiliation	Victims	Offenders	Total
African origin	99	1	100
Evangelicals	51	49	100
Catholic	69	31	100
Spiritist	87	13	100
Other	74	26	100

Source RIVIR, SDH, 2017; $n = 935$

Data analysis allows us to draw other conclusions. These include the profile of victims, whether the complaint was made by an individual victim or a group, by a religious community, that is a collective that is the victim, and the different manners in which the violation was voiced. Basically, in judicial processes, generally the aggressor is an institution, a school or the State. Within the ombudsmen's office, the aggressors are generally individuals as they provide a service in which individuals enter into contact to make complaints of an occasional and more defined nature. The judicial processes represent those that decide to take opposition to and denounce institutions through judicial actions.

The first point to note about the aggressors is that in 83% of cases this information is not recorded. The number of judicial processes for which it is possible to access this information is very low. Across newspapers and ombudsmen, this information is absent for 70% of cases. For those cases where this is known, slightly less than 20% are Evangelicals, ignoring the internal diversity of this group. These are followed by Catholics, other religions, atheists, a few from religions of African origin and a handful of each of Jews, Spiritists and Jehovah's Witnesses.

Table 4 cross-references the victims and aggressors from each religious sector, where adherents of religions of African origin appear to be the victim in 99% of times across the three research sources and, only in 1%, the aggressor. Among Evangelicals, half are victims and the other half aggressors. Among Catholics, 70% are victims and 30% the aggressors, and among Spiritists, 87% and 13%, respectively. The other religions have approximate proportions of 70–30% (Table 4).

Of the 965 cases, for only 159 is it possible to identify the religion of both the victim and the aggressor. Simply put, individuals linked to Evangelical churches are predominant among those accused, especially in cases of violations against members of religions of African origin, but are also present in violations against all other religious segments. This is a serious issue that must be confronted. It is important to emphasise the heterogeneity of this religious group and the diverse segments that represent to "be Evangelical" in Brazil, a reality in which some groups identified in these cases would very likely not be considered Evangelicals by the majority of groups that belong to this segment.

In some cases, it was possible to identify the actions of groups associated with localised and recent initiatives that characterise themselves through practices of hate and intolerance and that self-denominate themselves as Evangelicals, but do not share the majority of practices or doctrines, beliefs or values followed by and generally associated with the segment.

There are numerous practices that are not shared, performed by independent groups not linked to recognised institutions with national reach. As no national representative body exists to unify the segment, it is necessary that various groups come together to discuss this issue within the segment itself. This invitation should be extended to various denominations, training centres, theological seminaries, universities, publications, representative entities and leaderships to permit serious and informed dialogue. Action is required from study and research groups, and forums of the Evangelical movement itself, as only from its own dialogue and decisions will it be possible, to use a term from the segment, to "separate the wheat from the chaff".

This point should also be considered by Catholicism, which also has aggressors against all other groups. This statistic should also be seen from a qualitative perspective, due to the small sample available, as an indicator that should certainly mobilise religious leaders, those primarily interested in the theme. At the level of the National Conference of Bishops of Brazil (CNBB), it is possible to identify some initiatives and reflections related to the topic of religious intolerance, being a theme which has been present in the concerns of the leaderships.

Another notable group are the atheists who have Evangelicals, Catholics and adherents of religions of African origin among their victims. Again, it is worth remembering that we are considering very small numbers, which may have far more weight individually than collectively, though I think it important to consider this data in promoting dialogues as it is indicative of certain movements and how the phenomenon of religious intolerance and violence in Brazil that warrants deeper analysis (Table 5).

On this issue, it is also important to highlight that a significant number of victims of religious intolerance are also identified among Evangelicals. This is very present in the educational environment, but also in other spaces, and may be related to the fact that religion is most present among poorer and black populations. As a result, its followers come to suffer intolerance in various situations due to different prejudices that characterise the popular understanding of this group that has historically suffered different intolerances, since its establishment in Brazil by Pentecostal groups at the beginning of the twentieth century.

Table 5 Religious affiliation of victims and aggressors by religious segment in a single case (n)

Victims	Offenders					
	African origin	Evangelicals	Spiritists	Catholics	Atheists	Total
African origin	2	74	0	15	4	95
Evangelicals	0	14	2	3	1	20
Catholics	0	22	0	6	2	30
Spiritists	0	11	0	3	0	14
Total	2	121	2	27	7	159

Source RIVIR, SDH 2017; $n = 159$

The data also reveals that generally religious groups are intolerant with their own religious group: Catholics intolerant with other Catholics, Evangelicals intolerant with Evangelicals, adherents of Afro-Brazilian religions intolerant with adherents of Afro-Brazilian religions. This is widespread: intolerances that also represent disputes and divergences of interpretation that become conflicts beyond the level of ideas and convictions.

4 Conclusion

One of the first issues identified by the RIVIR is the difficulty of the Brazilian State in dealing with religious intolerance and violence both in the process of monitoring and in identifying these violations. This was noticed not only in relation to the State but also observed in the Brazilian media. The manner in which they are communicated are, requiring educational processes aimed at journalists and managers that discuss this issue. This is a process that has already occurred in relation to the issue of violence against women and against the LGBT population. The theme of religious intolerance is still fragile, still seen as something colourful that affects some or others, generally understood only to affect the black population and adherents of religions of African origin and that forget the importance of religious freedom in the formation and consolidation of democracy in Brazil.

Religious intolerance has affected the Brazilian population as a whole since 1500. In this sense, it is also important to see more spaces opened to receive victims of religious intolerance. There are some initiatives along these lines, whether of public bodies, of civil society or of the Order of Attorneys of Brazil in some States. It is necessary to consider spaces and create flows and processes in which victims of religious intolerance can be received, can have somewhere to turn to, can have a network of social support and can receive support in psychological, social, economic and judicial issues.

Brazil has a society that is increasingly plural, and in which religious diversity is a fact, an issue that is here to stay. Brazil is a diverse country. There are indicators through which the national census has not been able to capture the diversity in its breadth nor to produce sufficient information to understand, in a concrete manner, the religious phenomenon in its complexity. There is today a diversity of beliefs and non-beliefs, often combined, that require the State to have awareness and reflect, with civil society, with public bodies, religious organisations, universities and research institutes, with a view towards producing knowledge that supports development of actions that promote respect of religious diversity.

The concept of the secular State confirms for us the possibility of experiencing the new social rights. It is the confirmation that it is possible to have interaction between different. No one is against the concept of the secular State. Nobody, in principle, demands that all people have the same religion. This logic, which is accepted in a more or less coherent manner, is a very powerful example to society of what can be constructed, in terms of respect for difference and the promotion of human rights.

The religions of African origin, a religious minority, but a cultural majority, have a quantitative presence smaller than that of Catholics or Evangelicals in Brazilian society according to official statistics. Even so, in the RIVIR, they appear with significant regularity among those that most suffer violation of their rights because of their religion. In the case of schools, for example, it is unacceptable to come across children that hold positions of leadership in Candomblé or Umbanda and that are forced to hide their religious identity when they enter school.

Another issue is the necessity for space for mediation of conflicts, a point that becomes particularly relevant in view of the high presence of religious intolerance in the home and relationships between closely related individuals. The ombudsmen receive these psychological complaints, aggressions that are verbal, that involve fights between neighbours, between individuals that know each other, but that also represent serious conflicts. It is exactly these fights and quarrels that give origin to the physical aggressions and murders that feature in the pages of the newspapers. As a society, considering the various abuses that occur in the domestic context, it is necessary to develop processes for training, for meetings between groups, and varied experiences of dialogue and mediation, forums such as those developed by the Federal Government with the creation of the National Committee for the Respect of Religious Diversity or through initiatives like the Deliberative Workshops on Human Rights and Religious Diversity (de Fonseca et al. 2016). These spaces of social participation, of dialogue, are fundamental in the breaking down of prejudices, to establish an environment of respect for religious diversity.

The phenomenon of religious intolerance and violence is extremely complex, and various other elements, not considered in this text due to its scope, cannot be ignored. It is however important to underline the presence of this phenomenon associated with the existence of racism, homophobia and a series of prejudices and of financial and property-based disputes, issues often present in episodes of religious intolerance. It is possible to understand religious intolerance as an additional dimension that conforms to a narrative that establishes processes of invalidation of the others, denial of the others, denial of their capacity to exist and practice what they believe.

Returning to the educator Freire (1995), who provides the epigraph to this section, tolerance should be understood as a virtue of human coexistence, an instance of the existence. Tolerance is something to be created and cultivated by and between us, while intolerance is no more than an addictive distortion. The challenge posed and which I believe to be fundamental, as a society, is the increase of groups that calmly discuss this so complex theme through a relationship of respect, promoting the inclusion of the maximum number of people that could certainly contribute to a new reflection and a change to the construction of a culture of peace in Brazil.

References

Bastide R (1971) As religiões Africanas no Brasil. Pioneira & Edusp, São Paulo

Bruneau T (1974) Catolicismo brasileiro em época de transição. Loyola, São Paulo

Casali A (1985) Elite intelectual e restauração da Igreja. Vozes, Petrópolis
Casanova J (1994) Public religions in the modern world. University of Chicago Press, Chicago
Conde E (1960) História das Assembleias de Deus no Brasil. Rio de Janeiro
Cunha LA (2017) A Educação Brasileira na Primeira Onda Laica: Do Império à República, self-publi. Rio de Janeiro
Fonseca ABC (2011) Relações e privilégios: Estado, secularização e diversidade religiosa no Brasil. Novos Diálogos, Rio de Janeiro
Fonseca ABC, Adad C (2016) Relatório sobre Intolerância e Violência Religiosa (2011–2015): resultados preliminares. Brasília
Fonseca ABC, Conrado F, Gilson G et al (2016) Direitos Humanos e Diversidade Religiosa: experiências de diálogo. Brasília
Damazio S (1994) Da elite ao povo: Advento e expansão do espiritismo no Rio de Janeiro. Bertrand, Rio de Janeiro
Lustosa OF (1990) A Igreja Católica no Brasil e o Regime Republicano: Um aprendizado de liberdade. Loyola & CEPEHIB, São Paulo
Deiros PA (1994) História del Cristianismo en América Latina. FTL, Buenos Aires
Della Cava R (1975) Igreja e Estado no Brasil do século XX: sete monografias recentes sobre o catolicismo brasileiro – 1916/1964. Novos Estud – CEBRAP 5–52
Dias R (1996) Imagens de Ordem: a doutrina católica sobre autoridade no Brasil (1922–1933). Unesp, São Paulo
Farias D (1998) Em defesa da ordem: Aspectos da práxis conservadora católica no meio operário em São Paulo. Hucitec, São Paulo
Fonseca AB (2004) A função da religião no pensamento de Rui Barbosa. Intellèctus 4:1–11
Freire P (1995) Pedagogia da tolerância. Paz e Terra, Rio de Janeiro
Hervieu-Leger D (2001) The twofold limit of the notion of secularization. Peter Berger and the study of religion. Routledge, London, pp 111–125
Huntington SP (1996) The clash of civilizations and the remaking of world order. Simon & Schuster, New York
Leonard É (1963) O protestantismo brasileiro. Aste & Juerp, São Paulo
Maggie Y (1992) O medo do feitiço. Relações entre magia e poder no Brasil. National Archive, Rio de Janeiro
Martin D (1978) A general theory of secularization. Blackwell Publishers, Oxford
Miceli S (1988) A elite Eclesiástica Brasileira. Bertrand, São Paulo
Moura SL, Almeida JMG (1978) A Igreja na Primeira República. História Geral da Civilização Brasileira. Difel, São Paulo, pp 321–374
Negrão L (1996) Entre a cruz e a encruzilhada: Formação do campo umbandista em São Paulo. Edusp, São Paulo
Oliveira L (1986) Ilha de Vera Cruz. Universidade de São Paulo, Terra de Santa Cruz
Pierson P (1971) The younger church in search of maturity. Princeton
Schwarcz L (1998) As barbas do Imperador: D. Pedro II, um monarca nos trópicos. Cia das Letras, São Paulo
Serbin K (1996) Church-state reciprocity in contemporary Brazil. The convening of the international eucharistic congress of 1955 in Rio de Janeiro. Notre Dame
Silva E (2000) Rui Barbosa e o quilombo do Leblon. In: Estudos históricos sobre Rui Barbosa. Edições Casa de Rui Barbosa, Rio de Janeiro, p 256
Sydow EM (2015) Produto da consultoria para o Projeto 914BRA3034. Brasília
Taylor C (2007) A secular age. Harvard University Press

Mexican Law of Religion at 28 Years of the Constitutional Reform on Religious Matters

María Concepción Medina González

Abstract In the framework of the centenary of the promulgation of the Political Constitution of the United Mexican States (1917), the current directions of Mexican Law of Religion are addressed. The starting point is the constitutional reform of January 28, 1992, to Articles 3, 5, 24, 27, and 130, which are the basis for the development of a Law of Religion in a positive sense. This reform contains the principles that guarantee the freedom of religion in Mexico: separation between State and churches and Laicity of State. "Mexican Law of Religion" means the totality of state legal norms that include the religious factor linked to individual, corporate, and collective religious needs and interests under the fundamental principles of religious freedom, secularism (*laicity*), and separation of the State and religious communities. In this sense, the holders of the religious factor are not only the individual person and the religious communities or religious associations but also the indigenous peoples. For the analysis, I will focus my remarks on some fundamental topics: the amendments to Articles 24 and 40 of the Political Constitution and the New Constitution of Mexico City; development and legal protection of the dimensions of religious freedom; management of religious diversity as public policy and recent cases, such as the Native American Church case and the Blood Transfusion case, since these illustrate the Supreme Court's readiness to protect the right of religious freedom. One of the most difficult issues to resolve with respect to the register of religious associations has been how to define "*notorio arraigo*." The Basic Law strives to protect religious freedom and to establish a society tolerant of religious difference. Furthermore, increased protection of religious minorities may signal a change in Mexican cultural perceptions of religious minorities.

Keywords Freedom of religion · Secularity of state · Mexican law of religion · Religious associations · Religious pluralism

M. C. Medina González (✉)
National Autonomous University of Mexico, Mexico City, Mexico
e-mail: mariamarianita@hotmail.com

© Springer Nature Switzerland AG 2020
R. V. S. Alves (ed.), *Latin American Perspectives on Law and Religion*, Law and Religion in a Global Context 3,
https://doi.org/10.1007/978-3-030-46717-3_7

1 Introduction

Mexico is not a place of religious monoculture. In Mexico, there is true religious pluralism. Although a majority of Mexicans declares to profess the Catholic religion, the presence of other religions is extensive. The Mexican secular (lay = *laico*) State has the enormous task of managing the religious diversity, and with the Mexican law of religion,[1] to take up the challenge of guarantying the full exercise of religious freedom, without constituting ghettos or any type of segregation, to make peaceful religious coexistence possible.

The basis for the legal relationship between State and church is to be found in the Mexican Constitution of 1917. Since that date, there have been amendments to Articles 24 and 130 on few but important occasions. Before constitutional reform of January 28, 1992, Articles 24 (at the time freedom of belief) and 130 (at the time Supremacy of State on Church) contained anti-clerical provisions, religious associations could not obtain legal personality and the principle of Supremacy of State on church predominated.

With the constitutional reform of January 28, 1992 to Articles 3 (right of education), 24 (at the time freedom of belief), 27 (right of property) and 130 (at the time Supremacy of State on church), several anti-clerical provisions were derogated, religious communities and churches could obtain legal personality as "religious associations" (*asociaciones religiosas*) by the Ministry of Interior.

This constitutional reform showed several processes such as: construction of laicity on the recognition of religious diversity, the visibility of the "religious minorities" at the possibility to be registered as religious associations and obtain legal personality, and recognition of religious diversity within a framework of inclusion and tolerance.

In particular, Article 130 (today, Principle of Separation of State and churches) allowed the churches and religious communities to acquire legal personality once they obtained their registration as religious associations by the Ministry of Interior.

Now, the last constitutional reform to Article 24 on July 19, 2013, implied the substitution of the expression "every man" for "every person," the introduction of the right to freedom of ethical convictions, conscience, and religion. It makes clear that this freedom includes the right to participate individually or collectively, both in

[1]It is worth noting that the concept of "Mexican ecclesiastical law" is formally limited, because it refers to the ecclesiastical, to the institutional, to the churches, but not all religious communities are erected in this way, as churches; for example, the case of Jewish, Buddhist, Hindu communities. For that reason, among others, I prefer to refer to the "Mexican Law of Religion" as the set of rules of the State concerning the religious factor that attends to the religious needs and interests at the individual level (individual juridical person), corporate level (religious communities and religious associations), and collective level (indigenous peoples, with respect to their religious practices and customs), under the principles of religious freedom, laicity (laicidad), and separation of state and churches (or religious communities). Under Mexican law of religion is to be understood the "totality of state juridical norms, which regulate the religious factor related to religious needs and interests of its holders at the individual level, the corporative level (religious communities and religious associations) and the collective level (indigenous people, in the case of their religious usages and customs), and under the fundamental principles: laicity of the State, religious freedom and separation between State and religious communities" (Medina González 2005).

public and in private, in ceremonies, devotions or acts of worship, provided they do not constitute an offense punishable by law. Although a prohibition is incorporated: "No one can use the public acts of expression of this freedom for political purposes, proselytism or propaganda."

Before this reform, several civil and non-Catholic religious associations demonstrated in about 20 states in the Mexican Republic to warn that they would not allow the reform of Article 24 of the Constitution, because it threatens the secular nature of the Mexican State and it gives privileges for Catholics. They expressed three arguments: (I) The intention of the reform is the dismantling of the secular state. It is intended to use it to demand clerical privileges: mainly replacement of secular education for religious instruction in public schools and control of mass media. (II) The handling of the reform in the concept of "freedom of religion." The redefinition of "freedom of religion" that the Catholic hierarchy seeks to establish offers a tendentious and biased concept of that freedom to provide religious education in public schools as a religious privilege. (III) The consequences of reform are an affectation of the freedoms of religious minorities. For example, religious education in public schools will cause that children and adolescents who profess a different faith then Catholic become victims of acts of intolerance and discrimination. Religion is also represented as a factor of division among students professing different faiths and as an element of social polarization that will damage seriously the living together.

On the other side, the constitutional reform to Article 40 on November 30, 2012, to include the "lay character" of State was not really necessary to know that "laicity" is the scenario and presuppose for the effective exercise of fundamental freedoms. Laicity and religious freedom are not opposed and are not mutually excluded. Reference to an "open laicity," "positive laicity," or even "healthy laicity" is made. For example, religious freedom includes the teaching of religion too, and the state has to guarantee it. The current dimension of laicity is particularly in the field of cultural identities and protection of minorities. The issue of laicity is not only "political" but also related to the "minorities," who defend their "vulnerability." The concept of the secular (lay = *laico*) state is dynamic, and is linked to social processes. In the debate on laicity are present new actors, and not only the traditional State–church or churches but also women, academics, homosexuals, and indigenous people. Certainly, the "pathology" of laicity would be to reduce religion to the private sphere alone. The formula "for greater religious freedom" less "lay state" is a fallacy.

However, the exercise of religious freedom recognizes limits.

There is no doubt that the "recent" constitutional reforms involve two key elements of the rule of law (*Estado de derecho*): (I) Popular sovereignty, under Article 40 of the Constitution (linked to Article 39). (II) Human rights, including the right to religious freedom established in Article 24 of the Constitution.

For the following analysis, I will focus my remarks on four fundamental aspects: binomial "Law and Religion"; analysis of the amendments to Articles 24 and 40 of the Constitution; approaches to public policy management of religious diversity; and cases.

2 Law and Religion

This conceptual binomial gives me the opportunity to analyze the amendments to Articles 24 and 40 and their constitutional implications, from the perspective of the *Mexican Law of Religion*, whose core is religious freedom, and it grounds the dignity of the human person, so that I will not focus only in the so-called "church-State relations," which at least in its formal name apparently may be restrictive and not open to religious communities that are not churches.[2]

Here, I want to refer to the important intervention of *François Houtart* in the Assembly of the United Nations in 2008,[3] which noted that the world needs alternatives and not merely regulations, since it is not sufficient to rehabilitate or maintain a system but to transform it.

It is a question of permitting all forms of knowledge, including traditional forms of all philosophies and cultures, to participate in the construction of alternatives[4] "in breaking the monopoly of Westernization." This author considers various aspects among religions:

> the wisdom of Hinduism in relationship to nature, the compassion of Buddhism in human relations, the permanent quest for utopia in Judaism, the thirst for justice which defines the prophetic current in Islam, the emancipatory power of the theology of liberation in Christianity, the respect for the sources of life in the concept of the land itself among the indigenous peoples of the Americas, the sense of solidarity expressed in the religions of Africa, can all make important contributions in the context of mutual tolerance guaranteed by the impartiality of political society.

This consideration has its own specific weight to the topic at hand, since to democratize society within a framework of laicity (*laicidad*) is to allow multiculturalism to be expressed through religious freedom. A lay (*laico*) State that renounces religious freedom, renounces the claim of this human right in all its dimensions; it loses its right to exist as such, i.e., as a lay (*laico*) State.

3 Analysis of the Amendments to Articles 24 and 40 of the Mexican Constitution

This second aspect focuses primarily on distinguishing between the justification for the existence of the constitutional reform to Article 24 of January 28, 1992, and

---

[2]I mean Jewish, Buddhist and Islamic religious communities.

[3]Cf. General Assembly of the United Nations. Panel on the financial crisis, October 30, 2008.

[4]Here, I want to refer to an indigenous representative Chamula, expert in Tsotsil, indigenous language of the National Commission for the Development of Indigenous Peoples, who—in December 2010—questioned the application of human rights in indigenous communities, since in these—he says—"there is no freedom but complementarity, there is no equality but reciprocity, there is no fraternity but relatedness." How to translate the Universal Declaration of Human Rights into the indigenous context? It is a challenge for the indigenous peoples themselves.

the reason for the existence of the recent amendments to Articles 24 and 40 of the Constitution.[5]

Regardless of the political nature attributed to the constitutional reforms of January 28, 1992, about a "search for legitimacy of the Federal Executive," it was rather to combat obvious anachronism and open simulation with:

(a) The adequacy of the rules in religious matters to social reality, to prevent thereby any simulation;
(b) The updating of the regulations on religious freedom. It demands that the Mexican government complies with international treaties signed by the Mexican state to ensure that fundamental right; and
(c) The need to promote, in the awareness of Mexican society, respect for the legal system and proper implementation of the law on religious matters.

With this constitutional reform and the subsequent issuance of the *Law on Religious Associations and Public Worship* (July 15, 1992), several processes took place:

(a) The construction of laicity (*laicidad*) on the recognition of religious diversity.
(b) The visibility of religious minorities, which may be registered as religious associations before the *Ministry of Interior* to obtain juridical personality.[6]
(c) The recognition of religious diversity that creates conditions for inclusion and tolerance that are essential for peaceful coexistence among different believers, religious communities, and religious associations.

3.1 Amendment to Article 40 of the Constitution

Article 40, in close connection with Article 39 of the Mexican Constitution,[7] establishes the fundamental characteristics adopted by the political organization of the Mexican people.

---

[5]Amendments to Articles 24 and 40 of the Mexican Constitution were approved by the Senate on March 28, 2012. The amendment to the first paragraph of Article 24 received 72 votes in favor and 35 votes against; while the amendment to Article 40 was approved by 97 votes in favor, 3 against, and one abstention. The amendment to the first paragraph of Article 24 of the Mexican Constitution was published on July 19, 2013, in the DiarioOficial de la Federación. The amendment to Article 40 of the Mexican Constitution was published on November 30, 2012, in the DiarioOficial de la Federación.

[6]In the year 1992, were registered as religious associations only three communities of Catholic orientation (the Catholic, Apostolic, and Roman Church in Mexico, the Mexican Episcopal Conference, and the Primatial Archdiocese of Mexico); in 1993 and 1994 were registered diverse religious associations, mostly, different than Catholic.

[7]"Article 39. National sovereignty is vested essentially and originally in the people. All public power derives from the people and is instituted for their benefit. The people have at all time the inalienable right to alter or amend their form of government".

One reason, apparently, "*to raise the lay (laica) nature of the State to constitutional rank*"[8] was the reaction to assumed acts that "violated" this *lay* nature (for example: *to allow religious services at public hospitals*;[9] *to deny minority rights; to impose the beliefs of the majority;*[10] and *to dictate public policies based on religious criteria for 110 or 120 million Mexicans as if they were Catholics*).[11]

Generally, in the case of the amendment to Article 40 of the Constitution, it was argued that this reform was made to ratify, to reaffirm the lay (*laica*) nature of the Mexican State, even to defend, and strengthen it against the *backward and obscurantist temptation*,[12] and against attacks on laicity (*laicidad*), and that "*postponing the fullness of secularity of the State*" means the "*risk of a successful [attack] from the rhetoric of intransigence.*"[13]

In sum, this constitutional reform was rather "confirmatory," "declarative," and not "foundational" or "constitutive" in character. Therefore, even if there had not been any constitutional reform to Article 40, the laicity (*laicidad*) of the Mexican state would have remained intact.[14]

---

[8]And here I want to ask: was the Mexican state not lay (laico) already? And if this is so, then the article 3 of the Law of Religious Associations and Public Worship, which establishes "The Mexican state is lay (laico)," was unconstitutional.

[9]"Deplora el Senado que el carácter laico del Estado haya sido vulnerado," La Jornada, February 18, 2010, p. 10.

[10]"Intelectuales piden a senadores ratificar el carácter laico del Estado mexicano," Carlos Monsiváis censura cerrazón de la derecha, La Jornada, February 19, 2010, p. 10.

[11]"Censuran a Rivera por su postura sobre el Estado laico," *Rumbo de México*, February 19, 2010.

[12]See Footnote 11.

[13]Cf. "Navarrete confía en que el Senado apruebe reforma para Estadolaico," *La Crónica*, February 19, 2010, p. 9.

[14]The Mexican state is lay (laico), not confessional, and does not subscribe to any religion or religious denomination as its own. The conception of a lay (laico) State is dynamic, also linked to social processes.

Precisely, one of the dimensions of laicity (laicidad) is in the field of cultural identities and the defense of minorities, of course in attention to the following guiding principles: (1) religious freedom. (2) Separation of State and churches (or rather, religious communities). (3) No intervention by the authorities in the internal affairs of religious associations (linked to respect for the right of self-determination of religious communities). (4) Authorities may not attend in an official character any religious act of public worship. (5) Churches and other religious communities should not interfere in the functions of the state. (6) State laicity (laicidad). On November 6, 2012, the Senate declared approved the amendment of Article 40 of the Constitution, establishing formally the lay (laica) nature of the Mexican State, as follows: "Article 40. It is the will of the Mexican people to constitute a representative, democratic, lay (laica), and federal Republic composed by States, free and sovereign in all matters concerning their internal affairs; but united in a federation established according to principles of this fundamental law." (The underlined is mine). This can be assumed to be a platform to strengthen the management of religious diversity.

Here, I would refer comparatively, while maintaining a proper sense of proportion, the case of the German law of religion, where, although there is no principle of laicity (*laicidad*), there is the principle of neutrality. The *Fundamental Law* of the Federal Republic of Germany does not explicitly contain the word "neutral," this nature of the German State has been recognized and developed by the jurisprudence of the Federal Constitutional Court.[15]

In my opinion, the "laicity" is a scenario, which may be presupposed, where the effective exercise of fundamental freedoms—including the freedom of religion—takes place.[16] Therefore, "*laicity*" and "religious freedom" are not opposed and are not mutually excluded, since a lay (*laico*) state must ensure full enjoyment of religious freedom.

Certain documents such as the *Universal Declaration of Laicity (laicidad) of XXI* Century[17] and the *Lay (laica)* Charter[18] do not address in its true size, at least explicitly, religious freedom; rather, they include it only by reference, for example, this is related to "freedom to adhere to a religion", "free choice in matters of religion" and the "right to profess or not to profess religious beliefs." The "*Alphabet of the lay (laica) Republic*"[19] simply refers to "freedom of worship" or "to exercise any religious option or not practice any one." But it is evident that religious freedom in its complexity implies this and much more.

---

[15]From the freedom of belief, Article 4, paragraph 1 of the Fundamental Law, derives the principle of neutrality towards different religions and confessions. The ideological-religious neutrality is a binding mandate for the State. The State's obligation to neutrality implies that the State must conduct itself equally before various religious orientations; the State cannot generate religious indifferentism. The State is prohibited from favoring certain denominations, also from making distinctions between religious communities and valuing the belief or non-belief of its citizens, and noting their convictions as correct or false. Cf. BverfGE 24, 236 (246), BVerGE 32, 98 (106), BVerfGE 33, 23 (28), BVerfGE 93, 1 (16).

[16]"Pathology" of the laicity (laicidad) is to reduce religion to the private sphere.

[17]See Libertades laicas. Red Iberoamericana por las Libertades Laicas. Programa Interdisciplinario de Estudios sobre las Religiones. El Colegio Mexiquense, A.C.

[18]Cf. Extraordinary Chair "Benito Juárez" of UNAM, January 14, 2013.

[19]José Woldenberg, ex-counselor of the Federal Electoral Institute introduced this alphabet during the Forum „Laicidad y democracia: 150 aniversario de la libertad de pensamiento."

3.2 *Amendment to Article 24 of the Constitution (Freedom of Religion or Belief)*

Article 24 by decree published on January 28, 1992	First paragraph amended by decree published on July 19, 2013
Article 24. Everyone is free to embrace the religion of his choice and to practice all ceremonies, devotions, or observances of his respective faith, either in places of public worship or at home, provided they do not constitute an offense punishable by law The congress cannot dictate laws that establish or prohibit any religion Every religious act of public worship must be performed strictly inside places of public worship, which shall at all times be under governmental supervision	Article 24. Every person has the right to freedom of ethical convictions, conscience and religion, and having or taking, as the case may be, whichever they like. This freedom includes the right to participate, individually or collectively, both in public and in private at ceremonies, dedications or acts of worship, as long as they are not a crime or transgression penalized by the law. Nobody can use public expression acts of this freedom with political purposes, proselytism or political propaganda

3.2.1 An Approach to the Three Argued Reasons for Rejecting the Amendment to Article 24 of the Constitution

There were several groups,[20] which expressed different reasons for rejecting the amendment to Article 24 of the Constitution and these were linked to[21]:

(a) The **intent of reform**. It was argued that this was "*the dismantling of the lay (laico) State*".
(b) The **manipulation of reform**. It was argued that redefining "freedom of religion" was offering a *tendentious and biased concept of that freedom.*
(c) The **consequences of reform**. There was reference, in this respect, to the *effect on the freedoms of religious minorities.*

---

[20] A large majority was evangelical groups, as shown by the various demonstrations that occurred in more than 20 states of the Mexican Republic.

[21] Approximately, 50 organizations and associations publicly opposed the amendment to Article 24, among which are Pentecostal churches, the Light of the World, Apostolic Church of Mexico, Presbyterian churches, and Masonic Grand Lodge. Moreover, it was expressed that some small religious groups are in opposition to this reform, because they considered that the reform would benefit the Catholic associations. Historic churches—such as the latter—and Jewish, Orthodox, Anglican or traditional evangelical churches supported the amendment to Article 24.

It was noted that reference to the supposed "danger" of religious teaching in public schools was common in these three reasons.

The reference to religious freedom only as "*teaching religion in public schools*" represented, rather than a serious approach to the dimensions or areas of religious freedom, a manipulation of the discourse on religious freedom that prevented a serious analysis of its real scope.

3.2.2 Analysis of Article 24 of the Constitution

The Article 24 in force provides that:

> Every person has the right to freedom of ethical convictions, conscience and religion, and having or taking, as the case may be, whichever they like. This freedom includes the right to participate individually or collectively, in public or private, in the ceremonies, devotions and acts of worship, provided they do not constitute a crime or an offense punishable by law. No one may use the public acts of expression of this freedom for political purposes, proselytism or propaganda.[22]

Although the new version of this Article uses an inadequate legislative technique, the substance of the constitutional reform of Article 24 focuses on: (1) Replacement of "every man" by "every person" in accordance with the terminology adopted by all international instruments on human rights. (2) The formal introduction of the right to freedom of ethical convictions.

(a) freedom of ethical convictions. Its inclusion—it seems to me—was linked *mutatis mutandis* to a formulation used in Article 4 of the *Fundamental Law* of the Federal Republic of Germany, which refers to the profession of religious and ideological beliefs (or non-religious worldview) called *Weltanschauung*,[23] whose translation into Spanish is complex, but in the case of Article 24 was adopted simply as "ethical convictions," which creates some confusion especially when this is disassociated from the "freedom of religion."

---

[22]The text of Article 24 of the Constitutional Reform from January 28, 1992, establishes: "Every man is free to embrace the religion of his choice and to practice the ceremonies, devotions and acts of worship, provided they do not constitute a crime or an offense punishable by the Law" (first paragraph). "The Congress of the Union may not enact laws establishing or prohibiting any religion" (second paragraph). "Religious acts of public worship must regularly be performed inside the temples. Those extraordinarily performed outside of them shall be subject to the Law" (third paragraph).

[23]"Art und Weise, wie jemand die Welt und ihren Sinn sowie sein Dasein betrachtet und beurteilt" (Mode and form how someone observes and judges the world, its reason and its existence), (Wahrig 1997). Gerhard Anschütz considers Weltanschauung as the doctrine comprising the total and universal world that seeks to recognize and to value the position of man in the world.

(b) freedom of conscience.[24] Various international instruments establish, unanimously, freedom of conscience as a fundamental right, where "consciousness" is precisely its subject.

Note that within the elements of freedom of conscience are: (1) "Freedom of formation of consciousness" as the right guaranteed to every person to follow his own representations in the formation of concepts of religious-moral value or dis-value without any influence of State coercion or social pressure, and perform this purpose under the constitutional legal order (Listl and Dietrich 1994) (2) "Freedom of realization of consciousness" implies "to omit" the legal prescribed behavior and "not to observe" the legally established rules of "not to do." It is here that the "right of conscientious objection" is linked with the fundamental right to "freedom of conscience."

The *International Covenant on Civil and Political Rights* does not explicitly refer to a right of conscientious objection, however, in *General Comment No. 22* to Article 18 of the *Covenant,* it considers that such right can be derived precisely from Article 18, paragraph 1, and there shall be no differentiation among conscientious objectors on the basis of the nature of their particular beliefs.

At the bottom of the issue about conscientious objection,[25] there is a relationship of tension between constitutional freedom and equality.[26]

Of course, freedom of conscience does not exclude or exempt, without further ado, the objector, of having to fulfill civic obligations, because a person who is recognized as a conscientious objector must perform, in principle, an alternative service (*servicio sustitutorio*), in order to reconcile precisely the right to freedom of conscience with the observance of common duties for all within the rule of law.

The *Mexican Law of Religion* provides what one might describe as "*conscientious objection secundum legem,*" for example, that the legislation itself establishes a certain "right to object" to justify the breach of a legal mandate.[27]

[24]While it is true that the Constitution of the United Mexican States did not establish expressly the freedom of conscience, this was considered by the Constituent Assembly of 1856–1857 in the sense that freedom of conscience, based on the most intimate convictions of the person, could not be subject to regulation by the State legal order. Meanwhile, the Constituent of 1916–1917 considered freedom of conscience as presupposed and included in Article 24 of the Constitution, since, in the opinion of the liberals of the period, Article 24 expressed, on the one hand, a large freedom of conscience and, on the other hand, limitation only for religious acts which constitute a crime or an offense punishable by law.

[25]"Conscientious objection" comes to be defined as "the attitude of a person who refuses to comply with a rule of law under a binding mandate from his consciousness, which is in radical opposition to the implicit ethical content of the legal norm. See Lima Torrado, Jesús. Desobediencia civil y objeción de conciencia, Mexico, Comisión Nacional de los Derechos Humanos, 2000, p. 25.

[26]See Die Rechtsstellung des Wehrdienstverweigerers aus Gewissensgründen in den Mitgliedsstaaten des Europarats, Ein vergleichender Überblick, Max-Planck-Institut für ausländisches Recht und Völkerrecht, 1967, p. 231.

[27]For example, this is the case of Article 10 of the Military Service Law (Ley del ServicioMilitar) and Article 38, paragraph III of its Regulation (Reglamento) concerning the ministers of worship, who may be exempted from compulsory military service; also this is the hypothesis in the case of

In addition, it is essential to examine carefully the second paragraph of Article 1 of the *Law of Religious Associations and Public Worship*,[28] in order to align its content with the current Article 24 of the Constitution, which expressly guarantees freedom of conscience.

(c) freedom of religion. Notwithstanding the constitutional reform on human rights from June 10, 2011 (the rules on human rights shall be interpreted in accordance with the Constitution and international treaties on this matter, favoring to the people all the time the more extensive protection), and in addition to the requirements of the *New Law of Amparo*,[29] (the sphere of protection of rights is extended, the human rights established within international treaties are subject of direct protection) still, the reform of Article 24 reinforces full religious freedom, from the interpretation of this in international instruments and from the contributions of comparative law.

Religious freedom consists of an *internum forum* and an *externum forum*.

The *internum forum* relates to the freedom of belief. "Positive freedom of belief," i.e., to have or to adopt[30] a belief of one's choice "or preference" (*International Covenant on Civil and Political Rights*) as well as to maintain or to "change his belief"[31] (*American Convention on Human Rights*); this *internum forum* includes the "negative freedom of belief," which is summarized in not having any belief.

The *forum externum* relates to the "freedom to profess a belief." "Positive freedom of profession" involves the right to say what one believes, which includes the freedom to propagate one's belief, and also the freedom of dispreading other beliefs (what is known as a missionary activity) and to say that one does not believe at all.

"The negative freedom of profession" guarantees the right to keep what one believes secret, or the right to silence (*Schweigerecht* in German law of religion).

Moreover, the freedom of exercise of religion in any form involves exercising it alone, in a community, in private (for example, the called *devotio domestica simplex*—private devotion without the intervention of a minister of worship of one's religious confession—and *devotio domestica qualificata*—private devotion involving a minister of worship of one's religious confession), and in public (the called *exercitium religionis publicum*) (Listl and Dietrich 1994).

Article 59, Health Law for the Federal District, where it is provided that doctors, for reasons of a religious nature, may refuse to perform an abortion.

[28]This establishes: "Religious convictions do not exempt in any case from complying with laws of the country. No one may invoke religious motives to evade the responsibilities and obligations established in the laws."

[29]Published on April 2, 2013, in the Diario Oficial de la Federación.

[30]The "freedom to adopt a belief" consists usually in search of a community of believers, learn about it, and take its doctrine.

[31]The "freedom to change one´s religion" implies in the background "the right to abandon or to resign from being a member from a community of believers and to enter another." This formulation has been considered in many cases instead of "to change one´s religion" because it has been objected usually by Islamic countries, such as Saudi Arabia. See Nowak (1989).

Moreover, the manifestations of the exercise of religion include, for example (Listl and Dietrich 1994), *Religious service*: as the typical form of religious adoration or proclamation, for example, worship. *Religious uses*: among which are processions, wearing/carrying of religious clothing or (a certain style of) beard, circumcision, prayers, tolling of bells, flying of church banners; in short, rites and rituals of different religions. *Praxis (practice)*: conducting religious assemblies, foundation and support of charities and humanitarian institutions; manufacture or acquisition of ritual objects; collecting donations; training of religious leaders; observance of days of rest and specific holidays; missionary activity; sustaining religious hospitals; implementation of development projects; distribution of flyers; pacifists, motivated by a pacifist spirit. *Teaching*: transmission of content from one religion or worldview in religious schools, in public schools, in various forms of non-formal education and in missionary work.

Also freedom of religious association is part of the fundamental right of religious freedom in its positive and negative aspect.

In this regard, religious freedom in Mexico should not be a taboo subject. Hence, the importance of serious and open debate on issues such as: the right to self-determination of religious communities, as well as freedom of expression of their ministers of worship; mass media in the ownership or possession of religious associations; the right of parents to ensure the religious and moral education of their children in conformity with their own convictions, even in public schools; the protection of cultural property of a religious character; and, attention to the problems of displaced indigenous people because of "religious intolerance."

It clarifies that **this freedom includes the right to participate individually or collectively, in public or private, in ceremonies, devotions, or acts of respective worship, provided they do not constitute a crime or an offense punishable by law**.

In this respect, it is not that "*this freedom includes the right* ...", but rather "*this right includes freedom* ..." (in accordance with Article 18 of the *International Covenant on Civil and Political Rights*,[32] and Article 12 of the *American Convention on Human* Rights[33]). In addition to the observation about the inadequate legislative technique used, it is considered that such provision falls far short in scope, at least formally, when it refers only to ceremonies, devotions and acts of respective worship.

Finally, a prohibition is incorporated: **no one can use the public acts of expression of this freedom for political purposes, proselytism or propaganda**. The questions are: who is the addressee of this? Any person? What specifically does "**using public acts of expression of this freedom**" mean? What does "this freedom" mean?

---

[32]Article 18 of the Covenant: (1) "Everyone shall have the right to freedom of thought, conscience and religion. This right shall include freedom to have or to adopt a religion or belief of his choice, and freedom, either individually or in community with others and in public or private, to manifest his religion or belief in worship, observance, practice and teaching."

[33]Article 12 of the Convention: "Everyone has the right to freedom of conscience and of religion. This right includes freedom to maintain or to change one's religion or beliefs, and freedom to profess or disseminate one's religion or beliefs, either individually or together with others, in public or in private."

The "freedom of ethical convictions, conscience and religion" or the "freedom to participate individually or collectively, in public or private, in ceremonies, devotions, or acts of respective worship"? Is this prohibition is applicable during an electoral campaign and also in non-election times? What would be the sanction for contravening this provision?

By reading this provision, suddenly came to my mind the image of the presidential candidates who gathered at the Mass celebrated by Pope Benedict XVI in Silao Guanajuato in 2012,[34] where some of them even took communion publicly.

President Enrique Peña Nieto also received communion at the Mass celebrated by Pope Francisco on February 12, 2016, at the Basilica of Guadalupe during his visit to Mexico.[35]

If at the time a prohibitive provision like this had been in force, would this prohibition have been applicable to presidential candidates or why could it not be applicable to the president of Mexico?

Moreover, prohibitions against ministers of worship engaging in politics matters existed before, for example, to hold public offices and not be elected for public offices,[36] those who have ceased being ministers of worship with anticipation and in the manner established by law, may be elected (Article 130 of the Constitution d) and Article 14, first paragraph, LARCP); to associate for political purposes, to proselytize in favor of or against any political candidate, party or association (Article 130 of the Constitution, and Articles 12 and 29 LARCP); to celebrate political meetings in temples (Article 130 of the Constitution and Article 21 LARCP); in developing public acts of their own ministry, to induce the electorate to vote or not to vote for a particular candidate or political party (Article 404 CPF).

To these, it has been added: "***no one can use the public acts of expression of this freedom for political purposes, proselytism or propaganda***" as a "burden" additional to the bans for ministers of worship, especially if this prohibitive requirement seems an "openletter" to the exercise of discretional activity of governmental authorities in its application.

4 Public Policies for Managing Religious Diversity

The *laicity* (*laicidad*) of the State, as a scenario and presupposed, where the effective exercise of religious freedom and other fundamental freedoms occurs, also

---

[34] Papal Mass held on March 23, 2012, at Bicentennial Park in Silao, Guanajuato.

[35] See https://www.sdpnoticias.com/nacional/2016/02/13/comulgo-pena-nieto-en-misa-de-el-papa-en-la-basilica and http://www.animalpolitico.com/2016/02/los-politicos-de-mexico-en-primera-fila-para-ver-al-papa-francisco/.

[36] In the doctrine, it is discussed the legal nature of this constitutional impediment of the ministers of worship to exercise a passive vote, placing it within three possible explanations: (1) An incompatibility on the basis of the principle of State–churches separation. (2) A mutilation of human rights of ministers of worship, or (3) A discriminatory treatment.

involves the generation of appropriate public policies for the management of religious diversity.

At the **legislative level**, it is necessary to legislate without discrimination, as happened with the derogation of the word "sect" in federal regulations. This word was removed from the *Federal Code of Electoral Institutions and Procedures* (COFIPE)[37] but this has not been done in case of the *Federal Civil Code*, because Article 1330 still includes the word "sect".[38]

Moreover, the *National Council to Prevent Discrimination* (CONAPRED) published a *Handbook for lawmaking without discrimination*, which will undoubtedly contribute to that purpose.

At the **jurisdictional level**, the interpretation of "religious freedom and their different facets"[39] and "differences of religious freedom and freedom of worship"[40] is developed.

At the **federal executive level**, it is necessary to comply with the generation of an appropriate public policy of management of religious diversity.

Among the public policies for management of religious diversity are the following.

4.1 Political-Administrative Attention for the Transformation

Regardless of the circumstances that involved a significant shift of the administrative body of the federal executive in charge of religious affairs before 1992, it was called "*Underdirectorate of Religious Worship, Firearms and Explosives*"; and with the reform from January 28, 1992, the situation changed toward the formation of a

[37]The COFIPE was abrogated and the General Law of Electoral Institutions and Procedures (LGIPE) came into force, which does not contain the term sect. The LGIPE was published on May 23, 2014 in Diario Oficial de la Federación.

[38]It is recommended to carry out this derogation also in local regulations (electoral codes and civil codes), where the word "sect" is present.

[39]"Libertad religiosa. Sus diferentes facetas," in Semanario Judicial de la Federación, NinthEpoch, FirstChamber, Thesis 1a. LX/2007, Subject: Constitutional, isolated thesis, February 2007. "Freedom of worship" means "freedom to practice the ceremonies, rites and meetings associated with the cultivation of certain religious beliefs."

[40]"Libertad religiosa y libertad de culto. Sus diferencias," in Semanario Judicial de la Federación y su Gaceta, NinthEpoch, FirstChamber, Thesis 1a LXI/2007, Subject: Constitutional, isolatedthesis, February 2007. "Acts of public worship" as "the acts specifically oriented to develop collectively rites, ceremonies and practices of different religions recognized as institutionalized or formalized expressions of religious faith, defined and governed by pre-established rules by them."

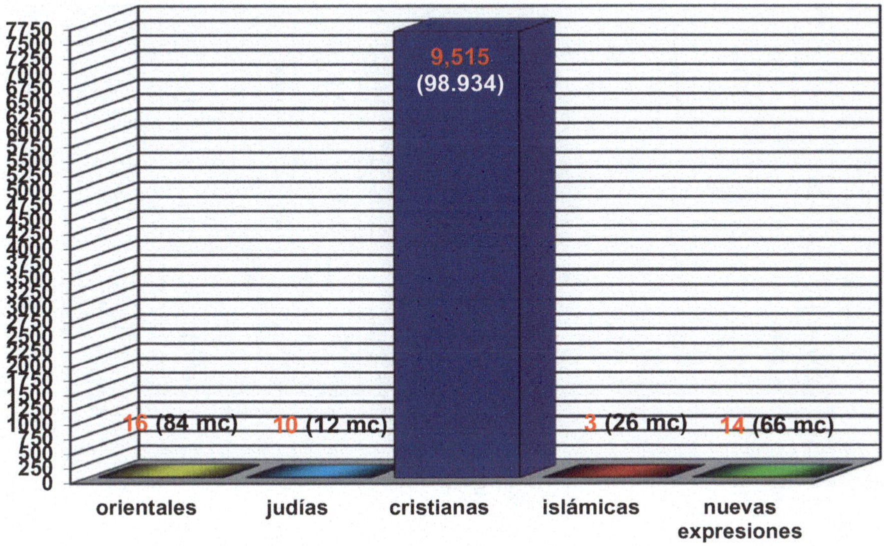

Fig. 1 Registered religious associations (9.558) and ministers of worship (ministros de culto = mc, 99.122) (April 31, 2020)

General Directorate of Religious Associations, within an "*Undersecretariat for Population, Migration and Religious Affairs*" and today an "*Undersecretariat of Democratic Development, social participation and religious affairs.*" Here, it is expedient to review the vision, mission and objectives of this Undersecretariat (Fig. 1).

While the services offered by the *General Directorate of Religious Associations* formally involve administrative attention to religious diversity, this is only part of public management policy (Table 1).[41]

Since the last administration took office on December 1, 2012 an the new administration on December 1, 2019, a rethinking of public policy for the management of religious diversity under the last *National Development Plan* 2013–2018 and today under the *National Development Plan 2019–2024* is expected, and depending mainly on the implementation of the constitutional reform of Article 24.

Finally, the Law of Religious Associations and Public Worship has had important reforms:

[41]The management of the Federal Executive relations with religious associations (churches and religious communities), with full respect for the lay (*laico*) spirit of public institutions, formally has had as guidelines: (a) Improving the relationship with religious communities, religious associations and religious traditions existing in the country; (b) Greater openness and fairness for different religions; (c) Assumption of a positioning of "non-control" by the authority on religious associations; (d) Respect of the internal life of religious associations and religious pluralism; (e) Strengthening of interfaith dialogue and coexistence; (f) Permanent dialogue with religious organizations and ministers of worship; (g) Transparency and access to information on religious matters; (h) Improving the administrative service to attend the religious associations; (i) Application of modern technology for recording and processing information in religious matters.

Table 1 Procedures and services offered by the DGAR in religious matters

Procedures and services offered by the DGAR in religious matters (September 2006–August 2012)

Procedure or service	2006–2007	2007–2008	2008–2009	2009–2010	2010–2011[a]	2011–2012[b]
Offered advisories to the general public on religious matters	3108	4063	3600	1730	3177	2345
Emitted opinions for the admission and legal stay in the country of ministers of worship from abroad	7100	6938	5266	6213	6118	6395
Proceeded declarations and registration of immovable property owned by religious associations[c]	1487	1234	1280	1602	2017	2164
Certificates of constitutive registration given to new religious associations	305	157	211	220	233	140
Accumulated constitutive registration of religious associations	6791	6964	7174	7394	7624	7719
Advices to celebrate acts of public worship outside the temples	5982	8963	6848	6163	70,705	53,376
Authorization for transmissions of acts with religious content in mass media (radio and television)	5181	5446	9300	14,884	15,096	113,960

Procedures and services offered by the DGAR in religious matters (September 2012–August 2019)[d]

Procedure or service	2012–2013	2013–2014	2014–2015	2015–2016	2016–2017	2018–2019
Offered advisories to the general public on religious matters	748/1118	1346/1555	1680/1811	2084/2291	2076	966
Emitted opinions for the admission and legal stay in the country of ministers of worship from abroad	3189/4492	4566/4514	3225/3447	3059/3331	2865	2366
Proceeded declarations and registration of immovable property owned by religious associations	1398/2026	1599/1555	1736/1884	1565/1746	1461	919
Certificates of constitutive registration given to new religious associations	80	184	260	409/429	94	74

(continued)

Table 1 (continued)

Procedures and services offered by the DGAR in religious matters (September 2012–August 2019)[d]

Procedure or service	2012–2013	2013–2014	2014–2015	2015–2016	2016–2017	2018–2019
Accumulated constitutive registration of religious associations	7870	8053	8313	8722/8736	8830	9359
Advices to celebrate acts of public worship outside the temples	7736/24,152	44,346/38,499	466/478	483/554	944	471
Authorization for transmissions of acts with religious content in mass media (radio and television)	69,332/313,039	270,674/380,263	232,923/233,088	362,152/362,387	409,302	283,510

Source Based on data from the Sixth Work Report of the Ministry of Interior 2017–2018

Source Based on data from the Sixth Work Report of the Ministry of Interior 2017–2018, and the First Work Report of Presidency of the Republic 2019

[a]The numbers for the period 2010–2011 were modified to actual ciphers, because for the previous report, were used approximate ciphers for the months of July and August 2011

[b]Data included until June 2012 and estimated data for the months July and August

[c]From November 2009, the procedure "Declarations of proceeded for incorporating of immovable property into patrimony of religious associations" registered in the Federal Commission of Regulatory Improvement, was merged with that of the "registration of immovable property titles owned by the religious associations" adopting the name of "proceeded declarations and registration of immovable properties owned by religious associations," being also a change in the frequency of the ciphers

[d]When two numbers appear together in this table, the first refers to what the Presidency of the Republic reports, and the second corresponds to what the Ministry of the Interior reports

(a) April 24, 2006, to incorporate dialogue and tolerance as an obligation of religious associations (Article 8, fraction III).
(b) August 19, 2010, to include full respect for human rights (Article 3, first paragraph, article 8th, fraction IV) and the protection of children and adolescents (article 12 Bis, Article 29 fractions XII and XIII, Article 31 fraction V).
(c) May 25, 2011, on the immigration status of religious ministers (Article 13).
(d) December 17, 2015, to incorporate the Ministry of Culture instead of the National Council for Culture and the Arts (CONACULTA) (Article 20 first paragraph), before which it will register those responsible for the temples, property of the nation.

4.2 *Extraordinarily Acts of Public Worship Are not "Public Spectacles"*

It must be insisted that in the case of holding acts of extraordinarily public worship of religious associations, provisions that strictly correspond to "public performances"[42] should not be applied since it is not possible to fulfill the same requirements for implementation and because "extraordinarily acts of public worship" are not "public spectacles."

4.3 *Spiritual Assistance*

It is required further to facilitate spiritual support in health, social care, and rehabilitation institutions, making this effectively one of the dimensions of the right to religious freedom of internal people and users.[43]

After the earthquake of September 19, 2017, dioceses, bishops, priests, and lay people attended the emergency in different ways, not only arranging parishes and seminars, as refuge and collection centers, making special collections in the parishes, and channeling everything through Cáritas Nacional (Mexicana) but also offering spiritual accompaniment and psychological attention to the people in need.

For its part, the Central Commission of the Jewish Community of Mexico also helped those affected by the earthquake by establishing collection centers. Churches and religious communities are organized to help the society in the health contingency due to Covid-19. For example, the Mexican Episcopate Conference promotes the "Families without Hunger" campain.

---

[42]Cf. Law for holding public events in the Federal District (Ley para la celebración de espectáculospúblicosen el Distrito Federal), Article 4, V. Public spectacle; Article 25, VII, Requirements of permissions to hold public spectacles.

[43]Based on Article 6 of the Regulation of the Law on Religious Associations and Public Worship, published on November 6, 2003, in the DiarioOficial de la Federación.

4.4 Prohibition of Discrimination on Religious Grounds

The constitutional and legal normativity on religious matters assumes the principle of non-discrimination in favor of religious diversity.

Article 1 of the Constitution explicitly prohibits discrimination based on religion and establishes that the authorities have the obligation to promote, protect, and ensure the human rights of all people.

Article 2 of the *Law of Religious Associations and Public Worship* recognizes the right of individuals to be free from discrimination, coercion or hostility because of their religious beliefs and the prohibition to restrict the exercise of any work or activity for religious reasons.

Article 4 of the *Federal Law to Prevent and Eliminate Discrimination* prohibits all discriminatory practice. This law establishes the following in Article 9 as discriminatory behaviors: to hinder freedom of religion, religious practices or customs, provided they do not violate public order (paragraph XVI), and to deny religious assistance to persons deprived of liberty, serving in the armed forces or interns in assistance or healthcare institutions (paragraph XVII).

4.5 Conscientious Objection

Education authorities have refrained from punishing students—Jehovah's Witnesses—because of their religious beliefs, who refuse to salute the flag and sing the national anthem at civic ceremonies that take place in schools, according to the *General Recommendation Nr. 5*, issued by the *National Commission of Human Rights* (May 14, 2003).

However, in the case of basic education teachers, for example, Jehovah's Witnesses are required, in respect of their right to conscientious objection to honoring national symbols, to complying instead of this with an alternative service, so that they should not be separated from their charges—as this happens at the present—because they "*do not inculcate love for the country in their students.*"

4.6 Coordination Agreements in Religious Matters[44]

It is necessary to review the status of coordination agreements on religious matters signed by the *Ministry of Interior principally* with the governments of the states

[44] Agreements—that were ready to be signed—are those corresponding to the states of Coahuila, Jalisco, Puebla and Veracruz. Agreements in process of elaboration, in case of the states: Campeche, Guerrero, Queretaro, San Luis Potosi, Sonora, Tamaulipas, Tlaxcala.

of Zacatecas,[45] Chiapas,[46] Chihuahua,[47] Michoacan,[48] Nuevo Leon[49] and Quintana Roo,[50] to update them, and to promote the signing of agreements with the remaining states.

4.7 Translation of the Law of Religious Associations and Public Worship *and Its* Regulation *into Indigenous Languages*

The Ministry of Interior has promoted the translation of the *Law on Religious Associations and Public Worship* into various indigenous languages in at least six states. These languages are: *Tsotsil, Tseltal, Tojolab'al, Zoque, Cho'l* (in Chiapas); *Mazahua* (in State of Mexico); *Náwatl* (in Puebla); *Náhuatl, Tenek* (in San Luis Potosí); *Náhuatl, Totonaca* (in Veracruz), *Purhépecha* (in Michoacán)[51]; however, translation of the law by itself is not enough, there should also exist informed knowledge about its content, so this topic must be observed too (Table 2).

Table 2 Translation

Federative entity	Indigenous language
Chiapas	Tsotsil
	Tseltal
	Tojolab'al
	Zoque
	Cho'l
Estado de México	Mazahua
Puebla	Náwatl
San Luis Potosí	Náhuatl
	Tenek
Veracruz	Náhuatl
	Totonaca
Michoacán	Purhépecha

[45] Published on January 28, 2005, in the DiarioOficial de la Federación.

[46] See Footnote 45.

[47] Published on March 9, 2005, in the DiarioOficial de la Federación.

[48] Published on April 25, 2005, in the DiarioOficial de la Federación.

[49] Published on April 28, 2005, in the DiarioOficial de la Federación.

[50] Published on May 3, 2005, in the DiarioOficial de la Federación.

[51] The translation of the law into indigenous languages took place in states that have concluded a coordination agreement with the Ministry of Interior in religious matters: Chiapas, Michoacán, Nuevo León, Puebla, Querétaro, San Luis Potosí, State of Mexico, and Veracruz.

4.8 *Interreligious Dialogue*

The State must encourage the development of the work of interreligious dialogue at different levels, for example, (1) At national level: the *Interfaith Council of Mexico* (founded in 1992 and as a civil association in 1995). (2) At state level: the Interreligious Councils of Chiapas (founded in 1992), Guerrero (founded in 2005), Nuevo León (founded in 2012), Michoacán (founded in 2016), Querétaro (founded in 2017), Veracruz (founded in 2017); and (3) At municipal level: the Municipal Evangelical Interfaith Council in Larrainzar (founded in 2007).

Also with respect to those who, exercising their right of self-determination, have decided not to belong to any interfaith council, as has been the case of the *Christian Congregation of Jehovah's Witnesses*.

On April 14, 2016, was inaugurated the first Encounter between Deputies and Interfaith Councils.[52] Where the deputies pronounced themselves to elaborate a political agenda and initiatives to advance in a regulation of the Article 24 of the Constitution, whereas representatives of interreligious councils manifested the necessity to legislate in the matter of freedom of conscience and to improve the Law of Religious Associations and Public Worship, as well as its Regulations, in order to defend and promote religious freedom. Finally, it was assumed that Mexico has much to learn about religious freedom, since the 1992 reforms, although they recognized that right, said reforms "are still far from what Mexico has signed on human rights issues."[53]

4.9 *Migration*

It should support religious associations that make use of their right to bring into the country ministers of worship and associated religious persons to participate in pastoral interchanges, as well as for international events held in Mexico, so it is necessary to reduce administrative obstacles on matters of inviting foreign ministers of worship into the country.

A positive aspect of the Mexican lay (*laico*) State has been to allow special diets in migration centers for people who, for religious reasons, make such request (*Immigration Law*,[54] Article 107, II, second paragraph). This shows more openness to guaranteeing religious freedom.

---

[52]Proposals: (A) Develop a political agenda with these issues and advance in the constitution of a better society. (B) In no public school should be imposed or tought any religious line of thought. (C) Legislate on conscientious objection; improve both the Law of Religious Associations and Public Worship, and its regulations to defend and promote religious freedom. (D) That religious associations may own and operate radio and television stations. (E) That a fiscal legislation be elaborated according to the aims and objectives of the religious associations and churches, because they are not economic companies with the objective of trading.

[53]Promote secondary legislation on religious freedom and worship, which strengthens social values. See Bulletin No. 1341.

[54]Published on May 25, 2011, in DiarioOficial de la Federación.

It requires greater collaboration between government and religious associations for the defense and the protection of the rights of migrants, especially of unaccompanied migrant children.

Finally, members of the Tohono otham indigenous people, as it is written on the other side of the Rio Grande; "tojonoo'otam," as pronounced on the Mexican side, are part of the 82,000 indigenous people, of whom some 42,000 reside in Mexico and around 40,000 in the United States, in the desert territory of Sonora and Arizona, divided by 120 km of border that was imposed without having been consulted. To that is added the construction of the "wall," proposed by Donald Trump, which represents a double offense for this indigenous population.[55]

4.10 *Official Recognition of Studies in Religious Institutions*

Since 1995, there has been a policy of openness by the *Ministry of Education* to recognize studies in religious matters, such as theology or religious sciences. Provided, they comply with the established legal requirements.

For example, official validity was recognized by the *Ministry of Education* for the curriculum in Judaic at the upper level (October 2012), which is unprecedented in the history of the Jewish Community of Mexico.

4.11 *Tax Matters*

The tax treatment of religious associations is regulated through a "general resolution" for all of them. However, the religious associations are not yet considered "nonprofitlegal entities" (*personas morales sin fines de lucro*)[56]; they are not authorized to receive donations deductible from income tax[57]; so this situation should be changed.

[55]See http://www.proceso.com.mx/488808/pueblo-indigena-separado-la-frontera-va-contra-muro-trump.

[56]Although the Law of Income Tax (Ley del Impuestosobre la Renta) does not expressly refer to religious associations, it establishes that: "For the purposes of this Law, are considered non-profit legal persons (…) the following: XVI. Civil associations or societies with political, sporting or religious purposes."

[57]Cf. Tax Administration System (SAT). Rules for Religious Associations for the Fiscal Year 2019, of March 25, 2019.

4.12 Donations in Kind from Abroad

Various religious denominations in Mexico, especially evangelical churches,[58] have close relationship with churches from the USA who are willing to support them with donations in kind, especially: food, used clothing in good condition, medicines, toys, medical equipment, among others.

The current problems, in this case, are customs procedures that carry a high cost, which often turns out to be more expensive than the amount donated, and churches or religious communities do not have sufficient financial resources to cover such costs.

It seeks to guide religious associations to find the most appropriate way to receive donations from abroad. At present, they do this through civil associations for welfare; however, it insists that religious associations as "non-profit legal entities" also should come to be considered authorized donees.

4.13 Labor Matters

In this item, it is necessary to determine that ministers of worship are not employees or workers of religious associations, because there is a general assumption that considers religious associations as their employers, who therefore have to pay patronal contributions to the *Mexican Social Security Institute* (IMSS). That is a mistake.

4.14 Security

State authorities have recognized that religious associations, churches, and religious communities have much to contribute to Mexican society, to rebuild the social net (*tejido social*), especially in prevention matters, so their specific involvement in the *National Security Plan* of the federal government must be known.[59] For now, they work on voluntary disarmament programs[60] that are usually carried out in the atrium of Catholic churches.

It is important to highlight that "voluntary disarmament" has already been institutionalized by reforming the *Law on Social Prevention of Crime and Violence for the Federal District*, which was added with an Article 25 Bis, published on July 5,

---

[58] For example, in the State of Tamaulipas.

[59] Cf. Speech of Enrique Peña Nieto, Second Special Session of the National Public Security Council, December 17, 2012.

[60] For example, since 2007 voluntary disarmament programs are developed in the Federal District under different names: "Entrega voluntaria de armas de fuego" (voluntary handing over of firearms) and "Portufamilia, desarmevoluntario" (For your family, voluntary disarmament).

2017, in the Official Gazette[61]; as well as the *Organic Law of the Public Security Secretariat of the Federal District*, whose article 3 was added with a fraction XXX Bis, published on July 5, 2017, in the Official Gazette.[62]

Finally, on August 25, 2015, for example, the government of the state of Veracruz and religious organizations signed an agreement to prevent crime.

4.15 Reservations to International Treaties

It is necessary to review and to update the interpretative declarations and reservations made at the time by the Mexican State in concluding international treaties relating to religious freedom and ministers of worship.

4.16 Religious Tourism

At the federal level, the *Ministry of Tourism* (SECTUR) has conducted coordinated actions with state governments and non-governmental agencies to strengthen religious tourism in Mexico. This *Ministry* reported that Mexico is one of the most visited nations of the world thanks to the architectural, artistic, and cultural wealth of its sanctuaries, comparable in the arrival of tourists to other world religious centers.[63]

At the local level, on June 14, 2014, the "religious tourism program" was presented by the Federal District Government. The program involves three routes for visitors: (1) The Guadeloupian way (*El caminoguadalupano*), (2) Bastions of Catholicism (*Baluartes del catolicismo*), and (3) Ways of faith (*Caminos de la fe*). This program considers not only Catholic, but also Buddhist, Jewish, Methodist, Mormon and Orthodox temples.

---

[61] Ley de Prevención Social del Delito y la Violencia para el Distrito Federal. Artículo 26 Bis. El Gobierno de Ciudad de México, atenderá el desarme voluntario, a través de las acciones y/o Programas conforme a los lineamientos que la Secretaría de Desarrollo Social emita para su implementación.

[62] Ley Orgánica de la Secretaría de Seguridad Pública del Distrito Federal. Artículo 3°—Corresponden a la Secretaría las siguientes atribuciones: XXX BIS. Coadyuvar con la Secretaría de Desarrollo Social de la Ciudad de México en el desarrollo de la Acción Interinstitucional denominada "Por Tu Familia, Desarme Voluntario" y su modalidad "por Tu Familia, Desarme Voluntario te Acompaña Desde Tu Casa", para generar un ambiente de paz, con la finalidad de establecer acciones de prevención delictiva a través de promover la cultura de la paz y no violencia.

[63] https://www.gob.mx/sectur/prensa/mexico-entre-los-paises-mas-visitados-por-turismo-religioso-sectur.

4.17 Environmental Education for Sustainability

The *Ministry of Environment and Natural Resources* (SEMARNAT), in coordination with the *Ministry of Public Education* (SEP), has developed since 2008 a program to encourage the called "green schools," which perform actions and environmental management strategies to combat climate change.

In 2012, for example, the Tarbut Hebrew College was recognized as "*Green school. Environmental leader*" and the Israeli College of Mexico as "*Green school,*" implying that in the field of environmental sustainability, institutions representing a diversity of religions are taken into consideration for such programs.

4.18 Resolution of Religious Conflicts

The *General Directorate of Religious Associations* must address in a more timely and prudent manner the conflicts on religious intolerance matters that are characterized by the combination of several factors, including political, partisan, economic and agrarian, also caciquism (*cacicazgo*). These have even instrumentalized religion to cover up political actions or justify violence, making it difficult to identify intolerance as purely religious and to achieve an immediate peaceful solution to the conflicts.

5 Cases

According to a typology of violations of religious and ideological freedom by State and non-State agents (2016)[64] we want to highlight here only two recent aspects for the case of Mexico, related to: constitutive register of religious associations and conscientious objection.

[64]Cfr. Report of the German federal government on the world situation of religious freedom (June 9, 2016): (a) Criminal sanctions. (b) Administrative obstacles. (c) Legal sanctions in family and inheritance matters. (d) Limitations to the public exercise of religion. (e) Prejudices and social stigmatization. (f) Obstacles in recognition and registration of religious associations. (g) Religious praxis and way of life. (h) Religious education. (i) Care of real estate intended for religious purposes. (j) Religious freedom of the indigenous peoples. (k) Conscientious objection to military service. (l) Religious freedom and freedom of opinion. (m) Discrimination based on religion and ideology. (n) Access to public service and public positions. (o) Access to education. (p) Access to the private economy. (q) Limitations to religious freedom based on family law and inheritance.

5.1 Constitutive Register and Native American Church of Mexico

The General Directorate of Religious Associations, of the Ministry of the Interior, denied registration to the Native American Church of Mexico as a religious association, for failing to comply with requirements and deadlines. This decision was based in Article 9 of the Regulations of the Law of Religious Associations and Public Worship.

Faced with the refusal to register, the Supreme Court of Justice of the Nation in the *amparo* under revision 267/2016, determined that the formal requirements required by the law for the constitutive registration as a religious association cannot be understood as insurmountable barriers, through which the validity is questioned or the ideological content of a certain religious belief. That study would imply invading an area alien to its powers as authority. In other words, the authority is not entitled to question the content or practices that give life to a certain religious ideology, but must limit itself to verify the formal requirements imposed by the law for registration.

5.2 Conscientious Objection to Blood Transfusions

In the weighing of the right to religious freedom with the human right to life, a federal judge[65] (Eighth District Court in the State of Chihuahua) ordered that a minor suffering from leukemia received a blood transfusion once the alternative medical treatments had been exhausted, by virtue of which the minor professed the religion Jehovah's Witnesses.

With the sentence, the fundamental right of religious freedom was revised, as well as the rights to a second opinion, informed consent and decision making, regarding medical treatments. However, due to the lack of maturity of the girl to understand the scope of the medical act on her health, the right to life was privileged; so the doctors were authorized to perform the necessary treatments to protect the life of the minor, including blood transfusion.

It was also determined that the corresponding reforms were made for the creation of a protocol and procedure so that the doctors, in case of the refusal of the consent of the parents to administer treatments to minors, appear before a judge to argue the case, and it is that judge who analyzes the circumstances, listens to the parties and resolves the corresponding.

[65] Judge Mauricio Fernandez de la Mora, head of the Eighth District Court in the State of Chihuahua, granted the "amparo" to a woman of the Rarámuri ethnic group, who professes the religion Jehovah's Witnesses, for blood to be transferred to her five-year-old daughter, affected by leukemia, provided other means or alternative treatments have been exhausted, such as those proposed by various doctors, including oncologists at the Cancer Center of Chihuahua. See Nota Informativa: DGCS/NI: 45/2017, Poder Judicial de la Federación. Ciudad de México, a 13 de julio de 2017.

6 Conclusion

With the amendments to Articles 24 and 40 of the Mexican Constitution, it is clear that a truly secular State (lay/*laico* State) has to facilitate the effective exercise of religious freedom. The State has to generate a public policy that engages a significant change in the way in which it manages the religious diversity, which makes it comprehensible to decision makers that this field is not in the sphere of persuasion or negotiation but in the necessary observance of rules that ensure religious freedom effectively.

This management is expressed in developing actions and strategies for the implementation of in force legal instruments, consistent with Mexico's international obligations in this regard; plus informed dialogue between State authorities and religious actors in the meaning of full religious freedom and the responsibility that implies its exercise in the context of a secular State (lay/*laico*), respectful of religious diversity.

References

Lima Torrado J (2000) Desobediencia civil y objeción de conciencia, 1st edn. National Commission for Human Rights, Mexico

Listl J, Dietrich P (1994) Handbuch des Staatskirchenrecht des Bundesrepublik Deutschland, 2nd edn. Duncker & Humblot, Berlin

Medina González MC (2005) Das Religionsrecht in Mexiko. Volumes I and II. LIT, Münster

Nowak M (1989) UNO-Pakt über bürgerliche und politische Rechte und Fakultativprotokoll. CCPR-Kommentar, Engel, Norbert P, Strassburg

Wahrig G (1997) Deutsches Wörterbuch. Bertelsmann Lexikon, Gütersloh

Colombia as a Secular State

Vicente Prieto

Abstract In contrast to the previous constitution (1886), the Colombian State fully adopted the principle of secularity with the Constitution of 1991. This is demonstrated by the debates of the National Assembly in 1991, the text of the Constitution itself, and subsequent legislation and case law. However, it was not until the Religious Freedom Act (Act 133 of 1994) that the secularity of the Colombian State was explicitly affirmed for the first time. The Constitutional Court has played the leading role in the concrete development of the principle of secularity through its case law. Throughout the years, since it was created in 1991, there have been many occasions in which it has ruled on issues related to religious freedom and to the "secular state." Although it is possible to identify concepts that can be considered consolidated, there have been different approaches and differences of judgment depending on the specific case and the personal convictions of the judges. The issue of the importance of the religious factor in public life has been raised in close relation to this. Most of the relevant decisions of the Constitutional Court have had the Catholic Church as their reference point, due to the historical and social reality of the country. The process in recent years has insisted on the equality of all religious denominations before the Law and on the elimination of any form of privilege or discrimination. Nonetheless, there are difficulties in explaining the relationship between equality and secularity on the one hand and between secularity and pluralism on the other. This article examines these issues in light of the right to religious freedom as the fundamental principle of both secularity and equality.

Keywords Secularity of the state · Freedom of religion or belief · Equality · Religion in Colombia

V. Prieto (✉)
Universidad de La Sabana, Chía, Colombia
e-mail: vicente.prieto@unisabana.edu.co

© Springer Nature Switzerland AG 2020

R. V. S. Alves (ed.), *Latin American Perspectives on Law and Religion*, Law and Religion in a Global Context 3,
https://doi.org/10.1007/978-3-030-46717-3_8

1 Background: Secularity in the Constitutional and Legal Texts

Colombia has been and continues to be mainly a Catholic country[1] where the social and cultural influence of Catholicism are manifested in diverse aspects of its artistic and cultural heritage, such as holidays that originated in Catholic religious festivities, names of cities and towns, traditional foods, and symbols displayed in public and private activities and ceremonies, both civil and military, that represent society in some way. The social reality of Catholicism and its influence in the life and culture of the country was clearly reflected in the Constitution of 1886 as well as in numerous laws and decrees, even if they were not the expression of a strictly denominational regime.

Certain reference points in the evolution that occurred in recent decades should be kept in mind in order to understand the rules that are now in force. The first of these is 1957, when the Liberal and the Conservative parties agreed to permit the military government then in power to call a plebiscite[2] that approved the following Preamble to the Constitution, the original text of which dated back to 1886: "In the name of God, the supreme source of all authority, and in order to strengthen national unity, one of the bases of which is the political parties' recognition that the Catholic, Apostolic and Roman Religion is that of the Nation, and that the public powers will protect it as such and see that it is respected as an essential element of social order, and in order to secure the goods of justice, liberty and peace, the Colombian people, in this national plebiscite, Decree: The Political Constitution of Colombia is that of 1886, with the permanent reforms introduced up to and including Legislative Act No. 1 of 1947, and with the following modifications (…)."

In addition to the Preamble, there was Article 53[3]: "The State guarantees freedom of conscience. No one will be harassed because of their religious opinions, nor compelled to profess beliefs or observe practices contrary to their conscience. The freedom of all religions that are not contrary to Christian morals or to the laws is guaranteed. Acts contrary to Christian morality or subversive of public order, undertaken on the occasion or pretext of the practice of a religion, are subject to common law. The Government may conclude agreements with the Holy See subject to subsequent approval by the Congress to regulate, on the basis of reciprocal deference and mutual respect, the relations between the State and the Catholic Church."

The Concordat between the Colombian State and the Holy See was signed in 1973. Article 1 of the accord states that: "The State, attending to the traditional Catholic sentiment of the Colombian Nation, considers the Catholic, Apostolic and Roman religion a fundamental element of the common good and integral development of the

---

[1]According to a recent study published by *Semana* magazine, 85% of all Colombians consider religion to be important in their lives. The distribution of the population by religion is as follows: Catholics, 72%; Evangelical Christians, 15%; other religions, 4% (http://www.semana.com/nacion/articulo/colombianos-consideran-a-la-religion-muy-importante-en-sus-vidas/530679).

[2]See Legislative Decree No. 0247 of 1957.

[3]Introduced into the Constitution through the Constitutional Reform of 1936.

national community. The State guarantees the Catholic Church and its members full enjoyment of their religious rights, without prejudice to the just religious freedom of other churches and their members, the same as for all citizens."[4]

Ever since the process of elaborating a new constitution was initiated in 1991, there was a clear will to substantially modify the model of Church-State relations, which meant eliminating any trace of privilege, special recognition or particular protection for any church or religious faith, and especially for the Catholic Church, which had been the only beneficiary of such recognition until then. The Preamble to the Constitution of 1991 therefore suppressed all references to the Catholic Church: "The people of Colombia, in exercise of their sovereign power, represented by their delegates to the National Constitutional Assembly, invoking the protection of God, and in order to strengthen the unity of the Nation and ensure to their members life, coexistence, labor, justice, equality, knowledge, liberty and peace, within a legal, democratic and participatory framework that guarantees a just social, economic and political order, and committed to promoting the integration of the Latin American community, decree, sanction and promulgate the following Political Constitution of Colombia…".

As deduced from the minutes of the deliberations of the National Constitutional Assembly, the invocation of God's protection was presented as a compromise solution. Instead of opting for either of the two "extreme" solutions (i.e., maintaining the 1957 text, or eliminating all reference to God, the Catholic Church, or Christianity in general), an "intermediate" or "aseptic" position was chosen, which was limited to a generic invocation of divine protection.[5] In any case, it seems clear that the delegates, including the non-believers, wanted to reflect the religiosity of the Colombian people by the invocation of God in the preamble, recognizing "the convictions of those who elected us."[6] Consequently, the Colombian Constitutional Court affirms that the totality of religious beliefs constitutes a "protected constitutional value" (Decision C-350 of 1994, n. VI, 6).

---

[4]Being the recognition of a fact, but with no mention of special State protection for Catholicism (unlike the Preamble to the 1886 Constitution then in force), the Constitutional Court, upon examining the constitutionality of the Concordat, in Decision C 027 of February 1993 determined that the Article did not compromise the principles of secularity and equality assumed in the Constitution of 1991. It is therefore a fully applicable law. Regarding the scope of Decision C 027/93 and the present state of the Concordat rules, see Prieto (2010). The text of the Constitutional Court decisions quoted in this paper is available at the Court's official website: http://www.corteconstitucional.gov.co/relatoria/. The internal enumeration of the decisions does not follow a uniform criterion.

[5]For information on the drafting of the new preamble, with useful references to the sources, see Prieto (2011).

[6]These are the words of María Mercedes Carranza, a member of the Constitutional Assembly who wished to include the invocation of God in the preamble proposal she presented with other delegates, and the text, which came to a vote on April 8, 1991, is substantially the same as the one that was finally adopted. She explained that the invocation was included, despite her personal disagreement, out of respect for "the convictions of those who elected us." During the debate, this condescendence was interpreted as the way non-believers sought to achieve consensus. In return, believers had to "yield" their own convictions, by renouncing the text of the previous preamble. See Prieto (2011).

The principle of equality was made clear from the beginning.[7] The same did not occur with secularity, however, which is not mentioned explicitly in the texts that were definitively promulgated, despite agreement among the delegates and the concrete proposals that they made.[8] The topic was omitted in the text presented by the respective Commission for the first Plenary Session debate,[9] although the following clause had been included in one of the draft bills: "There will be no official State religion. Without prejudice to the exclusive competencies of the State established in this Constitution, the Government may maintain relations of cooperation and conclude Accords or Agreements with both the Catholic Church and with other religions, on the basis of reciprocal deference and mutual respect" (*Gaceta Constitucional* n. 130, 18-X-91, p. 5).

The clause was not adopted. The reasons for its rejection are expressed in the words of one of the delegates: With respect to the Concordat, "it is not indispensable to include it in the Constitution (...); if the clause does not appear there, that does not preclude concluding Treaties with the Vatican. To establish it in the Constitution is an inappropriate way since any topic relating to any State would henceforth have to be dealt with the same way. The determination that no religion has official status arises from the present preamble, which contains explicit recognition of the Catholic religion. If this is going to be eliminated and there are no clauses in the Constitution granting privileges to the Catholic religion, that reference could be suppressed" (*Ibid.*, p. 3).[10]

The right to freedom of religion was established in Article 19 of the final text of the new Constitution: "The freedom of religion is guaranteed. Everyone has the

[7]See Articles 13 and 19 of the Constitution of 1991.

[8]Nonetheless, there has always been awareness that the Colombian State assumed the principle of secularity in 1991. To summarize, a recent Constitutional Court decision states: "The jurisprudence has emphasized that even though State secularity was not expressly incorporated into the Constitution through an explicit rule, it is a principle that is part of the constitutional order based on the systematic and genealogical interpretation of the changes produced by the Constitution of 1991 in relation to the Constitution of 1886, since the new constitution promotes the separation of church and State, the State neutrality regarding different religions, and the prohibition of favoritism towards any of them" (Decision C 570 of 2016, n. 4.4).

[9]It read as follows: "Freedom of religion and of worship. Every person has the right to freely profess his or her religion and to disseminate it individually and collectively. Freedom of worship is guaranteed. All religious faiths and churches are equally free before the law. The exercise of the priestly and pastoral ministry of any religion or form of worship is incompatible with holding public office, except in institutions providing education, or charity or spiritual assistance" (*Gaceta Constitucional* n. 82, 25-IV-91, p. 15). As is well known, the *Gaceta* was the official organ of the National Constitutional Assembly. We use the facsimile edition published in CD-ROM form by the *Imprenta Nacional de Colombia*.

[10]The Report-Paper for the first Plenary Session debate stated that "Having disappeared from the Preamble to the Constitution (...) the official status of the Catholic religion, there is full equality among religions and churches, which translates into freedom of religion" (*Gaceta Constitucional* n. 82, 25-IV-91, p. 12).

right to freely profess his religion and to spread it individually and collectively. All religious faiths and churches are equally free before the law."[11]

In summary, the discussions about what the definitive texts would be were inseparable in many ways from the debates about the Preamble. If there was agreement on anything from the beginning, it was that the reference in the 1957 text to special protection owed by the State to the Catholic Church would disappear. This decision undoubtedly reflected the purpose of assuming the principle of secularity. However, there may have been an impression that it was a "one-way" secularity (i.e., the Catholic Church). The concern for an explicit statement of State secularity in relation to all churches and religions was materialized in the Religious Freedom Act-RFA- (Act 133 of 1994): "No church or religious denomination is or will be official or established. However, the State is not atheistic, agnostic or indifferent to the religious sentiments of Colombians" (Article 2, 1).

It adds: "The Government will protect individuals, as well as churches and religious groups, in their beliefs and will facilitate their participation in achieving the common good. Likewise, it will maintain harmonious relations of common understanding with the churches and religious entities existing in Colombian society" (RFA, Article 2, 2).

These relations can materialize through the signing of cooperation agreements: "The State may conclude agreements on religious questions with churches and religious denominations, their federations, confederations and associations of ministers that have legal personality and guaranteed duration due to their statutes and membership, whether they be International Treaties or Internal Public Law Agreements, especially to regulate the provisions of Points d) and g) of Article 6, the second subsection of Article 8 of this Statute, and Article 1 of Act 25 of 1992. The *Convenios de Derecho Público Interno* (Internal Public Law Agreements) will be subject to prior verification of legality by the *Sala de Consulta y Servicio Civil del Consejo de Estado* (Civil Service Advisory Office of the Council of State) and will enter into effect once they are signed by the President of the Republic" (Article 15 of the RFA).[12]

Chapter IV of the RFA deals specifically with "the autonomy of churches and religious denominations." Article 13 states that "Churches and religious denominations have, in their religious affairs, full autonomy and freedom and they may establish their own rules of organization, internal rules and provisions for their members. In said rules, as well as in those governing the institutions they create for their own ends, they can include clauses to safeguard their religious identity and their own nature, as well as due respect for their beliefs, without prejudice to the rights and freedoms recognized in the Constitution, especially those of freedom, equality and nondiscrimination. Paragraph: The State recognizes the exclusive jurisdiction of ecclesiastical

[11]The Article relating to freedom of conscience is Article 18: "Freedom of conscience is guaranteed. No one will be harassed for his or her convictions or beliefs, nor be compelled to reveal them or obliged to act against his or her conscience."

[12]The references in this Article are to the civil effects of marriage, religious education in public schools, and religious assistance in hospitals, military facilities, and detention centers.

courts to rule on the validity of religious acts or ceremonies that affect or may affect the civil status of individuals."

We can conclude that the secularity implied in the Constitution and in the legal texts cited is an amicable, benevolent, or as it has often been called, a "positive" secularity.[13] The most notable manifestations of this are the invocation of God in the Preamble to the Constitution; State protection of all religious beliefs, harmonious relations with religious entities and their participation in the common good[14]; the possibility of celebrating Accords or Agreements with religious entities[15]; tax exemption[16]; recognition of civil effects for all religious marriages[17]; religious education in public schools[18]; exemption from military service for all religious ministries[19]; religious assistance in military, penitentiary, care-providing establishments,[20] etc.

2 Constitutional Court Case Law

To a good extent, the concrete application of the principle of secularity has been the work of the Constitutional Court. During the years that have passed since its creation in 1991, there have been many occasions on which the Court has spoken on questions related to religious freedom and the "secular State."

There first one is Decision C 088 of 1994, which states that the non-confessionality clause of Article 2 of the RFA "means that the State does not profess any religion" (Point E). In the same decision: "The fact that the State is not indifferent to different religious sentiments means that relations of cooperation can exist with all churches and religious creeds due to their own inherent transcendence, as long as such relations are developed within the equality guaranteed by the Constitution" (*ibid.*).

That same year, Decision C 350 of 1994 declared the unconstitutionality of Act 1 of 1952, which ordered the President of the Republic to renew the nation's official consecration to the Sacred Heart of Jesus each year. It states that secularity means "strict separation between the State and churches" (VI, n. 6). It is a "strict neutrality of the State in religious matters," as the only way to ensure "pluralism and the egalitarian coexistence and autonomy of different religious denominations" (*ibid.*).

In the 1990s, the Constitutional Court also ruled on two situations in which the meaning and scope of secularity typically come into play.

---

[13]See Prieto (2009).

[14]See the RFA, Article 2, 2.

[15]See *Ibid.*, Article 15.

[16]See *Ibid.*, Article 7.

[17]See Constitution, Article 42, and the RFA, Article 6, d).

[18]See Article 68 of the Constitution; Article 6, h) of the RFA, and Articles 23-24 of the General Education Law (Act 115 of 1994). The right of students to refuse the religious education offered to them is guaranteed in all of these laws.

[19]Act 48 of 1993, Article 28.

[20]See the RFA, Article 6, f), and Article 8.

The first was a plaint against the law establishing a whole series of Catholic holy days as civic holidays (Act 51 of 1983). In Decision C 568 of 1993, the Court held that these holidays stem from "a long cultural tradition" (Considerations of the Court) and do not affect the religious freedom of non-Catholics, since no one is obliged to participate in them as religious festivities. The purpose of the law, furthermore, is not of a religious nature, but "fundamentally patrimonial," intended to ensure that workers have "proper rest" and not to favor, protect, or sponsor any given religion in detriment to others (see *ibid.*).

The second was aimed at the procedural rules that permitted cardinals, bishops, and figures of similar hierarchy belonging to religious denominations other than the Catholic Church to issue their declarations by means of affidavits. Concretely, Decision C 609 of 1996 and, years later, Decision C 094 of 2007 upheld the constitutionality of the affidavits considering the social significance of religious hierarchy, which is analogous in Colombia to that of public officials for whom the same privilege is recognized.

An outstanding case at the beginning of the new century was Decision C 152 of 2003, which enumerated some of the consequences of secularity: "It is not only constitutionally forbidden for the State (1) to establish an official religion or church, but also (2) to identify itself formally and explicitly with any church or religion or (3) to perform official acts of adhesion, even if they are symbolic, to any creed, religion or church. Such actions on the part of the State would violate the principle of separation between church and State, would ignore the principle of equality in religious matters, and would undermine religious pluralism within the liberal non-confessional State. Neither can the State (4) take decisions or measures that have a religious purpose, much less if this constitutes an expression of preference for a particular church or creed, nor (5) adopt policies or develop actions that are primarily aimed to promote, benefit, or harm any particular church or religion compared to others that are equally free before the law. This would ignore the principle of neutrality that must orient the State, its organs and its authorities on religious matters (...); (6) the constitutionally prohibited religious connotations are those that have certain characteristics: they are unique and necessary and, therefore, promote a particular creed or religion. On the other hand, the Congress is not forbidden to adopt decisions offering various secular interpretations or arguments unrelated to any particular religion, even if for some members of society, from their own perspective, said decisions may have a religious connotation" (n. 4.2.3).

Decision C 1175 of 2004 resolved a lawsuit demanding the rule that required a representative of the Catholic Church on the *Comité de Clasificación de Películas* (Film Classification Committee).[21] According to said decision, the rule sought "to privilege Catholicism's particular vision of social and moral order, which is unacceptable in the light of the principles that sustain the Colombian State as a secular State"

[21] It involved Article 152 (partial) of Decree-Law 1355 of 1970. The demanded rule established that the Film Classification Committee would include a cinema expert, a lawyer, a psychologist, a representative of the Parents Association, and a representative of the Archdiocese of Bogotá as well. The purpose of said committee is to classify the films offered to the public in order to establish limitations, if needed, based on the age group of the viewers (protection of children and adolescents).

(VI, n. 19). The problem was not that the members of that Committee belonged, as a personal matter, to a specific church: "What does not harmonize with the establishment of a secular State is (…) that any citizen, priest or not, participates in the name and representation of a given religious denomination on a Film Classification Committee. Thus, what is to be excluded from the Committee is the confessional religious criterion and not the individuals that profess one or another religion" (*ibid.*). The demanded rule also undermined the principle of equality (see VI, n. 20). In summary, the law was declared unconstitutional: it "explicitly identifies the State with a given religion and consequently determine the making of decisions that express preferences for a particular religion" (VI, n. 21).

Along the same lines, Decision C 664 of 2016 declared the unconstitutionality of the rule contained in Act 199 of 1994 that required the presence of a representative of the [Catholic] Episcopal Conference on the National Governing Council of the SENA (National Learning Service). According to said decision, "The constitutional censure of the demanded rules is not due to having excluded other religions from said privilege, but rather to the confusion of functions and the attack on the separation of church and State that the rule entails (…); the participation of any religious denomination in the management of a public establishment that provides the secular service of education contravenes the constitutional principle of secularity, due to the confusion of functions it generates and is therefore not susceptible to being conferred on other creeds on equal terms" (n. 34).

In another area, there have been numerous Constitutional Court decisions related to what are known as laws of honors, commemorations, and institutional acknowledgements.[22] These laws are aimed to publicly exalt or extol certain individuals, deeds, or institutions because they are understood to promote values of constitutional interest; or in order to promote, support, and/or endorse certain goods (both material and immaterial), like monuments, events, or celebrations of recognized cultural, social or historical value.[23]

This is the context of Decisions C 766 of 2010 and C 817 of 2011, which have in common the fact that both declared the unconstitutionality of laws that exalted places and buildings belonging to the Catholic Church.[24]

[22] See Article 150, 15, of the Colombian Constitution.

[23] See Decision C 570 of 2016, n. 4.2.

[24] The former declared the unconstitutionality of the law commemorating the Jubilee of the Pontifical Crowning of the image of Our Lady of the Rosary of Chiquinquirá, in the municipality of La Estrella, Antioquia. The law designated the municipality a "Sanctuary City and Heritage of Cultural Interest," in recognition of its cultural and religious tradition. Furthermore, the nation committed itself to the "foment, dissemination, development of programs and projects undertaken by the municipality of La Estrella and its vital forces to exalt it as a Sanctuary City," and in support of the works that made known the history and cultural tradition of the municipality. Decision C 817 of 2011 declared the unconstitutionality of Act 1402 of 2010, "by which the Nation is associated with celebrating the 50th anniversary of the Diocese of El Espinal, and the Cathedral of El Espinal in the department of Tolima is declared a national monument. The National Government is authorized to allocate funds from the General Budget of the Nation to finance the execution of the necessary works for remodeling, repairing and conserving the cathedral located in El Espinal."

Decision C 766 of 2010 states that "neutrality" is the opposite "of the activity of State patronage or promotion of any religion." Consequently, the State is not supposed to "promote, sponsor, booster, favor or undertake any incentive activity with respect to any religious faith practiced in its territory" (A, n. 3). It adds that it is "contradictory to the principles of the secular State for any public decision to have as its main –and sometimes exclusive- purpose to promote, foster or exalt the values of any particular religion" (A, n. 1). This is what occurs with the Sanctuary-City qualification, which "has a predominantly religious meaning" (A, n. 4), "it is not used by the secular legal order", and "it leaves no place for doubt about the intimate relation it has with the practice of Catholicism" (*ibid.*). The fact of a city being named a Sanctuary by the State implies the "promotion of a particular religion" (*ibid.*), and from the economic viewpoint as well (State funds assigned for the purpose). The religious element predominates in the demanded rule, not as a mere accident or accessory, but as the main point.

Decision C 817 of 2011 uses similar arguments. In exaltation by the State of social manifestations that may have a religious component, the "secular factor" must be "sufficiently identifiable" and must have a "principal, rather than a simply accessory or incidental nature." The demanded law exalts an "institutional organization" of the Catholic Church (the Diocese of El Espinal), which "lacks any secular content, and would therefore prove contrary to the secular nature of the Colombian State." The cultural value of the diocese is made to depend on the fact that the majority of the population is Catholic, which "is not acceptable for the identification of a secular criterion and, instead, entails unjustified discrimination against persons who do not profess the same majoritarian creed (…); the simple demographic fact does not provide sufficient support for the link between religion and culture." It is necessary for "the legislator to show that the exalted practice or institution has implications, in any case verifiable and essential, which transcend the religious phenomenon and consequently welcome the non-religious members of the community" (VI, n. 21.3).

In conclusion, "the principal and verifiable purpose of the demanded rule is to promote a particular congregation of the Catholic faith" (*ibid.* n. 22). In this case, "it is not possible to identify a secular criterion"; on the contrary, the challenged law is "an act of public adhesion to and promotion of the practice of Catholicism in the municipality of El Espinal" (*ibid.*).

Nevertheless, when the starting point was not secularity but individual religious liberty, different conclusions were reached. We refer to some decisions resolving complaints against the National University and the ICFES[25] on the part of students who invoked their religious convictions to oppose having exams on certain days of the week.

At first one might think that the National University is a public entity that is not permitted to adjust its operation to the demands of any particular religion. The decisions of the Court, however, favored the plaintiffs, affirming the importance of the right to religious freedom even though its exercise could affect decisions made by public entities in the area of their jurisdiction.

[25] The Spanish initials for The Colombian Institute for the Foment of Higher Education.

That was the case, in the first place, of Decision T 448 of 2007.[26] According to said decision, "the Court safeguards the freedom of conscience and religion, not only with the protection of its private manifestations, but its external exercise as well, without ignoring that it has limits in the exercise of public guarantees and the fundamental rights of others" (III, 4).

A similar situation was resolved with Decision T 044 of 2008, which states that students should not face "the dilemma of choosing between acting contrary to their beliefs or sacrificing their academic aspirations of attending the nation's most important public university. Therefore, this Court deems it appropriate to caution the competent authorities of the National University to refrain from denying future petitions from members of the Seventh Day Adventist Church of Colombia to be permitted to take the entrance exams on a date and schedule that would not interfere with their observation of the *Sabbath*" (III, 7). It ruled to the same effect in relation to the ICFES in Decision T 493 of 2010.[27]

There was a notable turn in case law during the next few years in favor of a positive consideration of religion as a cultural element. The first instance of this was Decision C 948 of 2014, which examined the claim of unconstitutionality against Act 1710 of 2014 that "honors Mother Laura Montoya Upegui as an illustrious Colombian saint." The decision declared that the law is in keeping with the Constitution, except for some of its Articles and expressions. From the viewpoint of State secularity, there is no objection to expressions like those in Article 1: "On the occasion of her Sanctification, the Nation honors, exalts and extols the memory, life and work of Mother Laura Montoya Upegui for her lifelong dedication to the defense and support of the disadvantaged in Colombia;" or in Article 2: "The National Government and the Congress of the Republic of Colombia should honor the work and memory of Saint Laura Montoya in a special act of protocol, the date and time of which will be programmed by the Board of Directors of the honorable Congress of the Republic, with an invitation to the President of the Republic, in the municipality of Jericó, department of Antioquia." Article 5 orders the issuance of a coin in honor of Mother Laura, while Article 6 orders the production of a sculpture. Given the great touristic "and religious" impact of Mother Laura's canonization, Article 7 authorizes the National Government to make the necessary budget allocations to pave the Pueblo Rico-Jericó road. Finally, Article 8 "declares the municipality of Jericó to be of Great Potential for Touristic Development, especially in religious and

[26]The National University had scheduled its entrance exams for a Saturday. One candidate, who was a member of the Adventist Church, presented an *acción de tutela* (petition for guardianship or protection) in order to be given the exam on a day other than Saturday. The decision upheld the student's right to religious freedom and obliged the university to seek alternatives that would respect his religious convictions.

[27]It resolved the case of two Evangelical Christian students who refused to take the ICFES exams on Sunday for religious reasons. According to the decision, "Although administering the State exam is a necessary measure under Article 67 of the Political Constitution, carrying it out on a different day does not contravene the constitutional obligation of the defendant entity. In fact, the intention is not to refuse to give the exam, but to do it on a different day, since that would harmonize the individual's fundamental right to freedom of religion with the obligation of the ICFES to evaluate the quality of education in Colombia" (n. 3.3.1.2).

cultural products (museums and historic centers), for which the Government will promote investments in necessary touristic infrastructure to achieve the objective planned in this Article."

Decision T 139 of 2014 resolved the petition that sought to suspend work on an eco-park project near the city of Bucaramanga in the department of Santander. The project included a monumental statue more than thirty meters tall representing an anonymous "superior being." The plaintiff, an atheist, felt discriminated by what he interpreted as State enhancement of religious beliefs. The Court insists that the criterion for judging the secularity of the decision of the Government of Santander must be "a secular criterion to justify it" (n. 5.6.5). For the decision, according to the contract between the local government and the artist, "the sculpture does not represent a specific religion or particular deity. On the contrary, it seeks to idealize a superior being that will be interpreted by the observer according to his or her own criterion or belief." Furthermore, the secular criterion for the decision is guaranteed since "the project is aimed exclusively at promoting tourism in the Department through the creation of an Eco-park" (n. 5.6.6).

The common denominator in the latest developments of the principle of secularity has been the question of the constitutionality of laws declaring Holy Week ceremonies in certain Colombian cities to be cultural heritage, with the consequent allocation of funds.

In the first place, Decision C 224 of 2016 dealt with a claim of unconstitutionality against Act 1645 of 2013, "through which the Holy Week tradition of Pamplona, in the department of Santander, is declared Intangible Cultural Heritage of the Nation, and other provisions are enacted." Based on previous case law, the decision explains that "it is possible in a law for a religious dimension to converge with the recognition or exaltation of cultural, historic or social elements; for example, in those that aim to pay homage to citizens, celebrate municipal anniversaries, or hold institutional commemorations. However, in such events, to avoid infringement of the principles of secularity and State neutrality, the jurisprudence has been categorical in demanding that the religious foundation be "merely anecdotal or accidental in the *telos* of the exaltation." In other words, the main purpose of this type of regulations must never be religious exaltation, i.e., "the role of the State cannot be to promote, sponsor, drive, favor or undertake any incentive activity with respect to any religious faith practiced in its territory." That is why "the promotion and protection of cultural heritage, or any other constitutionally valid objective, with symbols predominantly associated with a religious faith is not reasonable" (n. 36).

Despite the above, in another decision in that same year (C 441 of 2016), with a similar object (budget allocations to foment, promote, and disseminate Holy Week in Tunja, department of Boyacá), the Court decided to declare the constitutionality of the demanded rules.

Decision C 567 of 2016 made explicit and explained in detail the reasons for the change in the jurisprudence. Once again, the issue involved was Holy Week, this time in the city of Popayán, department of Cauca. The Court states that "a rite or festivity may be religious and simultaneously form part of the cultural heritage of the nation or of humanity (…); the Constitution does not expressly prohibit safeguarding cultural heritage associated with religion. It certainly establishes the principles of religious pluralism, diversity and liberty, but none of its precepts explicitly establishes a rule that prevents the State from safeguarding cultural heritage linked to religion. On the contrary, the constitutional provisions previously reviewed are generic and contemplate a duty to provide ample protection, without distinctions, of diversity, wealth and cultural heritage (Articles 2, 7, 8, 44, 67, 70, 71 and 72). On the other hand, the Constitution does clearly prohibit discrimination for reasons of '*religion*' (Article 13), and it would be a form of discrimination to firmly and absolutely maintain that the State must protect the cultural heritage of the nation except when it is linked to religion, and only because of this fact, since in this case, the '*religion*' factor would be the detonator of difference" (n. 21).

In its analysis, the decision points out that in previous case law (mainly Decisions C 152 of 2003, C 766 of 2010, C 817 of 2011, C 224 of 2016 and C 441 of 2016) "There are (…) conceptual discrepancies" (n. 25). In order to overcome them, the analysis takes as its reference point the six requirements enumerated in Decision C 152 of 2003. It reaffirms the validity of the first five. With respect to the sixth, it corrects the excesses in interpretation in the previous cases, which not only required the secular element to play the main or leading role, but also insisted that the religious element had to be "merely anecdotal or accidental." This approach excluded the promotion and protection of cultural heritage predominantly associated with any religious faith, which in practice implied eliminating "a broad range of measures to safeguard the intangible cultural heritage of living religions" (n. 28). For Decision C 567 of 2016, in contrast, "religious neutrality is inclusive when it involves protecting culture, and State orientation is thus legitimate in order to guarantee public financing of cultural heritage even if it is narrowly or predominantly associated with a religious denomination" (n. 28).

Consequently, the criteria that should be kept in mind in the constitutional control of laws that promote and finance cultural manifestations linked to a given religious faith are summed up in the following statement: "The State cannot (1) establish an official religion or church; (2) formally and explicitly identify itself with a church or religion; (3) perform official acts of adhesion, even if symbolic, to a belief, religion or church; (4) take decisions or measures that have a religious purpose, much less if this constitutes the expression of a preference for any church or denomination; (5) adopt policies or develop actions, of which the real primary impact is to promote, benefit or harm any particular religion or church vis-à-vis others that are equally free before the law. To adopt rules that authorize public financing of goods or manifestations associated with religion (6) the measure must have an important, verifiable, consistent and sufficient secular justification and (7) must be susceptible to being conferred on other creeds, on equal terms" (n. 29).

Act 1754 of 2015 recognized "the religious and cultural importance of the monument to *Cristo Rey*, in the municipality of Belalcázar, in the department of Caldas" (Article 1). It also authorized "the National Government to contribute to the foment, promotion, protection, conservation, restoration, dissemination, development and financing required for recognition of the *Cristo Rey* monument located in the municipality of Belalcázar, Caldas" (Article 3). The foreseeable claim of unconstitutionality was resolved with Decision C 570 of 2016.[28] Despite its proximity to Decision C 567 of the same year, it does not incorporate the criteria applied in that case, but instead refers back to earlier case law, particularly Decisions C 766 of 2010 and C 817 of 2011. Despite this, the conclusion was favorable to the permanence of the monument in question. The reasoning, however, forces the reality of things, precisely because of the urgent need to ground the decision on "secular" reasons: "attending to its history and characteristics, the monument to *Cristo Rey*, more than a religious manifestation derived from its original relation to the Catholic faith, is in reality a symbol of peace and reconciliation and an important cultural, architectural, historical and touristic expression for the country. From that point of view, said monument has, above all, a secular or objective purpose" (n. 6.15).

Finally, Decision C 111 of 2017 resolved a new claim of unconstitutionality related to religious celebrations. This time the case was about patronal feasts of Saint Francis of Assisi in the city of Quibdó being declared a cultural heritage of the Nation. It refers repeatedly to Decision C 567 of 2016, and the conclusions are similar. It also recalls General Observations n. 13 and n. 21 of the United Nations Committee on Economic, Social and Cultural Rights (CESCR), which states that the concept of culture, as a human right, involves "systems of religion and beliefs" as well as their "rites and ceremonies" as long as they make it possible to identify a collectivity, give meaning to its existence, and configure a particular vision of the world (see n. 6.3.5). The conclusion is that "under certain conditions that aim to guarantee the constitutional principle of secularity, it is possible for the State to foment, support or develop actions of legal protection for manifestations related to a feast, event or religious figure" (n. 6.5.1). The conditions are those enumerated in Decision C 567 of 2016.

3 Final Reflections

3.1 Religion and Culture: Public Significance of the Religious Factor

The Colombian State is not "indifferent to the religious sentiments of Colombians" (Article 2 of the RFA). According to the same law, the principle of non-indifference is materialized in the protection of all faiths and in harmonious relations with religious entities that facilitate their participation in achieving the common good.

As is natural, the possibility of participating in the common good can be understood in very different ways. One of them—perhaps the most evident—consists of recognizing that religions promote initiatives of a beneficial, assistance-providing, and educational type, etc., that contribute to the common good. The fact that the State

---

[28]See also Decisions C 008 of 2017 and C 287 of 2017.

recognizes the legitimacy of these efforts, promotes them, and helps to sustain them economically, does not seem to pose problems from the viewpoint of secularity.

The difficulty arises when the religious factor is seen in itself, i.e., as specifically religious and not only as a promoter of social services. This is where the concept and practical scope of State secularity really comes into play. In other words, it is a question of determining whether religions contribute to the common good in themselves, or only when they develop activities that can be comprehended and assimilated from a secular perspective.

As we see it, the possibility of contributing to the common good implies recognizing the fact that religion in general, and churches and religious denominations in particular, actually constitute a good, positive reality. This means that the existence of individuals and institutions that profess sincere and profound religious convictions is an asset for society, and not some sort of "subculture"[29] or weakness typical of uneducated citizens.[30] Much less can it be understood that transcendental vital visions and their influence in the life of individuals and communities constitute a threat against which the State must defend itself, or a potential factor of conflict.

In this sense, Rhonheimer (2009) has pointed out what he calls the "civil function of religion." Religious faiths, if they develop their activity in a way that is compatible with respect for public order and the rights of others, and accept the secular political culture of the constitutional democratic State, fulfill an important role in civil life: they simply form part of the reality and vital heritage of a society, with positive consequences (individual and social) in multiple spheres of human life.

A first stage in recent jurisprudence of the Constitutional Court can be recognized between 2004 and 2014, in which religion and culture are seen as disconnected and somehow mutually exclusive realities. The State is called to promote and foment culture (history, art, literature, cinema, folklore), but not religion, the relevance of which should be limited to the private lives of individuals.

This insistence can lead to the extreme of ignoring the intrinsic value of religion. The fact is that religion is not only not opposed to the culture; it actually forms part of the culture in very diverse ways, ranging from holidays and popular celebrations to religious symbols displayed in public places. For this reason, instead of debating how far the secular sphere extends, where the religious sphere begins, and what predominates in any given situation (which is often hard to establish), we think it would suffice to recognize the value of religion as a specific cultural and social phenomenon, to protect and accept it as such. In any case, the most important thing is the guarantee of religious freedom on equal terms.

Along the same line, it is important to distinguish between State decisions grounded in religious precepts[31] and decisions that are not indifferent (i.e., they

---

[29] In this regard, see Pope Benedicto XVI (2006).

[30] When religious beliefs and practices are not only benevolently accepted but also recognized as something good in themselves, it is possible that "the destabilizing presumption of religion for democracy is inverted and becomes a benevolent presumption of its ethical and cognitive contribution to society" (Garzón Vallejo 2012).

[31] As would be the case, for example, in establishing that homicide is a crime because the Bible or other sacred texts says it is, rather than doing so because it infringes upon the dignity of human

take them into account) regarding the religious convictions of citizens (see Article 2 of the RFA). When religion is seen as naturally as other social phenomena (art, culture, education, sport...), it is possible to recognize that it has an analogous public relevance.

Some examples taken from Colombian jurisprudence may serve to illustrate the above. In the first place, the Decision that upheld the constitutionality of the establishment of holidays corresponding to religious festivities (C 568/93). It was argued that the Decision was based on the cultural tradition and on the guarantee of due rest for workers. Thus, they are "secular" arguments, capable of providing "secular" grounds for a decision that cannot be based on religious reasons.

The problem, however, can be focused from another angle: for an important portion of the population, certain days of the year have a particular religious significance that includes, among other consequences, a religious duty not to work. This is the reality, and it is somehow artificial to seek any other type of arguments that may be more in accordance with certain secular criteria. If the State "is not indifferent" and therefore keeps the phenomena in mind, in establishing those holidays, it is simply recognizing a social reality and working in consequence. In no way does it favor any particular religious creed if the same right is recognized for all churches and denominations.[32]

Decision C 1175/04 eliminated the inclusion of a representative of the Catholic Church on the Film Classification Committee. The reasons laid out at that time were: it is not admissible "to privilege the particular vision that the Catholic religious faith has of the social and moral order, which is unacceptable in light of the principles that sustain the Colombian State as a secular State." Again, the topic can be focused from a different perspective, which is that of Catholics whose lives are inspired by certain ethical and religious options. It is an undeniable social fact and does not seem contrary to the secularity that the State, in making decisions that directly affect public morality, has this fact in mind and decides that certain films cannot be presented because they offend the religious or moral sentiments of a significant number of citizens that express their convictions through a legitimate representative.

Other problems were of course raised, such as the balance between freedom of speech and the protection of religious sentiments, or the concrete way to put into practice the participation of religious creeds (not only of the Catholic Church) in that type of decisions. What we hope to underscore is the fact that the State does not

beings. The former is contrary to secularity, but not the latter, although it is an obvious fact that the majority of religious faiths condemn homicide. The secularity of the State does not mean, therefore, that so as to avoid encompassing religious doctrines in legislation, the State cannot prohibit theft, homicide, and rape simply because practically all religious doctrines do so see González del Valle (2005).

[32]This is what happened in Colombia with the Adventist Church, for which Saturday was officially recognized as the weekly day of rest (see Article XXIII of the *Convenio de Derecho Público* No. 1 of 1997, Decree 354 of 1998).

cease to be secular through the fact of taking into account a social reality of religious content.[33]

Although the State undoubtedly cannot assume canonical functions and declare a parish church a sanctuary, or the religious patron of teachers in Colombia a saint, considerations analogous to those of the above paragraphs can be made in relation to the decisions that declared the unconstitutionality of laws that decreed honors and economic support in favor of Catholic churches or sanctuaries. The basis can be that temples or sanctuaries satisfy (religious) needs that are very important to most of the population. Since there is no objection to the State promoting and financing other types of needs (probably less relevant for many) through, for example, sports or cultural facilities,[34] the same may occur with religious temples, depending on the situation and concrete needs of the population. There is no need to seek predominantly "secular" arguments (history, artistic value, etc.) that justify this type of aid: the consideration of its effective social and public relevance should suffice. True secularity undoubtedly prohibits the State from becoming the "secular arm" of a given church, in order to promote its particular spiritual objectives. What does not seem to be contrary to secularity is respect for and promotion of real social interests, among which religion occupies a primary place.[35]

In synthesis, the understanding that religion forms part of the culture helps to focus and resolve different problems. The latest jurisprudence of the Court seems to move along this line. From an approach to the question based on a distrust of religion and on the urge to seek that it does not surpass the limits of private life, it has moved on to an inclusive and positive vision.

With some precedents laid down since 2014,[36] the Decision that has most broadly developed the new tendency in the case law is undoubtedly C 567 of 2016. While previous jurisprudence had explicitly prohibited the promotion and protection of cultural heritage associated with any religious faith, the jurisprudence of recent years is more realistic and clearly states that "a rite or festivity can be religious and at the same time form part of the cultural heritage of the nation or of humanity." Furthermore, it holds that the exclusion of a cultural fact due to its linkage to religion is a form of discrimination and establishes the legitimacy of "public financing of cultural heritage even if it is narrowly or predominantly associated with a religious faith."

---

[33] On the other hand, the pretension of a "secular" or "neutral" morality is simply utopian. Decisions are made by concrete persons and can never be "neutral" since they correspond to a certain vision of life, which is more likely agnostic or atheistic than religious, but which takes sides in any case, so it is difficult to speak of neutrality. Navarro-Valls has noted that when religious beliefs are marginalized in the social sphere, the space has been occupied by ideologies that often tend to turn into "quasi-religions" that demonstrate the same intolerance for which some religious manifestations have been criticized (Navarro-Valls 2000).

[34] Which does not mean taking sides in favor of a given sports team or artistic group.

[35] See Navarro-Valls (2000).

[36] In Decision C 948 of 2014, for example, in addition to the "secular" motivations justifying homage to Saint Laura Montoya ("a whole life dedicated to the defense and support of the disadvantaged"), the impact of her canonization is recognized to be not only touristic (another undoubtedly "secular" reason), but religious as well. The religious factor therefore takes on its own specific significance.

3.2 Foundation of Secularity. Secularity and Equality

In the context of the Constitution of 1886, the State's commitment to protecting and ensuring respect for the Catholic religion, although explicable for sociological and historical reasons, was not congruent with the principles of secularity and equality. More consistent with said principles is the omission of such a commitment or its extension to all religious faiths. The Constitution of 1991 and the RFA move in the latter direction since they underscore the State's commitment to provide equal protection for all the different faiths professed by Colombians.

The insistence on equality has also served to support secularity. This is what occurred during the debates in the National Constitutional Assembly: by eliminating any explicit reference to the Catholic Church, all faiths were placed in a situation of equality. And secularity was also supposed to be guaranteed in this way.

The pretension of explaining and grounding secularity from the perspective of equality entails the risk of losing sight of the specific sense of secularity. In effect, the fact that all churches are, from the viewpoint of the State, on an equal footing, and therefore enjoy the same rights, is a distinct reality of State secularity. It could well occur, for example, that the State might want to intervene in churches (on matters of doctrine, internal organization, or clergy) thereby giving rise to churches *equally* controlled by the State, or to impose standardized forms of religiosity under the pretext of equality.

When the proper meaning of secularity is obscured, one might think that the confessional State "remedy" is a question of equality (all faiths must receive equal legal treatment from the State), when in reality the proper object of secularity consists of preventing the involvement of either the State or churches, to any extent whatsoever, in what is not their respective area of competence.

As we see it, the relationship between equality and secularity is illuminated when the starting point is religious freedom. Although there is undoubtedly a close relationship between secularity and equality (if all religious expressions are equally legitimate, the State cannot favor any of them), neither of these two principles is able to substantiate, from the human rights perspective, the legal treatment of the religious factor. The grounds for this must be sought directly in religious freedom, with its different dimensions (individual, collective, institutional).

Religious freedom, in effect, means that the State must recognize and guarantee full immunity from coercion in religious matters for individuals and denominations, on the part of the State itself, or of any other social element. Religious freedom thus implies recognizing a sphere of autonomy in which the State simply does not have competence.[37] Secularity is its logical consequence: the subjects of the right to religious freedom are persons and religious groups, not the State, which cannot be the subject of the act of religious faith. For this reason, it can neither assume nor commit itself to any church or denomination. Its authority is limited to dictating

[37] See Viladrich and Ferrer Ortiz (2004).

the necessary rules so that individuals and denominations can exercise their right to religious freedom without any coercion, within due limits.[38]

Something similar can be said about equality, which is always relative, in the sense that it does not possess an object of its own, but always exists in relation to the specific rights that are owed to everyone. In our case, it means that the right to religious freedom must be recognized for everyone because it is based on the equal dignity of all human beings, without privileges or discriminations.[39]

In summary, secularity and equality cannot be understood disconnected from religious freedom. Even more, they are at its service. Secularity therefore cannot be conceived as an end in itself, but rather as a means to guarantee and to facilitate the exercise of religious freedom on the part of individuals and groups, on equal terms. One consequence, pointed out by Palomino, is that the proper approach to possible problems and their solution is more accessible when secularity is assumed as a consequence of religious freedom, and not the other way around.[40] Put another way, the starting point should be the protection of religious freedom of all persons and groups, and not a particular model of Church-State relations.[41]

3.3 Secularity and Pluralism

For these reasons, it is religious freedom (and not secularity or equality) that performs "the function of the primary defining principle of the State in ecclesiastic matters." From this is derived "the civil identity of the State, its role in promoting the religious factor as part of the common good, the mutual independence between the State and churches, and (…) the full development of all rights related to religious freedom" (Viladrich and Ferrer Ortiz 2004).[42]

For some decisions of the Colombian Constitutional Court, the foundation of the system is not religious freedom, but rather secularity or even the pluralism of the Colombian State.[43] In addition to what has been said about secularity and equality, we think it is worthwhile to comment specifically on the affirmation that pluralism

---

[38]See Martín de Agar (1995). We follow the pagination of the version available at http://bibliotecanonica.net/docsaa/btcaai.pdf (visited 20 November 2017). Regarding the right to religious freedom in Colombia, Article 4 of the Religious Freedom Act declares that: "The exercise of rights connected to freedom of religion and of worship is limited only by protection of the right of others to exercise their public freedoms and fundamental rights, as well as safeguarding the safety, health and public morality, constituent elements of public order protected by law in a democratic society.". See also Prieto (2008).

[39]See Martín de Agar (1995).

[40]See Palomino (2011).

[41]See Martínez-Torrón (2014).

[42]Although the authors refer specifically to the Spanish system, we believe its considerations can easily be applied in the Colombian context.

[43]We recall some more significant statements. Decision C 350/94: "A State that is defined as ontologically pluralistic in religious matters and that also recognizes equality among all religions (Political Constitution, Articles 1 and 19) cannot at the same time establish an official religion or

fits in the category of founding "principle" in treatment of the religious question. The reference point is Article 1 of the Colombian Constitution[44] that lists among the characteristics of the Colombian State the fact of its being pluralistic.

As we see it, the term *pluralism* refers initially to a fact: the reality is that ideas, convictions, or beliefs do not exist alone in any given society; on the contrary, they are varied and multifaceted. But it may also indicate a "principle" or attitude, according to which variety is a value that should be recognized and promoted.[45] In relation to the religious factor, the term *pluralism* (as a principle) is used by the Court first of all in the sense that the State is not permitted to assume any particular religion, much less to impose it on the citizens or to deal with certain religious manifestations in a discriminatory way. If this is so, it is nothing other than religious freedom and the principles of secularity and equality. Consequently, establishing that pluralism is a principle in religious matters would be simply useless or superfluous.

If the meaning of pluralism is, on the other hand, that of "assuming and promoting the concurrence in society of diverse ways of understanding ethics, morality and, in general, different axiological scenarios" (Decision C 817/11), the result may be harmful to freedom of religion and to secularism in particular. Indeed, the State is not supposed to promote any particular "religious design" or to establish that it is better for many religious denominations to exist, instead of just a few or only one. The mission of the State is different: it is to take note of the social reality just as it is (recognition of pluralism as a fact) and to facilitate or promote the expression of the religious convictions that already exist in society—or that might exist—without taking sides in favor of or against any of them.

The promotion, by the State, of diverse or "alternative" religious or ideological visions (with the argument of favoring pluralism), implies ignoring the obligation

establish the legal preeminence of certain religious creeds. It is therefore a secular State;" Decision C 152/03: "By virtue of the principle of pluralism and cultural diversity, the State, in fulfillment of its functions, cannot place itself at the service of a particular religious faith. Nor can the State discriminate other religions when it intervenes to regulate the exercise of individual and collective rights regarding matters of religion and worship;" "Colombia is a State with a predominantly secular orientation, based on religious pluralism;" Decision C 1175/04: "In a secular State it is clear that the primary values imposed are those of plurality and tolerance;" Decision C 817/11: The "principle of pluralism," the "basis of fundamental rights, implies recognizing the equal validity of different ethical and moral formulas existing in society;" The "principle of religious pluralism (…) prevents the imposition of a particular creed or the recognition of any religion as that of the Nation;" The "mandate of democratic pluralism" means "to assume and promote the fact that in society there are different ways of understanding ethics, morality and, in general, different axiological scenarios, all of them equally valid and with no other limitation than the validity of fundamental rights" (*ibid.*). In summary, the "central concepts for resolving legal problems relating to the religious question are the lay or secular State and religious pluralism." This was repeated more recently in Decision C 224/16: "The Colombian State can be classified in the category of secular State (…), based on religious pluralism."

[44]The complete text reads as follows: "Colombia is a social state under the rule of law, organized in the form of a unitary republic, decentralized, with autonomy of its territorial units, democratic, participatory, and pluralistic, based on the respect of human dignity, the work and solidarity of the individuals who belong to it, and the prevalence of the general interest."

[45]See Hervada (1979).

of strict neutrality—secularity—in these matters. Committing itself to particular positions is not the role of the State, and it comes very close to being a type of "confessionality" that is no longer religious, but ideological or "secular" instead.

References

Benedicto XVI (2006) Encuentro con el mundo de la cultura en la Universidad de Ratisbona, 12 septiembre 2006. http://www.vatican.va/holy_father/benedict_xvi/speeches/2006/september/documents/hf_ben-xvi_spe_20060912_university-regensburg_sp.html. Accessed 15 Jan 2015

Garzón Vallejo I (2012) Deliberación democrática y razones religiosas: objeciones y desafíos. Co-herencia 9:81–117

González del Valle JM (2005) Derecho Eclesiástico Español, 6th edn. Thomson-Civitas, Cizur Menor (Navarra)

Hervada J (1979) Pensamientos sobre sociedad plural y dimensión religiosa. Ius Canonicum 63–76

Martín de Agar JT (1995) Libertà religiosa, uguaglianza e laicità. Ius Ecclesiae 199–215

Martínez-Torrón J (2014) Símbolos religiosos institucionales, neutralidad del Estado y protección de las minorías en Europa. Ius Canonicum 107–144

Navarro-Valls R (2000) Los Estados frente a la Iglesia. In: Palomino R, Navarro-Valls R (eds) Estado y Religión. Textos para una reflexión crítica, Ariel, Barcelona, pp 315–362

Palomino R (2011) Neutralidad y factor religioso: mito, principio y significado. In: Mazzola R, Zuanazzi I (eds) Aquitas sive Deus. Studi in onore di Rinaldo Bertolino, Giappichelli, Torino, pp 948–971

Prieto V (2008) Libertad religiosa y confesiones. Derecho Eclesiástico del Estado Colombiano. Temis-U. de La Sabana, Bogotá

Prieto V (2009) La laicidad positiva del Estado colombiano. Pensam y Cult 12:39–65

Prieto V (2010) El Concordato de 1973 y la evolución del Derecho Eclesiástico colombiano. Rev Gen Derecho Canónico y Derecho Eclesiástico del Estado 1–50

Prieto V (2011) Estado laico y libertad religiosa. Antecedentes y desarrollos de la Constitución colombiana de 1991. Universidad de La Sabana-Diké, Bogotá

Rhonheimer M (2009) Cristianismo y laicidad. Historia y actualidad de una relación compleja. Rialp, Madrid

Viladrich PJ, Ferrer Ortiz J (2004) Los principios informadores del Derecho Eclesiástico Español. In: Ferrer Ortiz J (ed) Derecho Eclesiástico del Estado español, 5th edn. Eunsa, Pamplona, pp 87–113

The manufacturer's authorised representative in the EU is Springer Nature Customer Service Centre GmbH, Europaplatz 3, 69115 Heidelberg, Germany. If you have any concerns regarding our products, please contact ProductSafety@springernature.com

Printed and bound by CPI Group (UK) Ltd, Croydon, CR0 4YY

05/10/2026

02228156-0003